COMPLETE

GRILLING

COOKBOOK

WILLIAMS-SONOMA

COMPLETE
GRILLING
COOKBOOK

GENERAL EDITOR

Chuck Williams

RECIPES

John Phillip Carroll, Barbara Grunes
Brigit Binns, and other contributors

PHOTOGRAPHY

Allan Rosenberg, Noel Barnhurst,
and Joyce Oudkerk Pool

First published in the USA, 1992–1999,
by Time-Life Custom Publishing.

Recipes originally published in the
Williams-Sonoma Kitchen Library and
Williams-Sonoma Cookware series
(© 1992–1999 Weldon Owen Inc.).

OXMOOR HOUSE INC.
Oxmoor House books are distributed by Sunset Books
80 Willow Road, Menlo Park, CA 94025
Phone: 650·321·3600 Fax: 650·324·1532

Vice-President/General Manager: Rich Smeby
Director of Special Sales: Gary Wright

Oxmoor House and Sunset Books are divisions of
Southern Progress Corporation

In collaboration with Williams-Sonoma Inc.
3250 Van Ness Avenue, San Francisco, CA 94109

WILLIAMS-SONOMA
Founder & Vice-Chairman: Chuck Williams
Book Buyer: Cecilia Michaelis

PRODUCED BY WELDON OWEN INC.
Chief Executive Officer: John Owen
President: Terry Newell
Chief Operating Officer: Larry Partington
Creative Director: Gaye Allen
Vice President International Sales: Stuart Laurence
Sales Manager: Emily Jahn
Associate Publisher: Val Cipollone
Editor: Sarah Lemas
Copy Editor: Sharon Silva
Consulting Editors: Judith Dunham, Norman Kolpas
Original Design: John Bull, The Book Design Company
Design Director: Paul Morales, Onyx Design Inc.
Art Direction: Sarah Gifford
Production: Chris Hemesath, Stephanie Sherman, Linda Bouchard
Proofreader: Desne Border
Indexer: Ken DellaPenta
Food Photographers: Noel Barnhurst, Joyce Oudkerk Pool,
    Allan Rosenberg
Illustrations: Thorina Rose
Front Cover Photographer: Daniel Clark
Front Cover Food Stylist: George Dolese
Front Cover Prop Stylist: Amy Denebeim

The Williams-Sonoma Complete Cookbook series
conceived and produced by Weldon Owen Inc.
814 Montgomery Street, San Francisco, CA 94133

A Weldon Owen Production

First printed in 2001
10 9 8 7 6 5 4

Library of Congress Cataloging-in-Publication Data is available.
ISBN 0-8487-2592-1

Separations by Colourscan Overseas Co. Pte. Ltd.
Printed in China by Leefung-Asco Printers Ltd.

A Note on Weights, Measures, and Temperatures
*All recipes include customary U.S., U.K. and metric measurements.
Conversions are based on a standard developed for these books
and have been rounded off. Actual weights, grilling times, and
temperatures may vary.*

CONTENTS

INTRODUCTION 8

SEAFOOD 20

Fish 22
Shellfish 52

POULTRY 68

Chicken 70
Other Birds 98

BEEF, PORK & LAMB 114

Beef   116

Pork   146

Lamb   166

VEGETABLES, SIDES & SALADS 182

On the Grill   184

From the Kitchen   224

DESSERTS 246

On the Grill   248

From the Kitchen   262

Basic Recipes   292

Glossary   296

Index   300

Introduction

We've entered a new era in the way we cook outdoors. Gone are the days when the backyard chef would simply build a fire in a grill, slip on a hamburger or steak, turn it once, and then call out, "Come and get it!"

Adventurous cooks have learned that, with a little attention to detail, almost all of the same foods regularly cooked on a stove top or in an oven can be cooked outdoors. Thus, the pleasures of preparing food in the open air, of savoring the flavor from the smoke of a live fire, have expanded dramatically.

Bringing together recipes from the best-selling *Grilling, Outdoor Cooking,* and other titles in the Williams-Sonoma Kitchen Library, along with recipes from Williams-Sonoma's *Grill Cookbook* and 31 new recipes, this book explores the world of outdoor cooking. It covers the full range of grilled main dishes, from quick-cooked fish fillets or duck breasts to a slow-roasted whole beef brisket or whole chicken. The book also includes recipes for salads, vegetables, and other side dishes and nearly 30 desserts, some of them grilled outdoors and some of them prepared in the kitchen. In other words, this is the only book you will need to put together a complete meal whenever you fire up the grill.

How to Use This Book

On these introductory pages, you'll find discussions of everything you need to know to grill successfully, including descriptions of various grill options, tools and accessories, and fuels and sources of fragrant smoke. You'll also learn how to build fires to suit different cooking methods—including direct and indirect heat—and how various marinades, bastes, and sauces can enhance flavor. The recipes are organized into chapters by featured ingredients: seafood; poultry; meats; vegetables, side dishes and salads; and desserts. The concluding sections offer recipes for wet and dry marinades and sauces, a glossary of commonly used ingredients, and a detailed index.

Once you've carefully read the basics, look through the recipes, letting the many full-color photographs help guide you in your selection. Prepare a few meals in the open air and you'll soon join the ever-growing ranks of experts on outdoor cooking.

Choosing a Grill

The dizzying array of outdoor cooking equipment available today might lead you to believe that there are many different ways to grill outdoors. Basically, there are only two, direct heat and indirect heat (see page 11), and almost any outdoor grill can be used for both methods with some success. The differences in equipment come down to matters of size, sturdiness and durability, types of fuel, and optional features, all of which will affect the cost of the product you choose.

The smallest outdoor grills, such as square or rectangular Japanese-style hibachis, are easily portable. Bear in mind that they will limit the quantity and size of the foods you cook and that the smallest ones lack a fire bed or cooking rack of sufficient size to accommodate indirect-heat cooking. These small grills are sometimes made of less durable materials and may not last beyond one summer.

Larger, sturdier grills will accommodate enough burgers or sausages to feed a crowd and are commonly designed to handle the cooking of a large cut of meat or whole poultry by indirect heat. They will last season after season if properly cared for (see Caring for Your Grill, page 10). Some of the largest models, whether fueled by charcoal or gas, may even be built into brick or stone bases to become permanent backyard features.

Charcoal Grills

Consisting of a metal pan that holds a bed of glowing charcoal beneath a metal rack or grid, charcoal grills come in many shapes and sizes. These include the small, inexpensive, cast-iron Japanese hibachi and the flat-bottomed brazier, which starred in many backyard barbecues in the 1950s. More versatile than the brazier is the popular kettle grill, whose deep, hemispherical fire pan and domed cover make it fuel efficient and suitable for cooking with direct or indirect heat. Vents on the fire pan and cover allow control of the fire temperature.

Usually square or rectangular in shape, hibachis are especially convenient for balcony or patio use. They are adequately sized to cook for two or three people.

Rotisserie Grills

Whether it comes built into your gas or charcoal grill, or is available as an attachable accessory, a rotisserie consists of a large spit positioned above the fire bed, slowly rotated at a constant speed by an electric motor. Evenly balanced on the spit and held securely in place with adjustable pronged forks that clamp firmly to the spit, a large meat roast or whole poultry cooks slowly and evenly on a rotisserie. Look for models with sturdy spits and strong, reliable motors. The key to successful mastering of this technique is to understand the center of gravity of the item you wish to spit roast. If the food is not well balanced, the motor will strain and jerk, resulting in uneven cooking, lost juices, and undue stress on the motor. Most rotisseries come with a counterweight system, which can be adjusted to compensate for the awkward shape of certain food items. It is preferable to have two people on hand for ease when mounting any food item onto a rotisserie spit. Truss whole poultry and tie roasts with linen kitchen string. Build the fire for indirect-heat cooking (page 11), positioning a drip pan beneath the food. The food will baste itself as it turns, but, if you like, you can baste it using the drippings from the pan.

Gas Grills

Whether fueled by a natural-gas line run from the house or by propane in refillable tanks, the flames of a gas grill burn beneath a bed of heat-absorbent crushed lava rock or ceramic briquettes, which in turn cook food placed on the rack or grid above them. More sophisticated models include multiple controls, allowing only parts of the bed to be heated for indirect-heat cooking; separate burners for cooking sauces or heating griddles; and built-in metal boxes that hold and heat wood chips for smoking.

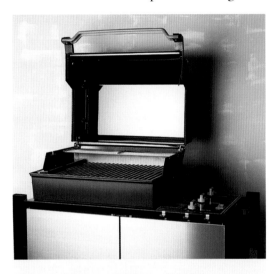

A gas grill gives off the same kind of heat as glowing coals. It also vaporizes drippings to produce smoke and channels off excess grease to prevent flare-ups. The high grill hood allows roasting as well as grilling.

Electric Grills

For easy indoor grilling, the electric countertop grill has stick-resistant metal grill surfaces that are electrically heated to three preset temperatures. Two hinged cooking surfaces allow foods to cook quickly on two sides at once or may be opened flat for a larger cooking surface. The electric smoker, reproducing the effects of a traditional pit barbecue, cooks food on wire shelves by indirect heat from fragrant wood smoldering in an electrically heated box.

Caring for Your Grill

Grills are low-maintenance tools but do require some attention. With a little regular care, your grill will cook efficiently and cleanly for many years.

• Before you begin to cook, brush the rack or grid with oil to help keep food from sticking and to make cleanup easier.

• While the grill is still hot after cooking, use a long-handled wire brush to scrape off any food particles stuck to the rack.

• Don't let ashes accumulate in a charcoal grill. Clean out the fire pan frequently.

• After a gas grill has cooled completely, sort through its lava rocks or ceramic briquettes, dislodging and removing any bits of food that could clog the gas jets. Replace the rocks or briquettes if they are heavily soiled and no longer heat efficiently.

• Never line the fire bed or cooking rack with any material. Grills get very hot and any foreign substance presents a risk of catching fire. Lining a grill with aluminum foil can hinder the necessary flow of air.

• When it is not in use, protect your grill with a waterproof cover. If possible, store it in a roofed structure such as a garage.

Designed for cleaning grills, a long-handled brush has rustproof bristles and a stainless-steel scraper.

Fire-Building Basics

The most important thing to remember about building a fire for outdoor cooking is to allow yourself enough time for the fire to grow hot.

If you are using a charcoal grill, the coals need 25–30 minutes from the time you light them until they are ready for cooking. You can tell at a glance when they are sufficiently hot: they will be evenly covered in light gray ash or, in dim light at night, will glow red. Gas grills require lighting 10–15 minutes in advance, so that their lava-rock or ceramic-briquette beds heat up fully.

Charcoal Fire-Starting Options

A properly built charcoal fire ensures quick, even burning. The most basic method calls for laying a base of paraffin-saturated corn cobs or other fuel-soaked starting aids that can be ignited to start the fire. Alternatively, if an electrical outlet is safely close by, position the coil of an electric fire starter. (To avoid unpleasant fumes that can permeate food, and to limit your contribution to air pollution, do not use lighter fluid or charcoal that has been presaturated with lighter fluid.)

On top of the starting aids, arrange a compact pyramid of charcoal pieces, building it large enough to cover the bottom of the fire pan in an even bed adequate for the cooking method you'll be using. Then, use a match to ignite the starting aids, or plug in the electric starter.

Alternatively, try an efficient chimney-type fire starter. Put the vented sheet-metal cylinder on the fire-bed grate. Stuff crumpled newspaper into the bottom of the chimney and pile the charcoal on top. Then, light the paper. The coals should be ready in about 20 minutes.

Whichever method you use, once the coals are ready, they must be spread in the fire pan as required by the cooking method. Chimney starters have heatproof handles that let you dump and spread the coals. If you have ignited them in a pyramid, use long metal tongs with a heatproof handle to spread the coals while keeping yourself safely clear of them.

Various devices and methods may be used to start a fire in a charcoal grill (clockwise from left). A chimney fire starter offers one of the simplest, most ecologically sound ways to get coals glowing brightly. Paraffin-saturated corn cobs are buried in charcoal or wood and then are lighted for easy, nontoxic fire starting that is free of fumes. An electric starter, like the corn cobs, is placed under the coals. Long, sturdy, moisture-proof wooden kitchen matches that will strike on any surface are the best choice for outdoor cooking.

Firing Up a Gas Grill

For cooks using a gas grill, starting the fire is easy. First, open the lid of the grill and make sure that the burner controls are turned off. If you are using fuel from a propane tank, make sure the tank has fuel. Then turn on the valve.

Light the grill following the manufacturer's instructions. If your gas grill does not have an automatic spark-inducing ignition button, use long wooden fireplace matches to ignite the gas jets. Then close the lid and let the bed of lava rock or ceramic briquettes heat for 10–15 minutes.

Controlling Heat and Flare-Ups

Take care to check food during cooking, as the heat of the fire will affect cooking time. You can regulate the heat in a charcoal grill by moving the coals with long-handled metal tongs. Push the coals closer together to intensify the heat, or spread them out to cool down the fire.

Vents serve the same purpose. Open the vents on a charcoal grill to feed oxygen to the fire and thus increase the cooking temperature. Partially close the vents if you need less heat. Before you start cooking on a charcoal grill, make sure to adjust the air vents as suggested in specific recipes.

Regulating cooking temperatures on a gas grill is easier. Simply use its dials to raise or lower the heat as needed.

When dripping fat causes flames to flare up during grilling, some cooks control them by dousing them with water from a spray bottle. Bear in mind, however, that steam from flames sprayed too close to you can cause burns, plus cold water can crack the finish of a hot grill. A safer and more prudent method of halting flare-ups is simply to cover the grill and close its vents.

Direct Versus Indirect Heat

Before you begin grilling, determine whether you'll need direct or indirect heat. For either method, once the fire bed is ready, set the metal rack or grid on which the food will cook 4–6 inches (10–15 cm) above the heat.

Foods cooked with direct heat are placed directly over the hot coals or burners of a grill. Use this method for searing and for grilling small or thin food items that take less than 25 minutes to cook, including some poultry pieces, steaks, chops, burgers, sausages, fish fillets, and kabobs.

To set up a direct-heat fire in a charcoal grill, use long-handled metal tongs, a long poker, or another safe tool to spread hot coals evenly across the area of the fire pan directly below where the food will sit. For a direct-heat fire in a gas grill, heat the burners beneath the rack on which you plan to cook.

Indirect heat cooks foods by reflected heat, much like roasting in an oven. Use this method for grilling larger pieces of food such as a boneless leg of lamb or a whole chicken. Heat circulating inside the grill cooks the food more slowly and evenly, although you may turn the food partway through the cooking time to ensure uniform cooking and to distribute appetizing grill marks.

To set up an indirect-heat fire in a charcoal grill, place a drip pan (an aluminum-foil roasting pan is ideal) on the fire grate and use long-handled tongs to position the hot coals around the edge of the pan. Then put the food directly on the grill rack over the pan and cover the grill. For foods that require 40 minutes or more of cooking time, light a second batch of coals in another grill or other fireproof container and use them to replenish the fire as the first batch of coals dies out.

For an indirect-heat fire in a gas grill, first heat the grill using all the burners, then turn off any burners directly beneath where the food will cook and put a drip pan on the fire grate. Replace the grill rack, put the food over the drip pan, and adjust the burners on either side of the food to equal amounts of heat.

Fire Safety

Whenever you grill, keep the following important safety points in mind.

• From the moment you ignite the coals to the moment you dispose of the cooled ashes, never leave your grill unwatched or unattended.

• Always keep children and pets safely away from the grill.

• Do not wear loose clothing when grilling, and if you have long hair, tie it back.

• Always use your grill out in the open on a level surface, well clear of enclosures, overhangs, or anything combustible.

• Use only fire starters specifically designed for grill use. Other fuels, such as kerosene or gasoline, should not be placed anywhere near an outdoor grill.

• Do not use chimney or electric-coil starters with instant-lighting briquettes.

• If using an electric-coil starter, as soon as the coals are lit, unplug it and place it on a fireproof surface, well clear of anything flammable or of anyone who might accidentally touch it, until completely cool. Follow the same precautions for a chimney starter.

Direct-heat cooking is ideal for searing and for cooking relatively thin pieces of food. In this method on a charcoal grill, the hot coals are spread uniformly across the fire pan beneath the grill rack.

Indirect-heat cooking is used for large items of food, such as a whole chicken, that require long, slow, even grilling. The hot coals are placed along the perimeter of the fire pan, surrounding a drip pan, and the food is arranged in the center of the grill rack. The grill is usually covered so food cooks slowly in the radiant heat.

Fuels and Aromatics

An array of choices faces the outdoor cook when it comes to fuels and other sources of heat and fragrant smoke. Some knowledge of their properties will help you make a smart selection.

Options for Charcoal

The most widely available fuel choice for a charcoal grill is charcoal briquettes. These compact, uniform, square pillow-shaped lumps of fuel are made by compressing pulverized charcoal with binding agents and additives that facilitate lighting and burning. They make a good fire and are easy to use, providing steady, spark-free heat. But the binding agents they include can leave an unpleasant aftertaste in food. By all means, avoid self-igniting briquettes, which may violate air-quality control standards in your area.

Hardwood charcoal, also sold in bags, makes a hotter, cleaner-burning fire. These lumps of fragrant hardwood—such as hickory, alder, oak, apple, pecan, or cherry—have been burned until they are charred to almost pure carbon. Break large chunks of hardwood charcoal into

smaller, more uniform pieces before lighting the fire, to ensure that the charcoal heats evenly. Keep a careful eye on the fire, however, as the charcoal will throw off some sparks at first.

Options for Gas

For most gas grills, propane is the fuel of choice. You can find already-filled tanks of this clean-burning gas in hardware stores and specialty grill stores. One tank will last for many hours of cooking, but it's a good idea to have a spare tank on hand. Look for dealers who will refill empty tanks or exchange filled ones for empty ones at a reasonable price. When propane tanks are not in use, store them away from direct sunlight, but keep them out of garages or other enclosed storage areas. Read and follow all precautions printed on the tank or attached flyers.

It is also possible to hook up a gas grill to a natural-gas line in your patio. Note that gas grills need to be mechanically adapted to burn that type of fuel efficiently and provide adequate cooking heat. Have a professional from a specialty grill store do the hookup and adaptation for you.

Vine cuttings can be soaked and spread over hot coals to add fruity flavor to grilled foods.

Charcoal briquettes are the most common fuel used for kettle grills, hibachis, and other charcoal grills. Store them in a dry place.

Hardwood charcoal, consisting of already burned hardwood, makes a hot, clean-burning fire. Like briquettes, hardwood charcoal should be stored in a dry place.

Dried basil stems, soaked and then spread over hot coals, create basil-scented smoke.

Where There's Smoke, There's Flavor

Cooking on a grill itself contributes some flavor in the form of smoke that rises from small flare-ups caused by fat and juices dripping into the fire. More flavor still can be added through the smoke from aromatic wood chips or twigs, as well as from dried herbs scattered loose over the coals or packaged in special bags.

Chips of aromatic woods, first soaked in water, are spread over glowing coals to imbue food with their aromatic smoke. Each type has its own character: (clockwise from left) mesquite chips, hickory chips, apple wood chips, alder chips.

Choose aromatic additions to complement food as you would choose spices or herbs. Mesquite, hickory, alder, apple, and pecan woods, as well as grapevine trimmings, deliver wisps of rich, sweet flavor. Woody herbs such as rosemary, oregano, thyme, and dried basil stems also contribute their familiar flavors, whether used on their own or blended. Such herbs may sometimes be found packaged in bags resembling tea bags, for a mess-free addition to a fire. Consider, too, using large, sturdy rosemary twigs as skewers for kabobs.

Before use, soak wood chips or herbs in water for 30–60 minutes, then drain them well. With a charcoal grill, add them directly to the coals while the food cooks, timing the addition so the flavor of the smoke they generate enhances but does not dominate whatever you are cooking. Robust meats, for example, can take longer smoking, while just a few minutes of smoke toward the end of cooking may be sufficient for milder-tasting seafood.

To use wood chips or herbs with a gas grill, look for a small, vented metal smoker box into which the soaked aromatics may be put for placing directly on the lava rocks or ceramic briquettes. The box will prevent small particles from clogging the fuel ports.

Smoking herbs, used for creating scented smoke, come loose or bagged.

Accessories and Tools

Cookware shops and hardware stores offer a vast array of tools and gadgets designed to make grilling easier. A few are essential, some are quite useful, and others are just plain fun. Shown here are a handful of accessories to consider acquiring for your outdoor kitchen.

Oven Mittens to Thermometers

Everyone needs an oven mitt and a potholder made of heavy, quilted cotton, with one side treated for fire resistance, to protect hands from intense heat during cooking. A leather barbecue glove, with an extension that shields the cook's forearm from the heat, provides maximum protection from heat when cooking over large grills or intense fires. Although it has its drawbacks (see Controlling Heat and Flare-Ups, page 10), an adjustable sprayer filled with water for quick dousing of flames is indispensable to some outdoor cooks.

An instant-read thermometer will let you measure the doneness of large cuts of meat or poultry in seconds, and a grill thermometer attaches magnetically to a grill rack or grid to measure surface temperature. A flashlight with a high-intensity beam, for example, helps you see what you're cooking after dark.

A large, heavy-duty apron guards clothing from splatters, and its pockets may be used to hold small tools. A good-sized basket made of wicker or other sturdy materials will conveniently and efficiently hold all your outdoor cooking accessories together in one place.

Basting Brushes

Long-handled brushes make it easy and safe to coat food with marinades or sauces while they cook. Brushes with shorter handles work fine for coating foods with marinades or glazes in the kitchen, before they go on the grill. Select one or more brushes with long natural bristles that are well attached to a sturdy handle.

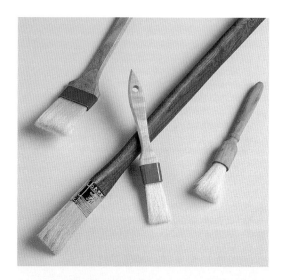

Basting brushes are useful for coating foods before and during grilling. Be sure to choose brushes with well-attached bristles.

Grill Screens

An incredibly versatile grilling tool, grill screens are ideal for cooking any foods that might otherwise fall between the spaces in your grill rack or grid. This might include shrimp (prawns) or scallops or small pieces of vegetables. They also work great for cooking pizzas on the grill. Made of fine wire mesh held together by a sturdy frame, or of heavy perforated metal, they are placed directly on top of the grill grid. Brush the screen with oil to help keep foods from sticking, then let it heat for a minute before adding the food.

Grill screens, placed directly on the grill rack, have small holes that allow heat to come through while preventing food from falling into the fire.

Skewers

A good set of skewers is essential equipment for grilling kabobs. If you've been frustrated by food spinning on traditional round skewers, you'll appreciate flat-edged metal ones that keep items in place when you turn them on the grill. Look, also, for double skewers, with parallel pairs of stainless-steel rods that anchor large, oddly shaped items.

If you use wooden or bamboo skewers, soak them in water for at least 15–30 minutes before loading to help prevent them from burning.

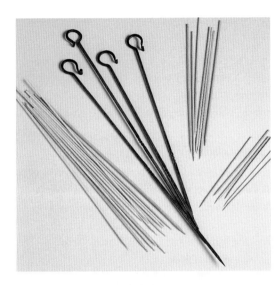

Various types of skewers, made from stainless steel, wood, or bamboo, are available for grilling. Also popular are double skewers, which stabilize large, awkward-shaped pieces of food.

Long-Handled Grill Utensils

Sturdy tools with long, well-insulated handles are used to turn and move food around on the grill while keeping your hands and arms at a safe distance from the heat. A two-pronged fork is handy for spearing and moving large or awkwardly shaped foods.

No grill cook should be without tongs, for placing on the grill such foods as chicken, ribs, and sausages, turning them, and removing them when they are done. A second pair of tongs is especially useful for rearranging or moving hot coals.

Spatulas are practical to have if you cook a lot of burgers, small steaks, fish fillets, or chops, and they are especially good for loosening foods stuck to the grill rack. Grill-cleaning brushes with rustproof metal bristles and stainless-steel scrapers scrape away residue from hot grill grids before or after cooking.

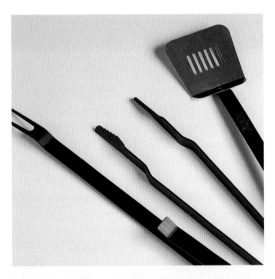

Tongs, spatulas, and other tools with long handles allow the cook to move foods on the grill while keeping hands safely away from the fire.

Grill Baskets

Made in a variety of shapes and sizes, with a pair of hinged wire grids that can be latched shut, these baskets simplify grilling delicate foods like large fish fillets or whole fish, which often stick to the grill and can fall apart when being turned. Use them, too, for grilling small foods such as cherry tomatoes and asparagus that might fall through the grid into the fire.

Choose grill baskets with long, heat-proof handles to facilitate safe turning. To help prevent sticking, brush the inside surfaces of their grids with oil before placing food inside.

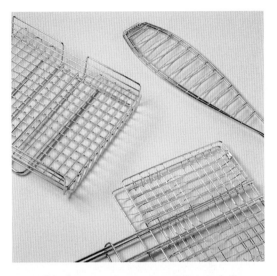

Grill baskets come in a variety of sizes, including elongated constructions that hold whole fish and small rectangles that secure hamburgers.

Grilling Times and Tips

The intensity of a grill's heat and the simple change of scene from kitchen to backyard can sometimes cause uncertainty over how long certain foods need to cook to the desired degree of doneness. The information and chart shown here provide some general guidelines for direct-heat grilling. For indirect-heat grilling, which takes longer, refer to instructions in specific recipes.

Remember that some simple tools and common sense can also help. For meats and poultry, arm yourself with an instant-read thermometer that will quickly gauge the internal temperature of a piece of food. And nothing beats the information you gain by cutting into a steak, chop, burger, or fish fillet with a sharp knife, or the edge of a spatula, to see if it is cooked through to your liking.

When referring to the chart that follows, always bear in mind that times will vary with the particular type of grill and fuel you are using and the particular ingredients you have chosen. No chart information is a substitute for what your own senses and judgment tell you.

Seafood

Fish should be cooked until it flakes when a knife is inserted into the flesh. Count on an average of 8–10 minutes per inch (2.5 cm) of thickness. Shrimp (prawns) should be cooked until uniformly opaque throughout. Clams, mussels, and oysters should be well scrubbed before cooking. Discard any that are not tightly closed. They should be cooked just until their shells open. Discard any that do not open.

Poultry

Chicken and turkey are done when they are cooked through completely, with no trace of pink remaining at the bone or at the center of boneless pieces. When pieces are pierced with a long-handled fork, the juices should run clear. The doneness of larger poultry pieces may also be checked with an instant-read thermometer inserted into the center of the meat, away from the bone; it should register 165–170°F (74–77°C) for white meat, 180°F (82°C) for dark meat.

Meat

To assess the doneness of meat on a grill visually, cut into the thickest part of one serving. Rare meat will look rosy pink in the center, medium-rare will be light pink in the center, and medium will have just a trace of pink. Cooking meat beyond medium runs the risk of it drying out and turning tough. (Burgers are an exception; for safety's sake, they should be cooked no less than medium, and many health experts say it is wiser to cook them at least medium-well.) If using an instant-read thermometer stuck into the thickest part of a piece of meat away from the bone, aim for 120–125°F (49–52°C) for rare meat, 130°F (54°C) for medium-rare, and 140°F (60°C) for medium. Pork should be cooked to 150–160°F (65–71°C).

Food Safety

To guard against food-borne illness from bacteria or molds, keep the following pointers in mind when cooking outdoors:

• Thaw wisely. If the food you plan to cook is frozen, defrost it completely in the refrigerator or microwave, never at room temperature.

• Inspect your ingredients. Throw out anything that looks or smells in any way suspicious. Check sell-by and use-by dates on packaging.

• Use clean equipment. Work with clean utensils, dish towels, and other accessories, both indoors and outdoors.

• Use clean hands. Especially before and after handling raw meat, poultry, or seafood, always wash your hands with lots of warm, soapy water, then dry with a clean towel.

• Avoid cross-contamination. Do not return cooked food to the unwashed platters or plates on which they sat when raw. If basting with a marinade in which raw food sat, bring the liquid to a boil in a saucepan before using or stop using the basting liquid at least 5 minutes before cooking concludes.

• Cook to doneness. Follow suggested cooking times, visual cues, and internal temperatures to make sure food is cooked long enough to kill any bacteria.

• Refrigerate leftovers. Don't leave leftover food standing at room temperature. Cover loosely and refrigerate promptly, then cover securely once it has cooled completely.

Grilling Chart

Seafood

TYPE	SIZE	HEAT	DONENESS	COOKING TIME
FISH FILLETS	½–1½ inches/12 mm–4 cm	Medium	Flesh just flakes	2–8 minutes per side
WHOLE FISH	¾–1½ lb/375–750 g	Medium	Flesh just flakes	6–15 minutes per side
SHRIMP	Medium (16–20/lb/500 g)	Medium	Opaque	2–4 minutes per side
	Jumbo (12–15/lb/500 g)	Medium	Opaque	3–6 minutes per side
SEA SCALLOPS	Medium (12–14/lb/500 g)	Medium	Opaque	2–4 minutes per side
LOBSTER TAILS	½ lb (250 g)	Medium	Opaque	8–10 minutes per side
OYSTERS, CLAMS, MUSSELS	Various	Hot	Until shells open	4–6 minutes

Poultry

TYPE	SIZE	HEAT	DONENESS	COOKING TIME
CHICKEN PIECES, BONE-IN				
Dark Meat	10 oz/315 g	Medium	Opaque, no pink at bone	12–15 minutes per side
Breasts	10 oz/315 g	Medium	Opaque, no pink at bone	10–12 minutes per side
CHICKEN BREAST HALVES, BONELESS	4–5 oz/125–155 g	Medium	Opaque throughout	6–8 minutes per side
TURKEY BREAST CUTLETS	4–6 oz/125–185 g	Medium	Opaque throughout	6–8 minutes per side
DUCK BREASTS	4 oz/125 g	Medium	Pink at center	5–6 minutes per side

Meat

TYPE	SIZE	HEAT	DONENESS	COOKING TIME
BEEF				
Flank Steak	¾–1 inch/2–2.5 cm thick	Medium	Medium-rare to medium	5–7 minutes per side
Other Steaks	1–2 inches/2.5–5 cm thick	Medium	Rare to medium	5–12 minutes per side
Hamburgers	1–2 inches/2.5–5 cm thick	Medium	Medium-rare to medium	5–12 minutes per side
VEAL CHOPS	1–1½ inches/2.5–4 cm thick	Medium	Medium to well done	9–15 minutes per side
LAMB CHOPS	1–2 inches/2.5–5 cm thick	Medium	Medium-rare to medium	5–10 minutes per side
PORK				
Chops	¾–1½ inches/2–4 cm thick	Medium	Medium (barely pink)	5–15 minutes per side
Cutlets	½ inch/12 mm thick	Medium-hot	Medium (barely pink)	3–4 minutes per side
Tenderloin	10–12 oz/315–375 g	Medium	Medium (barely pink)	12–15 minutes total
Sausages, Raw	4–6 oz/125–185 g	Medium	Cooked through	6–8 minutes per side
Sausages, Cooked	4–6 oz/125–185 g	Medium	Heated through	2–3 minutes per side
Ham Steak, Fully Cooked	1 inch/2.5 cm thick	Medium	Heated through	10–12 minutes per side

Menus

The recipes in this book can be combined in a variety of ways to make delicious outdoor meals. The menus suggested here offer only a handful of the many possible combinations. When planning any grilling menu, consider whether you'd like to grill more than one course or whether you'd prefer to accompany the grilled main dish with sides and salads from the kitchen. If you plan to grill a side dish or two, look for those that can be cooked at the same time as the main course. Grilled desserts, which generally require low heat, should be cooked after the other items, when the coals have died down. This book also includes make-ahead recipes for desserts from the kitchen to complete your outdoor menu.

Mediterranean Feast

Prosciutto-Wrapped Figs Stuffed
with Smoked Mozzarella
Page 157

Lamb and Eggplant Brochettes
with Provençal Dressing
Page 174

Couscous Salad with Cucumber,
Peppers, and Tomatoes
Page 228

Dark Chocolate Gelato
Page 285

Seafood Celebration

Oysters with
Soy-Citrus Vinaigrette
Page 60

Salmon with Sour Orange
and Red Onion Mojo
Page 35

Mixed Green Salad
Page 233

Pound Cake
with Raspberry Sauce
Page 250

Down-Home Barbecue

🔥 🔥 🔥

Hickory-Smoked Ribs
Page 158

Corn with Seasoned Butters
Page 204

Boston Baked Beans
Page 237

**Cabbage Salad
with Cumin Seeds**
Page 228

Vegetarian Supper

🔥 🔥 🔥

**Vegetable Skewers with
Romesco Sauce**
Page 197

Polenta Wedges
Page 210

Saganaki
Page 222

**Mixed Summer
Fruit Compote**
Page 270

Asian Flavors

🔥 🔥 🔥

**Pacific Rim Chicken
with Peanut Sauce**
Page 88

Red Ginger Slaw
Page 230

**Tropical Fruits with
Toasted Coconut**
Page 258

Seafood

Fish

When fish meets a hot grill, its delicate, translucent flesh becomes deliciously smoky and charred—the perfect partner for a vast array of sauces, relishes, and garnishes. You will find a recipe here to fit a menu for nearly every time of the year. Halibut with Red Pepper Butter would be a welcome centerpiece on any autumn table. In spring, Trout with Prosciutto and Sage makes a wonderful weekend lunch, while Greek-Style Whole Bass with Olives and Feta is ideal fare for dining under shade trees on a hot summer afternoon.

Halibut with Grilled Pipérade

SERVES 4

Pipérade *is a relishlike mixture of cooked vegetables from the Basque region of southern France. It is especially good with grilled tuna, swordfish, and chicken breasts, providing both garden-fresh color and flavor.*

FOR THE PIPÉRADE:

1 large yellow or red (Spanish) onion, cut crosswise into slices ½ inch (12 mm) thick
1 red bell pepper (capsicum), seeded, deribbed, and cut crosswise into rings ½ inch (12 mm) thick
1 green bell pepper (capsicum), seeded, deribbed, and cut crosswise into rings ½ inch (12 mm) thick
¼ cup (2 fl oz/60 ml) olive oil
salt to taste, plus ½ teaspoon freshly ground pepper to taste
2 tablespoons chopped fresh thyme or 1 teaspoon dried thyme
2 tablespoons chopped fresh parsley

FOR THE FISH:

4 halibut fillets, 6–8 oz (185–250 g) each and about 1 inch (2.5 cm) thick
4 teaspoons olive oil
salt and freshly ground pepper to taste

Prepare a fire in a grill.

To prepare the *pipérade,* arrange the onion slices and bell pepper rings on the grill rack. Brush lightly with some of the olive oil and sprinkle with salt and pepper. Grill for about 4 minutes, then turn and again brush lightly with oil. Continue to grill until lightly browned, about 4 minutes longer. Transfer the vegetables to a large bowl and add the ½ teaspoon salt, the thyme, and the parsley. Toss with a fork to combine, then set aside while you proceed immediately with the fish.

To prepare the fish, rub lightly with the olive oil and sprinkle with salt and pepper. Arrange on the grill rack. Grill, turning once, until just opaque throughout, about 10 minutes total.

To serve, spread the *pipérade* on a warmed platter or individual plates and top with the fish. Serve immediately.

Snapper with Cilantro Butter

SERVES 4

True red snapper comes from the Gulf of Mexico and the Atlantic coast, from the Carolinas south to Brazil.

FOR THE BUTTER:

¼ cup (2 oz/60 g) unsalted butter, at room temperature

3 tablespoons chopped fresh cilantro (fresh coriander)

1½ tablespoons fresh lemon or lime juice

1 teaspoon grated lemon or lime zest

¼ teaspoon salt

pinch of freshly ground pepper

FOR THE FISH:

2 lb (1 kg) red snapper fillets, cut into 4 equal pieces each about 1 inch (2.5 cm) thick

vegetable oil

salt and freshly ground pepper to taste

To prepare the butter, combine the butter, cilantro, lemon or lime juice and zest, salt, and pepper in a bowl and beat by hand with a wooden spoon. Shape into a rough log about 2 inches (5 cm) long and 1 inch (2.5 cm) in diameter, wrap in plastic wrap, and chill until firm.

🌿 Prepare a fire in a grill.

🌿 Rub the fish lightly with oil and sprinkle with salt and pepper. Arrange the fish on the grill rack. Grill, turning once, until just opaque throughout, about 10 minutes.

🌿 Transfer to a warmed platter or individual plates. Cut the cilantro butter into 4 equal slices and top each fillet with a slice. Serve at once.

Tuna with Beet Relish

SERVES 4

Cooked beet relish is reminiscent of a gingery sweet-hot chutney. Its flavor is a good match for turkey or pork, too.

FOR THE RELISH:

2 large beets

½ lemon, cut into chunks and seeds removed

1 piece fresh ginger, 3–4 inches (7.5–10 cm) long, peeled and thinly sliced

½ cup (4 oz/125 g) sugar

¼ cup (⅓ oz/10 g) chopped fresh parsley

FOR THE FISH:

4 tuna steaks, 6–8 oz (185–250 g) each and about 1 inch (2.5 cm) thick

2 tablespoons olive oil or vegetable oil

salt and freshly ground pepper to taste

lemon wedges

To prepare the relish, trim off the stems from the beets, leaving ½ inch (12 mm) intact; do not peel. Place the beets in a saucepan, add water to cover, and bring to a boil. Reduce the heat to low, cover, and simmer until tender when pierced, 30–40 minutes. Drain and, when cool enough to handle, cut off the stems and root ends and peel off the skins. Cut into large chunks and let cool.

🌿 In a food processor, combine the lemon and ginger and process until finely chopped. Scrape the mixture into a saucepan. Add the beets to the food processor, process to chop coarsely, and add them to the saucepan. Stir in the sugar.

🌿 Place the saucepan over medium heat and cook, stirring constantly, until the sugar has dissolved and the mixture has thickened slightly, about 4 minutes. Stir in the parsley. Transfer to a bowl to cool; cover and refrigerate until serving.

🌿 Prepare a fire in a grill.

🌿 To prepare the fish, pat dry with paper towels. Rub the steaks on both sides with the oil and sprinkle with salt and pepper. Arrange the fish on the grill rack. Grill, turning once, until just opaque throughout, 8–10 minutes, or less to your taste.

🌿 To serve, transfer to warmed individual plates. Place a spoonful of relish on each piece of fish and garnish with lemon wedges. Serve at once.

Swordfish with Tomatillo Salsa

SERVES 4

Because of its firm, meaty texture, sword-fish is perfect for grilling, and a zesty tomatillo salsa provides a nice contrast. Two or three ripe red tomatoes may be substituted for the tomatillos.

FOR THE SALSA:

6 fresh tomatillos
1 small red (Spanish) onion, cut into chunks
2 cloves garlic, cut into pieces
1 large Anaheim chile or other mild green chile, seeded and cut into pieces
½ red or green jalapeño chile, seeded and cut into pieces
4 or 5 fresh cilantro (fresh coriander) sprigs
salt to taste

FOR THE FISH:

4 swordfish steaks, 6–8 oz (185–250 g) each and about 1 inch (2.5 cm) thick
2 tablespoons vegetable oil
salt and freshly ground pepper to taste

To prepare the salsa, remove and discard the papery husks from the tomatillos. Chop the tomatillos coarsely. In a food processor, combine the tomatillos, onion, garlic, chiles, and cilantro. Process just until coarsely chopped and transfer to a bowl. Or chop all of the ingredients coarsely by hand and combine them in a bowl. Season with salt and set aside.

Prepare a fire in a grill.

Rub the fish steaks with the oil and sprinkle with salt and pepper. Arrange the steaks on the grill rack. Grill, turning once, until just opaque throughout, about 10 minutes.

Transfer to a warmed platter, place a spoonful of salsa on each steak, and serve. Pass the remaining salsa at the table.

Halibut with Red Pepper Butter

SERVES 4

Halibut has a delicate taste that contrasts nicely with this lively pepper butter. Peeled red bell peppers, available in jars, have sim-plified the preparation of anything calling for peppers "roasted and peeled." Serve with Polenta Wedges (page 210).

FOR THE BUTTER:

¼ cup (2 oz/60 g) unsalted butter, at room temperature
3 tablespoons chopped, roasted, and peeled red bell pepper (capsicum)
1 teaspoon chili powder
¼ teaspoon red pepper flakes
¼ teaspoon salt

FOR THE FISH:

4 halibut steaks, 6–8 oz (185–250 g) each and about 1 inch (2.5 cm) thick
vegetable oil
salt and freshly ground black pepper to taste

To prepare the butter, in a small bowl, combine the butter, roasted bell pepper, chili powder, red pepper flakes, and salt and beat by hand with a wooden spoon. Shape into a rough log 2 inches (5 cm) long and 1 inch (2.5 cm) in diameter, wrap in plastic wrap, and refrigerate until firm.

Prepare a fire in a grill.

Rub the fish lightly with oil and sprinkle with salt and black pepper. Arrange the fish on the grill rack. Grill, turning once, until just opaque throughout, about 10 minutes.

Transfer the fish to warmed individ-ual plates. Cut the pepper butter into 4 equal slices and top each fish steak with a slice. Serve at once.

Swordfish Drizzled with Balsamic-Butter Sauce

SERVES 6

The distinctive flavor of swordfish is enhanced here by the sweet-tart character of balsamic vinegar. Cod or grouper can be substituted for the swordfish. Serve with a salad of orzo flecked with dried currants.

¼ cup (2 fl oz/60 ml) balsamic vinegar
¾ cup (6 oz/185 g) unsalted butter, at
    room temperature, cut into pieces

6 swordfish steaks, 5–6 oz (155–185 g)
    each and ½ inch (12 mm) thick
olive oil
salt and freshly ground pepper to taste

Prepare a fire in a grill.

🔥 In a small saucepan over medium heat, bring the vinegar to a boil and boil until reduced to about 2 tablespoons, about 5 minutes. Remove from the heat and transfer to the top pan of a double boiler or a heatproof bowl placed over (not touching) hot water in a saucepan.

Whisk in the butter, a few pieces at a time, until it is fully incorporated. Keep warm until ready to serve.

🔥 Brush the fish steaks on both sides with olive oil and season with salt and pepper. Arrange the fish on the grill rack and grill, turning once, until just opaque throughout, 4–6 minutes total.

🔥 Transfer to warmed individual plates and spoon the balsamic sauce over the top, dividing evenly. Serve at once.

Greek-Style Whole Bass with Olives and Feta

SERVES 6

Grilled fish similar to this recipe are enjoyed in sun-drenched villages through-out Greece. Substitute red snapper or trout for the bass, if you like, and serve with warm pita bread and yogurt flavored with minced garlic.

½ cup (4 fl oz/125 ml) fresh lemon
  juice
⅓ cup (3 fl oz/80 ml) olive oil
1 tablespoon chopped fresh oregano
3 whole bass, about 1¼ lb (625 g)
  each, cleaned
leaves from 1 bunch fresh parsley,
  chopped
1 large yellow onion, chopped
1 cup (5 oz/155 g) Kalamata olives,
  pitted
½ lb (250 g) feta cheese, crumbled

Prepare a fire in a covered grill.

In a small bowl, stir together the lemon juice, olive oil, and oregano.

Make 2 diagonal slits on both sides of each fish, cutting into the fleshiest part. Brush the fish on both sides with the oil mixture. Place on the grill rack, cover, open the vents, and cook, turning once, until the fish are just opaque throughout, about 10 minutes total.

Just before the fish are ready, arrange the parsley and the onion on a warmed platter. Transfer the fish to the platter, placing them on top of the parsley and onion. Sprinkle the olives and cheese over the fish. Serve at once.

Fish in Indian Ginger Masala

SERVES 4

This zesty Indian spice rub will perk up the blandest white fish or stand up to a meaty fish like tuna. Do not marinate for more than an hour, or the acidity of the ginger will break down the texture of the fish. Serve with rice and lentils or cauliflower braised in a curried onion and tomato base. Or accompany with saffron rice and sautéed spinach.

4 meaty fish fillets such as tuna, shark, or swordfish, or firm white fish fillets such as halibut, sea bass, or flounder, 5–6 oz (155–185 g) each

1 piece fresh ginger, about 2 inches (5 cm) long, peeled and sliced

6 cloves garlic, chopped

2 or 3 jalapeño chiles, seeded and sliced

1 large yellow onion, chopped (about 1¼ cups/5 oz/155 g)

1 teaspoon ground turmeric

¼ cup (2 fl oz/60 ml) fresh lemon juice, white wine vinegar, or rice vinegar

¼ cup (2 fl oz/60 ml) olive oil, plus extra oil for brushing

salt and freshly ground pepper to taste

lime or lemon wedges

Place the fish fillets in a shallow nonaluminum dish.

In a blender or food processor, combine the ginger, garlic, chiles, and onion. Purée until smooth. Add the turmeric and lemon juice or vinegar and blend well. Transfer to a bowl and stir in the ¼ cup (2 fl oz/60 ml) olive oil; season with salt.

Pour this mixture evenly over the fish fillets. Cover and marinate for 1 hour at room temperature.

Prepare a fire in a grill.

Remove the fish fillets from the marinade and brush on both sides with olive oil. Sprinkle with salt and pepper. Arrange the fish on the grill rack. Grill, turning once, until just opaque throughout, about 8 minutes total. (If using tuna, it may be cooked less, to your taste.)

Transfer to warmed individual plates and serve immediately with lime or lemon wedges.

North African Fish Kabob

SERVES 4

You can use this spicy marinade for a whole fish as well: Cut a few shallow diagonal slashes in the fleshiest part on both sides of the fish and rub well with the marinade. Place in a shallow glass or ceramic dish, cover, and marinate for 1 hour at room temperature or 3–5 hours in the refrigerator. Serve the cooked fish with couscous or with roasted or fried potatoes sprinkled with a little ground cumin and freshly ground pepper.

3 cloves garlic, finely minced

1 tablespoon ground cumin

1 teaspoon freshly ground black pepper, plus pepper to taste

3 tablespoons fresh lemon juice

⅓ cup (3 fl oz/80 ml) olive oil, plus extra oil for brushing

¼ cup (⅓ oz/10 g) chopped fresh mint

2 tablespoons chopped fresh marjoram

pinch of cayenne pepper (optional)

1½ lb (750 g) fish fillets such as swordfish, snapper, mackerel, or tuna, cut into ¾–1-inch (2–2.5-cm) cubes

salt to taste

In a shallow nonaluminum dish, mix together the garlic, cumin, the 1 teaspoon black pepper, lemon juice, ⅓ cup (3 fl oz/80 ml) olive oil, mint, marjoram, and cayenne, if using. Add the fish cubes and toss to coat well. Cover and marinate for 1 hour at room temperature or in the refrigerator for 2–3 hours.

Prepare a fire in a grill.

Thread the fish onto skewers and brush with a little olive oil. Sprinkle with salt and pepper. Arrange the fish on the grill rack. Grill, turning once, until just opaque throughout, about 8 minutes total. (If using tuna, it may be cooked less, to your taste.)

Transfer to warmed individual plates and serve at once.

Anise-Marinated Fish

SERVES 4

The flavors of the Aegean permeate this dish. If you cannot find ouzo, the Greek anise-flavored liqueur, French Pernod will add a similar perfume. This marinade also would work well on a whole fish such as a 2½–3-lb (1.25–1.5-kg) snapper or rock cod. Cut a few shallow diagonal slashes in the fleshiest part on both sides of the fish, so that it can absorb the marinade, then cook for about 10 minutes on each side. Serve with panfried potatoes topped with crumbled feta cheese and chopped Kalamata olives.

5 tablespoons (2½ fl oz/75 ml) olive oil
1½ tablespoons finely minced garlic
1 tablespoon dried oregano
2 teaspoons chopped fresh thyme
grated zest of 1 lemon
2 tablespoons fresh lemon juice
¼ cup (2 fl oz/60 ml) ouzo or other
    anise-flavored liqueur
salt and freshly ground pepper to taste
4 firm fish fillets such as swordfish or
    sea bass, 5–6 oz (155–185 g) each
lemon wedges

In a small sauté pan over low heat, warm 4 tablespoons (2 fl oz/60 ml) of the olive oil. Add the garlic and oregano and simmer for about 2 minutes. Remove from the heat and transfer to a bowl. Stir in the thyme, lemon zest and juice, ouzo or other liqueur, salt, and pepper. Let cool completely.

Place the fish fillets in a shallow nonaluminum container and pour the cooled mixture over the fish. Turn the fish a few times to coat evenly. Cover and marinate for 2–3 hours in the refrigerator.

Prepare a fire in a grill.

Remove the fish from the marinade and brush with the remaining 1 table-spoon olive oil. Arrange the fish on the grill rack and grill, turning once, until just opaque throughout, about 8 minutes total.

Transfer to warmed individual plates and garnish with lemon wedges. Serve at once.

Fish in Grape Leaves

SERVES 4

In countries where grapes are grown, the vine leaves are used to wrap food cooked on the grill, imparting a smoky flavor and protecting delicate fish from breaking or sticking to the grill. Jars of grape leaves packed in brine can be found in stores selling Greek and Middle Eastern foods and in well-stocked food markets. Serve with rice pilaf or bulgar pilaf and grilled eggplant (aubergine) and bell peppers (capiscums).

½ cup (4 fl oz/125 ml) extra-virgin
    olive oil
4 tablespoons (2 fl oz/60 ml) fresh
    lemon juice
2 tablespoons chopped fresh dill, parsley,
    or oregano, plus extra for serving
4 fish fillets such as salmon, swordfish,
    sea bass, or rockfish, 5–6 oz
    (155–185 g) each
8 large grape leaves, rinsed, patted dry,
    and tough stems removed
freshly ground pepper to taste
1 cup (6 oz/185 g) peeled, seeded,
    and chopped tomatoes (optional)
2 teaspoons grated lemon zest
    or orange zest

In a shallow nonaluminum container, mix together ¼ cup (2 fl oz/60 ml) of the olive oil, 2 tablespoons of the lemon juice, and the 2 tablespoons chopped herb. Add the fish, turn to coat evenly, and marinate for about 30 minutes at room temperature.

Prepare a fire in a grill.

Wrap each fish fillet in 2 grape leaves. You may secure the leaves with toothpicks, but it is probably unnecessary. Sprinkle the wrapped fish with pepper and brush with some of the remaining olive oil. Arrange the fish on the grill rack and grill, turning once, until just opaque throughout, 6–8 minutes total.

Transfer the fillets to a warmed platter. Spoon the remaining oil and the remaining 2 tablespoons lemon juice over the fish packets. Top with the tomatoes, if desired, the citrus zest, and more herbs. Serve at once.

Salmon with Sour Orange and Red Onion Mojo

SERVES 4

FOR THE MOJO:

finely chopped zest of 1 orange
2 tablespoons fresh orange juice
1 tablespoon fresh lime juice
½ small red (Spanish) onion, sliced
2 large cloves garlic, minced
¾ cup (¾ oz/20 g) fresh flat-leaf
    (Italian) parsley leaves
½ teaspoon salt
¼ teaspoon freshly ground pepper
3 tablespoons extra-virgin olive oil

FOR THE FISH:

4 center-cut salmon fillets with skin
    intact, each 6–7 oz (185–220 g) and
    1¼ inches (3 cm) thick
olive oil
salt and freshly ground pepper to taste

Prepare a fire in a grill.

To prepare the mojo, in a food processor, combine the orange zest, orange and lime juices, onion, garlic, parsley, salt, pepper, and olive oil. Pulse briefly to combine the ingredients. There should still be some chunks of red onion visible. Transfer to a non-aluminum bowl and set aside.

To prepare the fish, brush lightly with olive oil and season generously with salt and pepper. Place the fillets, skin side down, on the grill rack and grill for 5 minutes. Using a metal spatula, turn and cook until firm, 3–4 minutes longer.

Transfer the fillets to warmed individual plates, scraping away the skin if it is charred and unsightly. Divide the mojo among small cups or ramekins and place one on each plate. Serve at once.

Middle Eastern Swordfish with Lemon and Thyme

SERVES 4

This fast and easy marinade for grilled swordfish can also be used with firm white fish such as sea bass or cod. Serve with rice pilaf and broiled eggplant (aubergine), zucchini (courgettes), or sautéed spinach.

1 yellow onion, coarsely chopped
2 cloves garlic, chopped
1 tablespoon ground coriander
2 teaspoons sweet paprika
pinch of cayenne pepper
¼ cup (2 fl oz/60 ml) fresh lemon juice
2 teaspoons coarsely chopped fresh
    thyme or oregano
½ cup (4 fl oz/125 ml) olive oil, plus
    extra oil
4 swordfish steaks, 5–6 oz (155–185 g)
    each
salt and freshly ground black pepper
    to taste

In a blender or food processor, combine the onion, garlic, coriander, paprika, cayenne pepper, and lemon juice. Purée until smooth and transfer to a bowl. Stir in the thyme or oregano and the ½ cup (4 fl oz/125 ml) olive oil.

Place the swordfish steaks in a shallow nonaluminum container and pour the mixture over the fish to coat evenly. Cover and marinate for 2–4 hours in the refrigerator.

Prepare a fire in a grill.

Remove the fish steaks from the marinade, brush on both sides with olive oil, and sprinkle with salt and black pepper. Arrange the fish on the grill rack and grill, turning once, until just opaque throughout, about 8 minutes total.

Transfer to a warmed platter or individual plates and serve at once.

Mediterranean Tuna Salad

SERVES 4

When you order tuna salad in a Mediterranean village, you will likely get canned tuna. If it is solid-pack albacore in good olive oil, it can be very good indeed. But since fresh tuna is generally available, why not take the time to cook a nice thick fillet? To achieve the correct balance of flavors, use a combination of mild-flavored pure olive oil and a fruitier extra-virgin oil. Take this salad in any direction you like by varying the optional additions to the vinaigrette.

FOR THE VINAIGRETTE:

2 teaspoons dried oregano or
  2 tablespoons minced fresh oregano

½ cup (4 fl oz/125 ml) mild-flavored
  olive oil

½ cup (4 fl oz/125 ml) extra-virgin
  olive oil

⅓ cup (3 fl oz/80 ml) red wine vinegar

3 tablespoons fresh lemon juice

2 cloves garlic, finely minced

¼ cup (⅓ oz/10 g) chopped fresh basil
  or mint (optional)

2 tablespoons capers, rinsed and coarsely
  chopped (optional)

2 tablespoons finely minced anchovy
  fillet (optional)

1 lb (500 g) tuna fillets

olive oil

12 small new potatoes, unpeeled, boiled
  until tender, drained, and cut in half
  or into thick rounds

4 ripe tomatoes, quartered

1 lb (500 g) green beans, trimmed,
  boiled just until tender-crisp, and
  plunged into cold water to halt
  the cooking

2 hard-boiled eggs, quartered

½ cup (2½ oz/75 g) Niçoise or
  Kalamata olives

2 green bell peppers (capsicums),
  seeded and sliced lengthwise

lettuce leaves (optional)

Prepare a fire in a grill.

To prepare the vinaigrette, if using dried oregano, place in a small, dry frying pan and toast over medium-low heat, shaking the pan occasionally, until fragrant, 2–3 minutes. Combine with all the remaining vinaigrette ingredients in a small bowl, including the basil or mint, capers, and anchovy, if using. Whisk thoroughly, then set aside.

Brush the tuna fillets on both sides with olive oil and arrange on the grill rack. Grill, turning once, to desired doneness, 4–6 minutes total for medium-rare.

Let the tuna cool completely, then cut into 1–2-inch (2.5–5-cm) chunks. Arrange the tuna, potatoes, tomatoes, drained beans, eggs, olives, and bell peppers on 4 individual plates, lined with lettuce if desired. Drizzle with the vinaigrette and serve.

Swordfish with Lime and Cilantro Sauce

SERVES 4

Firm-textured swordfish is perfect for outdoor cooking because it doesn't fall apart on the grill. This pleasantly spicy sauce enlivens the mild-flavored fish.

FOR THE SAUCE:

½ small jalapeño chile

⅓ cup (⅓ oz/10 g) chopped fresh cilantro (fresh coriander)

¼ cup (2 fl oz/60 ml) fresh lime juice

2 cloves garlic, minced

2 tablespoons vegetable oil

½ teaspoon salt

FOR THE FISH:

4 swordfish steaks, 6–8 oz (185–250 g) each and about 1 inch (2.5 cm) thick

2 tablespoons vegetable oil

salt and freshly ground pepper to taste

To prepare the sauce, remove any seeds from the chile half, then finely mince it. In a small bowl, combine the minced chile, cilantro, lime juice, garlic, vegetable oil, and salt. Stir with a fork to combine, then cover and refrigerate for at least 2 hours or for up to 2 days before serving.

Prepare a fire in a grill.

To prepare the fish, rub the steaks on both sides with the vegetable oil and sprinkle with salt and pepper. Arrange the fish on the grill rack and grill, turning once, until just opaque throughout, about 10 minutes total.

Transfer the fish to warmed individual plates. Place a small spoonful of sauce on each piece of fish and serve at once. Pass the remaining sauce at the table.

Fish with Walnut, Mint, and Basil Pesto

SERVES 4

This herb purée with the crunch of nuts is ideal for a firm white fish such as sea bass or halibut or a meaty fish such as tuna or swordfish. The pesto can be made 4–6 hours ahead (the color will darken over time), refrigerated, and brought to room temperature at serving time.

FOR THE PESTO:

⅔ cup (¾ oz/20 g) firmly packed fresh basil leaves

½ cup (½ oz/15 g) firmly packed fresh mint leaves

3 tablespoons walnuts, toasted and coarsely chopped

½ cup (4 fl oz/125 ml) olive oil

½ teaspoon salt

¼ teaspoon freshly ground pepper

2 tablespoons fresh lemon juice, or to taste

2 tablespoons grated lemon zest (optional)

4 fish fillets *(see note)*, 5–6 oz (155–185 g) each

olive oil

salt and freshly ground pepper to taste

Prepare a fire in a grill.

🔥 To prepare the pesto, in a blender or food processor, combine the basil, mint, and walnuts. Pulse briefly to combine. Add ¼ cup (2 fl oz/60 ml) of the olive oil and pulse briefly again just to combine. Add the remaining ¼ cup (2 fl oz/60 ml) oil and process to a coarse purée. Add the salt, pepper, lemon juice, and lemon zest, if using, and pulse to combine. You should have about 1½ cups (12 fl oz/375 ml) pesto.

🔥 Brush the fish fillets on both sides with olive oil. Sprinkle with salt and pepper. Arrange the fish on the grill rack and grill, turning once, until just opaque throughout, 6–8 minutes total.

🔥 Transfer to warmed individual plates, spoon the pesto over the fish, and serve.

Halibut, Veracruz Style

SERVES 5

If halibut is unavailable, substitute red snapper. Serve with tortillas wrapped in aluminum foil and heated on the grill.

3 boiling potatoes, about 1 lb (500 g) total weight, unpeeled

5 halibut steaks, 6–7 oz (185–220 g) each and ¾ inch (2 cm) thick

3 yellow onions, cut into slices ½ inch (12 mm) thick

6 tomatoes, quartered

olive oil

salt and freshly ground pepper to taste

1 tablespoon chili powder

¾ cup (4 oz/125 g) stuffed green olives

3 limes, cut into wedges

In a saucepan, combine the potatoes with salted water to cover and bring to a boil. Cook until not quite tender, 15–20 minutes. Drain, let cool, and cut into slices ½ inch (12 mm) thick.

🔥 Prepare a fire in a grill.

🔥 Brush the fish steaks, onions, tomatoes, and potatoes on both sides with olive oil and season with salt and pepper. Sprinkle the fish on both sides with the chili powder. Place the fish and vegetables on a grill screen on the grill rack. Grill until the fish is lightly browned, about 2 minutes. Turn the fish and continue to cook until opaque throughout, 5–10 minutes longer. Cook the vegetables, turning as necessary, until softened and warm throughout, about 5 minutes for the tomatoes and 10 minutes for the potatoes and onions.

🔥 Transfer the fish steaks to warmed individual plates. Scatter the vegetables and the green olives over the top and serve with lime wedges.

pepper. Arrange the fish in a single layer in a nonaluminum container. Pour the fennel mixture evenly over the fish and turn the fish to coat both sides. Cover and refrigerate for 30–60 minutes, turning once.

Trim off and discard the remaining fennel tops and cut each bulb in half lengthwise. Cook the fennel bulbs in boiling salted water until just tender when pierced, 7–10 minutes. Drain well and set aside.

Prepare a fire in a grill.

Remove the fish from the marinade, reserving the marinade. Arrange the fish and fennel bulbs on the grill rack and grill, turning the fish once and brushing it lightly with the reserved marinade and turning the fennel four or five times and brushing it lightly with the remaining ¼ cup (2 fl oz/60 ml) oil. The fish is done when it is just opaque throughout, about 10 minutes total, and the fennel will be ready at about the same time.

Transfer the fish and fennel to warmed individual plates and, if desired, top each piece of fish with a pat of the butter. Serve immediately.

Swordfish with Lemon, Garlic, and Olive Oil

SERVES 6

In Greece, Turkey, and Sicily, swordfish is greatly prized. While it is prepared in innumerable ways, grilling it on skewers is among the most popular. This recipe, which is enjoyed with variations in all of those locales, seasons the fish with lemon and garlic. Serve with rice pilaf or roasted potatoes, and broccoli, cauliflower, zucchini (courgettes), or eggplant (aubergine).

⅓ cup (3 fl oz/80 ml) fresh lemon juice
⅔ cup (5 fl oz/160 ml) extra-virgin olive oil

Fennel-Marinated Salmon

SERVES 4

If you can't locate fennel, use chopped fresh dill in place of the fennel tops and serve the fish with Radicchio and Belgian Endive with Shaved Parmesan (page 212) or sautéed cucumbers.

2 large fennel bulbs, with tops intact
½ cup (4 fl oz/120 ml) olive oil
3 tablespoons fresh lemon juice
½ teaspoon salt

¼ teaspoon freshly ground pepper
4 salmon steaks or fillets, 6–8 oz (185–250 g) each and about 1 inch (2.5 cm) thick
½ recipe Lime Butter *(page 204)* (optional)

Chop enough of the feathery fennel tops to measure about ¼ cup (⅓ oz/10 g). In a small bowl, whisk together the chopped fennel, ¼ cup (2 fl oz/60 ml) of the oil, the lemon juice, salt, and

2¼ lb (1.1 kg) swordfish fillets, cut into
    1½-inch (4-cm) cubes
salt and freshly ground pepper to taste
1 tablespoon minced garlic
2 teaspoons dried oregano (optional)
1 red (Spanish) onion
18 lemon slices and/or 18 bay leaves,
    plus lemon slices for garnish

In a bowl, combine the lemon juice and
olive oil. Place the fish cubes in a shallow
nonaluminum dish and sprinkle with salt
and pepper. Pour about ⅓ cup (3 fl oz/
80 ml) of the lemon juice mixture over
the fish and toss to coat evenly; cover
and refrigerate for 2–4 hours. Add the
garlic and the oregano, if using, to the
remaining lemon juice mixture. Set aside
to use as a sauce.

❧ Prepare a fire in a grill.

❧ Cut the onion through the stem end
into quarters and separate each quarter
into individual "leaves" or thin pieces.
Alternate the swordfish cubes with the
onion pieces and 18 lemon slices
and/or bay leaves on 6 skewers. Grill,
turning once, until the fish is opaque
throughout, about 6 minutes total.

❧ Transfer to warmed individual plates,
garnish with lemon slices, and serve
immediately. Pass the reserved
sauce at the table.

Lemon-Dill Salmon and Asparagus

SERVES 6–8

FOR THE ASPARAGUS:

16–20 large, thick asparagus spears, about 1 lb (500 g) total weight

⅓ cup (3 fl oz/80 ml) olive oil

2 tablespoons fresh lemon juice

2 tablespoons chopped fresh dill or 1 teaspoon dried dill

1 teaspoon salt

¼ teaspoon freshly ground pepper

FOR THE SALMON:

1 whole salmon, 3½–4 lb (1.75–2 kg), cleaned

3 tablespoons olive oil

salt and freshly ground pepper to taste

1 large lemon, thinly sliced, plus lemon wedges for garnish

1 bunch fresh dill, separated into large sprigs

To prepare the asparagus, snap off the tough stem ends. Using a vegetable peeler and starting about 2 inches (5 cm) below the tip, peel off the thin outer skin. Arrange in a shallow non-aluminum dish. In a small bowl, whisk together the olive oil, lemon juice, dill, salt, and pepper. Pour over the asparagus and turn to coat. Set aside for 30–60 minutes, turning once at the halfway point.

Prepare a fire for indirect-heat cooking in a covered grill (see page 11).

To prepare the salmon, pat dry with paper towels. Rub inside and out with the olive oil, then sprinkle liberally with salt and pepper. Place the lemon slices and dill sprigs in the cavity and stitch closed with a long wooden skewer or a trussing needle and kitchen string.

Place the fish on the center of the grill rack, cover, and open the vents halfway. Cook for 15 minutes. Using 1 large metal spatula at each end of the fish, flip the fish to its other side in one smooth movement. Don't worry if some of the skin sticks to the rack.

Remove the asparagus from its marinade and arrange around the fish. Re-cover and cook for about 12 minutes longer, turning the asparagus halfway through cooking. The fish is done when the flesh is opaque throughout, or an instant-read thermometer inserted into the thickest part registers 140°F (60°C). The asparagus should be just tender when pierced.

Transfer the fish to a warmed platter, arrange the asparagus around it, and serve with lemon wedges. Use 2 spatulas or 2 large spoons to remove the fish from its frame in serving-sized pieces.

Salmon Skewers

SERVES 4

Salmon stays moist and cooks quickly, so there's ample time to grill some vegetables or fruits over the same fire. The best cut to use for these skewers is a skinned and filleted salmon tail, which will have only a few errant bones, if any. Serve with Herbed Two-Potato Skewers (page 220) and Asparagus with Parmesan (page 208).

2 lb (1 kg) skinless salmon fillets

½ cup (4 fl oz/125 ml) olive oil

2 tablespoons chopped fresh dill
    or 2 teaspoons dried dill

2 tablespoons Pernod or other
    anise-flavored liqueur or brandy

½ teaspoon salt

½ teaspoon freshly ground pepper

2 lemons, sliced

fresh parsley or dill sprigs

lemon wedges

Cut the salmon into strips about 1 inch (2.5 cm) wide and 3 inches (7.5 cm) long. In a large bowl, stir together the oil, dill, liqueur, salt, and pepper. Add the salmon strips and toss to combine. Cover and refrigerate for about 30 minutes, tossing once or twice.

◖ Prepare a fire in a grill.

◖ Remove the salmon from the marinade. Boil the remaining marinade and reserve. Alternating them with the lemon slices, thread the salmon strips onto skewers, weaving each strip so that the skewer passes through it two or three times. Arrange the skewers on the grill rack. Grill, turning frequently and brushing with the reserved marinade, until the salmon is cooked through, 8–10 minutes.

◖ Transfer to a warmed platter and garnish with parsley or dill sprigs and lemon wedges. Serve at once.

Orange-and-Miso-Glazed Sea Bass with Cucumber Salad

SERVES 4

Some cooks may find the idea of marinating sea bass for 48 hours unthinkable, but the salt in the miso draws out moisture and transforms the exterior of the fillets into something approaching a dry-cured fish, while the center remains delicate and juicy. Sambal ulek is an Indonesian chile paste made from chiles, vinegar, and salt. Your favorite chile paste may be substituted.

FOR THE MARINADE:

1 orange

¾ cup (6 fl oz/180 ml) fresh
    orange juice

⅓ cup (2½ oz/75 g) firmly packed
    light brown sugar

⅔ cup (5 fl oz/160 ml) sake

1 cup (8 oz/250 g) white miso

1 tablespoon *sambal ulek* or other
    chile paste

4 skinless Chilean sea bass fillets, each
    about 7 oz (220 g) and ½–¾ inch
    (12 mm–2 cm) thick

FOR THE SALAD:

1 tablespoon canola oil

1 tablespoon seasoned rice vinegar

1 tablespoon mirin

2 teaspoons low-sodium soy sauce

2 teaspoons fresh lemon juice

1 English (hothouse) cucumber, halved,
    seeded, and cut into julienne strips
    1½ inches (4 cm) long and ¼ inch
    (6 mm) wide

3 green (spring) onions, including
    tender green tops, thinly sliced on
    the diagonal

1 tablespoon finely chopped fresh
    cilantro (fresh coriander)

To prepare the marinade, using a vegetable peeler, remove the zest from the orange, being careful not to remove any of the white pith, in about 6 wide strips. Then juice the orange and pour the juice into a small saucepan. Add the ¾ cup (6 fl oz/180 ml) orange juice, the orange zest, and the brown sugar. Bring to a boil over medium-high heat, stirring to dissolve the sugar, then reduce the heat to medium-low and simmer until reduced by about two-thirds, about 10 minutes. Reduce the heat to very low and stir in the sake, miso, and chile paste. Simmer, stirring occasionally to break up the miso, until smooth and thick, about 10 minutes. Remove from the heat, transfer to a bowl, and let cool to room temperature.

◖ In a large lock-top plastic bag, combine the fish and the marinade. Massage the bag gently to coat the fish evenly with the marinade. Press out the air and seal the bag securely. Refrigerate for 48 hours.

◖ Prepare a fire in a grill.

◖ To prepare the cucumber salad, in a bowl, whisk together the canola oil, vinegar, mirin, soy sauce, and lemon juice. Add the cucumber, green onions, and cilantro and toss well to combine. Set aside.

◖ Remove the fish from the plastic bag and place on a platter. Brush with a little of the marinade from the bag. Place the fish on the grill rack and grill for 3–4 minutes. Turn and grill on the second side until just firm, about 4 minutes longer.

◖ Transfer the fillets to warmed individual plates. Toss the salad one more time to be sure the dressing is evenly distributed, then divide among the plates. Serve at once.

Spicy Cuban Tuna Tacos

SERVES 4

The ideal way to eat these juicy, delicious tacos is standing alongside the grill. The grill master has company, and there is no need to arrange for a sit-down first course. Be sure to have all your ingredients ready on a tray to avoid last-minute dashes to the kitchen.

FOR THE MARINADE:

3 tablespoons olive oil

3 tablespoons fresh lemon juice

2 large cloves garlic, minced

1 large shallot, minced

1 teaspoon ground cumin

½ teaspoon salt

⅛ teaspoon cayenne pepper

¼ cup (⅓ oz/10 g) coarsely chopped fresh cilantro (fresh coriander)

1 tuna steak, about 8–10 oz (250– 315 g), 1¼ inches (3 cm) thick

FOR THE SALSA:

2 ripe plum (Roma) tomatoes, halved, seeded, and cut into ¼-inch (6-mm) dice

½ cup (3½ oz/105 g) canned black beans, rinsed and well drained

½ jalapeño chile, or to taste, seeded and finely minced

2 tablespoons finely chopped white onion

2 tablespoons finely chopped fresh cilantro (fresh coriander)

¾ teaspoon salt

¼ teaspoon freshly ground black pepper, or to taste

4 large flour tortillas

¼ head iceberg lettuce, shredded

1 ripe avocado, halved, pitted, peeled, and diced

2 limes, quartered

To prepare the marinade, in a shallow nonaluminum dish, combine the olive oil, lemon juice, garlic, shallot, cumin, salt, cayenne, and cilantro and mix well. Place the tuna in another nonaluminum dish and brush with enough marinade to coat completely. Cover and refrigerate for 1 hour. Boil the remaining marinade and reserve.

To prepare the salsa, in a bowl, combine the tomatoes, beans, chile, onion, cilantro, salt, and black pepper. Cover and refrigerate for up to 1 hour.

Prepare a fire in a grill.

Wrap the tortillas in aluminum foil and place on the edge of the grill rack to warm. Place the tuna steak on the center of the grill rack and grill, turning once, for 4–5 minutes on each side for medium-rare, or until done to your liking. Transfer the tuna to a cutting board and cut into 1-inch (2.5-cm) cubes, discarding any bones and skin. Toss the cubes quickly with the reserved marinade.

To serve, place the lettuce, avocado, and limes in small bowls. Set them out with the tuna, salsa, and tortillas. Each guest makes his or her own taco by placing equal amounts of the lettuce, warm tuna, salsa, and avocado on a warm tortilla, squeezing a little lime juice on top, rolling up to enclose the filling, and eating immediately out of hand.

Pasta with Fresh Tuna

SERVES 4

Italian cooks traditionally prepare a pasta sauce with canned tuna, but grilled fresh tuna is a delicious departure from custom. Garnish the pasta with lots of fresh parsley.

1 lb (500 g) tuna fillets, 1 inch (2.5 cm) thick

6 tablespoons (3 fl oz/90 ml) olive oil

salt and freshly ground black pepper to taste

1 lb (500 g) dried pasta such as penne, orecchiette, spaghetti, or linguine

1 cup (4 oz/125 g) chopped red (Spanish) onion

2 tablespoons finely minced garlic

2 teaspoons dried oregano

1 tablespoon red pepper flakes

2 cups (16 fl oz/500 ml) tomato sauce

12 Kalamata olives, pitted and coarsely chopped

6 tablespoons (½ oz/15 g) chopped fresh flat-leaf (Italian) parsley, plus extra chopped parsley for garnish

Prepare a fire in a grill.

Rub the tuna fillets with 2–3 tablespoons of the olive oil and sprinkle with salt and black pepper. Place on the grill rack and grill, turning once, 4–6 minutes total for medium-rare. (The tuna will cook slightly more in the sauce.)

Let the tuna cool slightly, then cut into strips 1 inch (2.5 cm) long and ½ inch (12 mm) wide.

Bring a large pot of salted water to a boil. Add the pasta, stir well, and cook until al dente. The timing will depend upon the type of pasta; follow the package directions.

Meanwhile, warm the remaining 3–4 tablespoons oil in a large sauté pan over medium heat. Add the onion and sauté until translucent but not soft, about 5 minutes. Add the garlic, oregano, and red pepper flakes and warm through. Add the tomato sauce and bring to a simmer. Add the tuna and warm through. Remove from the heat and add the olives and the 6 tablespoons (½ oz/15 g) parsley. Season with salt and black pepper.

Drain the pasta and place in a warmed pasta bowl. Add the tuna sauce, toss well, and garnish with parsley. Serve at once.

Flounder with Orange Salsa

SERVES 6

Flounder fillets are thin, so in this recipe they are quickly grilled on a bed of orange slices without turning. Serve them with couscous or white rice.

FOR THE SALSA:

3 large oranges
1 small red (Spanish) onion, chopped
2 jalapeño chiles, seeded and chopped
½ cup (¾ oz/20 g) chopped fresh
   cilantro (fresh coriander)
2 tablespoons fresh orange or lime juice

3 oranges
6 flounder fillets, 5–6 oz (155–185 g)
   each
vegetable oil or canola oil for brushing
1 bunch fresh chives, trimmed

To prepare the salsa, cut a slice off the top and bottom of each orange to expose the fruit. Place each orange upright on a cutting board and thickly slice off the peel in strips, cutting around the contour of the flesh. Holding the orange over a bowl, cut along both sides of each section, letting the sections drop into the bowl. Remove any seeds and discard, then cut up the sections and return them to the bowl. Add the onion, chiles, cilantro, and orange or lime juice and toss to mix. Cover and refrigerate until serving. Toss before serving.

Prepare a fire in a covered grill.

Peel the remaining 3 oranges in the same way as the oranges were peeled for the salsa, but do not section. Cut crosswise into thin slices. Arrange the orange slices on a grill screen and top with the flounder fillets in a single layer. Brush the fish with oil and lay the chives decoratively over the fish.

Put the screen on the grill rack, cover, open the vents, and grill until the fish flakes easily and is just opaque throughout, 7–10 minutes. Using a spatula, transfer the fillets, with the orange slices underneath, to individual plates. Serve immediately with the salsa.

Salmon with Mustard Glaze and Asian Vinaigrette

SERVES 4

Salmon has a rich flavor that calls for something piquant to balance it. Here, that contrast is provided by mustard. This dish has a pronounced Asian influence, and the sauce adds a touch of intense flavor.

FOR THE SAUCE:

2 green (spring) onions, including
   light green tops, thinly sliced
2 teaspoons seasoned rice vinegar
2 teaspoons mirin
2 teaspoons fish sauce
1 teaspoon low-sodium soy sauce
½ teaspoon Asian sesame oil
½ teaspoon fresh lemon juice

2 tablespoons dry mustard
2 teaspoons sugar
2 teaspoons water
4 center-cut salmon fillets, with skin
   intact, each 6–7 oz (185–220 g) and
   about 1¼ inches (3 cm) thick
sea salt and freshly ground pepper
   to taste

Prepare a fire in a grill.

To prepare the sauce, in a small bowl, stir together the green onions, vinegar, mirin, fish sauce, soy sauce, sesame oil, and lemon juice. Set aside.

In another small bowl, whisk together the mustard, sugar, and water until smooth. Season both sides of the salmon fillets generously with salt and pepper, and then brush both sides with the sauce. Place on the grill rack and grill until the skin begins to char and pull back, 4–5 minutes. Using a metal spatula, flip the salmon over. Continue to grill until the exterior is completely opaque but the center is still a little translucent, 2–3 minutes longer.

Transfer the fillets to warmed plates and drizzle with a little of the sauce. Serve immediately.

Trout with Prosciutto and Sage

SERVES 4

This northern Italian recipe couldn't be simpler, and it looks pretty, too. Ask your fishmonger to prepare the trout for cooking. Serve with fried potatoes and spinach, asparagus, or green beans.

4 trout or Coho salmon trout, about 10 oz (315 g) each, cleaned and boned with heads intact
salt to taste
freshly ground pepper to taste, plus 1 teaspoon
12 fresh sage leaves
4 large, thin slices prosciutto
olive oil
5 tablespoons (2½ oz/75 g) unsalted butter
grated zest of 1 lemon
2 tablespoons fresh lemon juice

Prepare a fire in a grill.

Using a sharp knife, cut shallow diagonal slashes in the fleshiest part on each side of each trout. Sprinkle with a little salt and pepper. Place 3 sage leaves in the cavity of each fish and then wrap each fish in a slice of prosciutto.

Brush each fish on both sides with a little olive oil and arrange on the grill rack. Grill, turning once, until the prosciutto is browned and the fish is just opaque throughout, 8–10 minutes total.

Meanwhile, in a small saucepan over low heat, melt the butter and stir in the lemon zest and juice and the 1 teaspoon pepper.

Transfer the fish to warmed individual plates and spoon a little of the butter sauce over each fish. Serve immediately.

Shellfish

Grilling shellfish can create a luxurious feast. You will need to take some care to prevent overcooking—the shell is nature's way of protecting the delicate morsels of flesh inside—but nearly every type of shellfish can be grilled and most are easy to prepare. Grilled Lobster with Citrus Butter is one of the ultimate treats of the shellfish repertoire, while Bacon-Wrapped Scallop and Salmon Skewers provide the best of farm, sea, and river in a single, appetizing package. Never grilled an oyster? It's time to put a batch over the coals.

Bacon-Wrapped Scallop and Salmon Skewers

SERVES 4–6

Blanching bacon—boiling it briefly in water—removes some of its fat and salt and tames its smoky flavor.

8 slices bacon, about ½ lb (250 g),
    cut into 3-inch (7.5-cm) lengths
1 lb (500 g) sea scallops
1 lb (500 g) skinless salmon fillets,
    about 1 inch (2.5 cm) thick,
    cut into 1-inch (2.5-cm) cubes
¼ cup (2 fl oz/60 ml) olive oil
2 tablespoons fresh lemon juice
2 tablespoons chopped fresh sage
    or 1 teaspoon dried sage
½ teaspoon salt
¼ teaspoon freshly ground pepper
lemon wedges

Fill a saucepan two-thirds full with water and bring to a boil over high heat. Add the bacon and blanch for 3 minutes. Drain, rinse with cold water, and pat dry with paper towels. Set aside.

🔥 In a bowl, combine the scallops and salmon. Add the olive oil, lemon juice, sage, salt, and pepper. Toss to combine and coat the scallops and salmon. Cover and refrigerate for about 30 minutes, tossing once or twice.

🔥 Prepare a fire in a grill.

🔥 Remove the scallops and salmon from the marinade. Boil the remaining marinade and reserve. Wrap a piece of bacon around each scallop and each piece of salmon. Alternate the bacon-wrapped scallops and salmon on 4 or 6 skewers.

🔥 Arrange the skewers on the grill rack. Grill, turning frequently and brushing two or three times during the first 4 minutes of cooking with the reserved marinade, until the bacon is lightly browned and sizzling and the scallops and salmon are just opaque throughout, about 8 minutes total.

🔥 To serve, transfer to a warmed platter and serve at once with lemon wedges.

Provençal Mussels with Garlic Bruschetta

SERVES 6

If your fishmonger can't supply you with seaweed, cook the mussels directly on a grill screen or rack. For an aromatic accent, soak a small handful of herbes de Provence in water for 5 minutes, drain, and scatter the herbs over the hot coals just before covering the grill.

FOR THE SAUCE:

2 tablespoons olive oil

2 large shallots, minced

3 cloves garlic, minced

4 large tomatoes, peeled, seeded, and chopped

½ cup (2½ oz/75 g) peeled and grated carrot

1 teaspoon dried herbes de Provence

salt and freshly ground pepper to taste

12 large cloves garlic, unpeeled

seaweed to cover grill screen (optional)

3 lb (1.5 kg) mussels, well scrubbed and debearded

6 slices French bread, cut on the diagonal

olive oil

Prepare a fire in a covered grill.

To prepare the sauce, in a saucepan over medium heat, warm the olive oil. Add the shallots and garlic and sauté, stirring occasionally, until soft, about 5 minutes. Stir in the tomatoes, carrot, herbes de Provence, salt, and pepper. Simmer until the tomatoes are soft, 5–8 minutes. Taste and adjust the seasoning. Reheat just before serving.

Place the whole garlic cloves on a piece of aluminum foil and wrap to enclose. Put the wrapped garlic on the grill rack and cook until soft, about 10 minutes (squeeze a clove to test). Transfer to a dish, unwrap, and discard the foil.

Spread the seaweed, if using, on a grill screen. Arrange the mussels on top in a single layer, discarding any mussels that do not close to the touch. Set the screen on the grill rack, cover, open the vents, and grill until the mussels open, 4–5 minutes. Transfer the mussels to a platter, discarding any that failed to open.

Brush the bread on both sides with olive oil and grill, turning once, until toasted, 3–5 minutes on each side.

Bring the mussels, garlic cloves, sauce, and toasted bread to the table. Serve hot. Have your guests squeeze the garlic cloves from their skins onto the hot bread for spreading.

Shrimp with Charmoula

SERVES 4

Charmoula *is an intensely flavored Moroccan marinade and sauce used on fish and shellfish. Here, it flavors shrimp.*

24–32 large shrimp (prawns)
¼ cup (2 fl oz/60 ml) fresh lemon juice
2 teaspoons sweet paprika
¼ teaspoon cayenne pepper
1 teaspoon ground cumin
3 cloves garlic, minced
¼ cup (⅓ oz/10 g) chopped fresh
    flat-leaf (Italian) parsley
¼ cup (⅓ oz/10 g) chopped fresh
    cilantro (fresh coriander)
½ cup (4 fl oz/125 ml) extra-virgin
    olive oil
salt and freshly ground black pepper
    to taste

FOR THE COUSCOUS:

3 cups (24 fl oz/750 ml) water
¼ cup (2 oz/60 g) unsalted butter
1 teaspoon ground cinnamon
1 teaspoon salt
2 cups (12 oz/375 g) instant couscous

Peel the shrimp, leaving the last shell segment with the tail fin intact, then devein. Slip the shrimp onto 8 skewers: For each serving, hold 2 skewers parallel and thread 6–8 shrimp onto them, so that 1 skewer passes through near the tail of each shrimp and the other skewer passes through near the head. Place in a baking pan large enough to hold the skewers flat.

In a bowl, whisk together lightly the lemon juice, paprika, cayenne, cumin, garlic, parsley, cilantro, olive oil, salt, and black pepper. Pour half of the mixture over the shrimp and turn the skewers to coat evenly. Cover and refrigerate for 2–4 hours. Reserve the remaining marinade to use for a sauce.

Prepare a fire in a grill.

Meanwhile, make the couscous: In a saucepan, combine the water, butter, cinnamon, and salt and bring to a boil. Spread the couscous evenly in a shallow, 9-inch (23-cm) square baking pan. Pour the hot water mixture over the couscous. Stir well, then cover and allow the couscous to absorb the liquid, 10–15 minutes.

Remove the skewers from the marinade and discard the marinade. Arrange the skewers on the grill rack and grill, turning once, until the shrimp turn pink, 6–8 minutes total.

Uncover the couscous and fluff with a fork. Spoon onto individual plates. Arrange the shrimp on the couscous, spoon on the reserved sauce, and serve.

Mixed Shellfish Grill with Lemon-Lime Butter

SERVES 6

1 lb (500 g) mixed sea scallops and large
  shrimp (prawns) in the shell
4 tablespoons (2 fl oz/60 ml) olive oil
salt and freshly ground pepper to taste
3 lb (1.5 kg) mixed live lobster(s) and
  fresh-cooked crab(s)
2 lb (1 kg) mixed clams and mussels,
  well scrubbed and mussels debearded
½ cup (4 fl oz/125 ml) dry white wine
⅓ cup (3 fl oz/80 ml) white wine
  vinegar
3 shallots, finely chopped
6 fresh parsley stems
pinch of fresh or dried thyme
1 bay leaf
1 cup (8 oz/250 g) unsalted butter,
  at room temperature, cut into
  1-tablespoon pieces
salt and freshly ground pepper to taste
1–2 teaspoons fresh lemon juice
1–2 teaspoons fresh lime juice
lemon and/or lime wedges

Place the scallops and shrimp in a bowl.
Stir in 2 tablespoons of the olive oil and
season with salt and pepper. Set aside.

Fill a large pot three-fourths full of
water and bring to a boil. Add salt to
taste and the lobster(s) and boil until
dark red and fully cooked, 6–10 minutes.
Using tongs, transfer to a plate to cool.
Bring the crab(s) to room temperature.
Discard any clams and mussels that do
not close to the touch, and place the
others in a bowl with the remaining
2 tablespoons oil, tossing to coat evenly.
Set aside.

Prepare a fire in a covered grill.

Thirty minutes before serving, in a
saucepan over high heat, combine the
wine, vinegar, shallots, parsley stems,
thyme, and bay leaf. Boil until reduced
to 3 tablespoons. Let cool slightly, then
reduce the heat to low. Add the butter,
1 tablespoon at a time, whisking vigorously until incorporated. When all of the
butter has been added, strain the mixture
through a fine-mesh sieve. Season with
salt, pepper, and the lemon and lime
juices. Place in the top pan of a double
boiler or in a heatproof bowl placed
over (but not touching) warm water.

Place the lobster(s) and crab(s) on the
grill rack and grill, turning once, until
hot, 4–5 minutes. Transfer to a platter.
Place the clams and mussels in a single
layer on a grill screen on the grill rack,
sprinkle with salt, cover, and cook until
they open, about 4 minutes. Discard any
that failed to open. Squeeze 2–4 lemon
and/or lime wedges over them and
transfer to the platter. Place the scallops
and shrimp on the grill screen on the
grill rack and grill, turning once, until
the shrimp turn pink and the scallops
are just firm to the touch, about 4 minutes. Add to the platter.

Just before serving, clean and crack
the lobster(s) and crab(s). Serve the shellfish at once with the lemon–lime butter.

Brochettes of Roasted Pepper–Wrapped Scallops

SERVES 6

Yellow bell peppers can be substituted for the red peppers. Grill your favorite vegetables to serve alongside the scallops. If you like, drizzle the brochettes with a good-quality pesto sauce in place of the vinaigrette.

1½ lb (750 g) sea scallops
2 tablespoons olive oil
grated zest of 1 lemon
freshly ground pepper to taste
4 large, long red bell peppers
  (capsicums)

FOR THE VINAIGRETTE:

2 tablespoons red wine vinegar
6 tablespoons (3 fl oz/90 ml)
  extra-virgin olive oil
1 tablespoon chopped fresh parsley
½ teaspoon chopped fresh oregano
  (optional)
salt and freshly ground pepper to taste

Prepare a fire in a grill.

In a bowl, combine the scallops, olive oil, lemon zest, and pepper. Toss to mix. Set aside.

Place the bell peppers on the grill rack and grill, turning as necessary until blackened and blistered evenly, 5–10 minutes. Transfer to a plastic or paper bag, close tightly, and let cool for 10 minutes. Using your fingers or a small knife, peel off the skin. Remove the stem, seeds, and veins and cut the peppers lengthwise into strips ¾ inch (2 cm) wide.

Wrap a pepper strip around a scallop, overlapping the pepper ends. Secure the strip in place by running a skewer through the scallop and pepper. Repeat

with the remaining pepper strips and scallops, dividing the wrapped scallops evenly among 12 skewers.

To prepare the vinaigrette, in a small bowl, whisk together the vinegar, olive oil, parsley, oregano (if using), salt, and pepper. Set aside.

Place the skewers on the grill rack and grill, turning once, until the scallops are just firm to the touch, about 2 minutes on each side.

Transfer the skewers to a platter and drizzle with the vinaigrette. Serve immediately.

Shrimp with Garlicky Tomato Glaze

SERVES 4

A spicy tomato marinade becomes a flavorful glaze for these shrimp, which acquire a smoky accent on the grill. Serve over rice.

3 tablespoons olive oil

2 tablespoons tomato paste

¼ cup (2 fl oz/60 ml) red wine vinegar

2 cloves garlic, minced

1 teaspoon dried basil

½ teaspoon red pepper flakes

½ teaspoon salt

1 lb (500 g) large or jumbo shrimp (prawns), peeled and deveined

In a large bowl, combine the olive oil, tomato paste, vinegar, garlic, basil, red pepper flakes, and salt. Stir until blended and smooth. Add the shrimp and toss to coat evenly. Cover and refrigerate for about 1 hour, tossing occasionally.

Prepare a fire in a grill.

Remove the shrimp from the marinade. Boil the remaining marinade and reserve. Thread the shrimp onto 4 skewers and place on the grill rack. Grill, turning two or three times and brushing once with some of the reserved marinade after 3 minutes, until the shrimp turn pink, 6–8 minutes total.

Transfer the skewers to a warmed platter or individual plates. Serve at once.

Thai Shrimp on Lemongrass Skewers

SERVES 6

6 thin stalks fresh lemongrass

FOR THE BRUSHING SAUCE:
¼ cup (2 fl oz/60 ml) fresh lime juice
1 tablespoon fish sauce
¼ cup (⅓ oz/10 g) chopped fresh mint
4 cloves garlic, minced
¼ teaspoon salt
¼ teaspoon red pepper flakes

2 lb (1 kg) jumbo shrimp (prawns), peeled and deveined
3 green (spring) onions, white part only, trimmed to 2-inch (5-cm) lengths

Using a small, sharp knife, shape the root end of each lemongrass stalk into a point. Soak the lemongrass stalks in water to cover for about 30 minutes. Drain.

To prepare the brushing sauce, combine the lime juice, fish sauce, mint, garlic, salt, and red pepper flakes. Taste and adjust the seasoning.

Prepare a fire in a covered grill.

Carefully thread the shrimp and green onions onto the lemongrass skewers and brush the shrimp with the sauce. Place on the grill rack, cover, open the vents, and grill, turning once, until the shrimp turn pink, 6–8 minutes total.

Transfer the skewers to warmed individual plates and serve at once.

Oysters with Soy-Citrus Vinaigrette

SERVES 4

FOR THE VINAIGRETTE:
1 lime
½ pink grapefruit (halved crosswise)
2 tablespoons extra-virgin olive oil
2 tablespoons low-sodium soy sauce
2 teaspoons sherry vinegar
pinch of cayenne pepper
¼ teaspoon celery salt
1 drop Tabasco or other hot-pepper sauce
¼ teaspoon salt, or to taste
¼ teaspoon freshly ground black pepper
1 tablespoon boiling water
7 pink peppercorns (optional)
2 teaspoons minced fresh ginger
2 tablespoons chopped fresh cilantro (fresh coriander)

12–16 oysters in the shell, well scrubbed

To prepare the vinaigrette, cut a slice off the top and bottom of the lime to expose the flesh. Steadying the fruit upright on the cutting board, slice off the peel in strips, cutting off the white pith and membrane to reveal the fruit. Holding the peeled fruit over a bowl to catch the juices, carefully cut on each side of the membrane to free each section, letting the sections drop into the bowl. Repeat with the grapefruit half, placing it cut side down on the cutting board and cutting a slice from the top. Dice the lime and grapefruit sections and return to the bowl with the juices. Set aside.

In a blender or food processor, combine the olive oil, soy sauce, vinegar, cayenne, celery salt, hot-pepper sauce, salt, and black pepper. Process for 30 seconds. With the motor running, add the boiling water and process for 30 seconds longer. Transfer to a serving bowl. Using a slotted spoon, transfer the diced citrus fruits to the vinaigrette. Add about 1 tablespoon of the citrus juices, and stir in the pink peppercorns (if using), ginger, and cilantro. Cover and refrigerate until serving. (The vinaigrette will keep for up to 12 hours.)

Prepare a fire in a grill. Have ready tongs, a kitchen towel, an oyster knife, and a serving platter.

Place the oysters, flat shell down, around the edge of the grill rack, discarding any that do not close to the touch. Grill just until the oysters open slightly, 3–6 minutes. Discard any oysters that failed to open. Working quickly (ideally with a helper), transfer the oysters to the platter with the tongs, turning them over so the larger, cupped side is downward, thus allowing the liquor to run out. Protecting your hand with the towel, grab each oyster and, using the oyster knife, finish removing the top of the shell by severing the side muscle. Run the knife under the oyster, detaching it from the shell but leaving it resting inside. Return the oysters to the platter and add 1 generous teaspoon of the vinaigrette to the top of each.

Serve the oysters immediately. To eat, simply tip an oyster along with the vinaigrette into the mouth. If correctly detached, the oyster will slip easily from its shell.

Shellfish with Romesco Sauce

SERVES 4

FOR THE ROMESCO SAUCE:

¾ cup (6 fl oz/180 ml) olive oil

1 large slice coarse country bread, about 1 oz (30 g)

¾ cup (4 oz/125 g) blanched almonds, toasted

½–1 teaspoon cayenne pepper

2–3 teaspoons minced garlic

1 large red bell pepper (capsicum), roasted, peeled, and roughly chopped

1 large tomato, peeled, seeded, and diced

1 teaspoon sweet paprika

salt and freshly ground black pepper to taste

¼ cup (2 fl oz/60 ml) red wine vinegar

2 live lobsters

16 large shrimp (prawns) or scallops

olive oil

lemon wedges

To prepare the romesco sauce, in a sauté pan over medium heat, warm 3 tablespoons of the olive oil. Add the bread and fry on both sides until golden, about 4 minutes. Roughly break up and place in a blender. Add the almonds, ½ teaspoon cayenne, and 2 teaspoons garlic. Pulse briefly to combine. Add the roasted bell pepper, tomato, paprika, salt, and pepper. Process to form a chunky paste. Add the vinegar and pulse once. With the motor running, slowly add the remaining oil in a thin, steady stream, processing until the mixture emulsifies. Taste and adjust the seasoning with cayenne, garlic, salt, and black pepper. Transfer to a bowl.

Prepare a fire in a grill.

Fill a large pot three-fourths full of salted water and bring to a boil. Drop in the lobsters, immersing completely, and cook for 6 minutes. Set aside to cool. Lay each lobster, underside down, on a cutting board. Insert a knife where the body meets the tail and cut the tail in half lengthwise. Turn the lobster and cut toward the head, cutting the lobster into 2 pieces. Remove the dark intestinal vein, the gravelly sac at the head, and any other organs and discard. Using a mallet, crack the claws and knuckles. If using shrimp, peel them, leaving the last shell segment with the tail fin intact, then devein. Thread the shrimp or scallops onto skewers.

Brush all the shellfish with olive oil. Arrange on the grill rack, with the lobster halves cut side down. Grill, turning once. The lobster meat should be firm to the touch within 6–8 minutes total. The shrimp should be pink within 3–4 minutes; the scallops should be just firm to the touch within about 6 minutes.

Transfer the shellfish to warmed individual plates. Serve with the lemon wedges and sauce on the side.

Tea-Smoked Shrimp with Sweet-and-Hot Pepper Relish

SERVES 4–6

Tea bags, soaked in water and then tossed on the hot coals, create an aromatic smoke in much the same way hickory chips do. Tea smoke is much milder, however, and therefore well suited to the delicate taste of fish and shellfish.

FOR THE RELISH:

¾ cup (4 oz/125 g) chopped green bell pepper (capsicum)

¾ cup (4 oz/125 g) chopped red bell pepper (capsicum)

½ cup (2 oz/60 g) chopped red (Spanish) onion

¼ cup (2 fl oz/60 ml) cider vinegar

1 tablespoon sugar

1 teaspoon mustard seeds

½ teaspoon celery seeds

½ teaspoon salt

⅛ teaspoon cayenne pepper

FOR THE SHRIMP:

2 black or green tea bags

2 lb (1 kg) large shrimp (prawns)

3 tablespoons olive oil

½ teaspoon salt

¼ teaspoon freshly ground black pepper

To prepare the relish, in a small bowl, combine the green and red bell peppers and the onion. In a small saucepan over high heat, combine the vinegar, sugar, mustard seeds, celery seeds, salt, and cayenne. Bring just to a boil, then pour over the pepper-onion mixture and stir to combine. Let cool, cover, and refrigerate for at least 2 hours or for up to 2 days before serving.

🌿 Prepare a fire in a covered grill.

🌿 To prepare the shrimp, soak the tea bags in cold water to cover for 10–15 minutes. Peel the shrimp, leaving the last shell segment with the tail fin intact, then devein and pat dry. In a large bowl, toss together the shrimp, olive oil, salt, and black pepper.

🌿 Using your hand, squeeze the tea bags to remove any excess water, then drop them onto the fire. Arrange the shrimp on the grill rack, cover, open the vents halfway, and cook for about 3 minutes. Turn the shrimp, re-cover, and cook until they turn pink, 3–4 minutes longer.

🌿 Transfer the shrimp to warmed individual plates and serve at once. Pass the relish at the table.

Lobster with Citrus Butter

SERVES 6

Dousing the embers with water gives the finished lobster a pleasantly smoky flavor. To offer this dish as a first course, split one lobster for two people. If you like, garnish with citrus wedges and sprigs of flat-leaf (Italian) parsley. Provide plenty of lobster crackers or nutcrackers for breaking open the heavy lobster claws.

4 qt (4 l) water
2 tablespoons salt, plus salt to taste
6 live lobsters, 1½ lb (750 g) each
½ cup (4 oz/125 g) plus 2 tablespoons
   unsalted butter, at room temperature
¼ teaspoon grated lemon zest
¼ teaspoon grated lime zest
¼ teaspoon grated orange zest
2 tablespoons chopped fresh parsley
½ teaspoon herbes de Provence
freshly ground pepper to taste

In a large stockpot, bring the water to a boil. Add the 2 tablespoons salt and 2 of the lobsters, immersing completely, and boil until the shells turn red, about 4 minutes. Using tongs, remove the lobsters and place under cold running water to cool. Repeat with the remaining lobsters, 2 at a time.

Prepare a fire in a covered grill.

Lay a lobster, underside down, on a cutting board. Insert a knife into the lobster at the point where the body meets the tail and cut the tail in half lengthwise. Turn the lobster around and cut toward the head, cutting the lobster into 2 pieces. Remove the dark intestinal vein and any other organs and discard.

In a small saucepan over medium heat, melt the butter and stir in the lemon, lime, and orange zests, parsley, and herbes de Provence. Season with salt and pepper. Remove from the heat.

Place the lobsters on the grill rack, cut side up. Cover and cook for 2 minutes. Pour ½ cup (4 fl oz/125 ml) water over the coals to create smoke and continue to cook, covered, for 2 minutes. Remove the cover and drizzle the lobsters with half of the citrus butter. Re-cover and cook until the meat is almost firm to the touch, about 2 minutes.

Transfer the lobsters to individual plates, cut side up, and drizzle with the remaining citrus butter. Serve hot.

Oysters with Orange-Cognac Butter

SERVES 6

If you've never grilled oysters before, you're in for a treat. Because they steam in their own juices, with nothing to dilute their flavor, they have an intense taste of the sea. Just be sure to grab the oysters off the grill as soon as their shells pop open. The point is simply to warm them slightly, not to cook them all the way through.

FOR THE BUTTER:
¾ cup (6 oz/185 g) unsalted butter,
   at room temperature, cut into pieces
1 tablespoon grated orange zest
3 tablespoons Cognac or other brandy
3 tablespoons ground almonds

24 oysters in the shell, well scrubbed

Prepare a fire in a covered grill.

To prepare the butter, in a food processor, combine the butter, orange zest, brandy, and almonds. Process until blended. Alternatively, combine the ingredients in a bowl and beat together with a wooden spoon. (The butter can be made up to 1 day in advance; cover and refrigerate, then bring to room temperature before serving.)

Arrange the oysters, cupped shell down, on the grill rack, discarding any that do not close to the touch. Cover, open the vents, and grill just until the oysters open, 3–6 minutes, depending on their size. Discard any oysters that failed to open.

Using long-handled tongs, transfer the oysters to a serving platter and remove and discard the top shells, being careful not to spill the liquid. Spoon a dab of butter on top of each oyster and serve.

Lobster Tails, Catalan Style

SERVES 6

FOR THE SAUCE:

1 ripe tomato, peeled, seeded, and chopped

3 cloves garlic, crushed

3–4 tablespoons (¾–1 oz/20–30 g) ground almonds

¼ teaspoon red pepper flakes

¼ teaspoon salt

¾ cup (6 fl oz/180 ml) olive oil

¼ cup (2 fl oz/60 ml) dry sherry

2 tablespoons red wine vinegar

6 lobster tails, 8–10 oz (250–315 g) each, thawed if frozen
unsalted butter, melted

To prepare the sauce, in a blender or food processor, combine the tomato, garlic, almonds, red pepper flakes, and salt. Process until a smooth purée forms. In a small bowl, whisk together the olive oil, sherry, and vinegar. With the motor running, slowly drizzle in the oil mixture, processing until smooth and thick. Taste and adjust the seasoning. Pour into a bowl and set aside. You should have about 1 cup (8 fl oz/250 ml).

Prepare a fire for indirect-heat cooking in a covered grill (see page 11).

Using scissors and working with 1 lobster tail at a time, split the tail shell open lengthwise. Brush the lobster meat with melted butter.

Place the lobster tails on the grill, cut side up. Cover, open the vents, and cook, without turning, until the shells turn red and the meat is just opaque throughout, about 10 minutes.

Transfer the lobster tails to warmed individual plates and serve at once. Pass the sauce at the table.

Shrimp and Mushroom Skewers

SERVES 4–6

The grilled lemon slices have a mildly bitter flavor that pairs nicely with grilled shrimp. If you want to toss an aromatic wood on the fire, use a subtle one such as applewood or grapevine cuttings. Serve the skewers atop polenta or orzo.

2 large lemons

½ cup (4 fl oz/125 ml) olive oil

¼ cup (2 fl oz/60 ml) dry white wine

1 tablespoon chopped fresh thyme, plus thyme sprigs for garnish

¾ teaspoon salt

¼ teaspoon freshly ground pepper

18 large or jumbo shrimp (prawns), about 1 lb (500 g) total weight, peeled and deveined

18 large fresh white mushrooms, about 1 lb (500 g) total weight, brushed clean and stems removed

Using a sharp knife, cut the lemons into 18 slices about ⅛ inch (3 mm) thick. Save the ends for another use. Using the tip of the knife, pry out any seeds in the slices. Set the lemon slices aside.

In a large nonaluminum bowl, whisk together the olive oil, wine, chopped thyme, salt, and pepper. Add the lemon slices and shrimp and toss to coat evenly. Cover and refrigerate, tossing once or twice, for about 45 minutes.

Prepare a fire in a grill.

Add the mushrooms to the lemons and shrimp and again toss to coat. Let stand for 10–15 minutes.

Thread the shrimp, lemon slices, and mushrooms onto skewers in the following manner: Place a lemon slice against the inside curve of a shrimp. Bend the shrimp in half, so that the head end nearly touches the tail end, enclosing

the lemon slice in the center. Insert a skewer just above the tail, so that it passes through the body twice. Next, slip a mushroom onto the skewer. Repeat until all the ingredients are used, loading 6 skewers in all. Boil the remaining marinade and reserve.

Arrange the skewers on the grill rack and grill, turning frequently and brushing once after 3 minutes with the reserved marinade, until the shrimp turn pink and the mushrooms are tender and lightly browned, 8–10 minutes total.

Transfer to a warmed platter, garnish with thyme sprigs, and serve.

Poultry

Chicken

The smell of chicken sizzling over hot coals is a universally appealing aroma. From the beaches of Italy to the ranchland of Texas to the spice-scented cities of India, people love to grill chicken. The versatile bird marries well with such diverse ingredients as garlic, fruit, and herbs. A classic like Lemon-Rosemary Chicken is delicious in any season, while Chicken Breasts with Double-Garlic Aioli seem made for a summertime dinner party. Chicken Kabobs are the quickest option imaginable and pick up lots of smoky flavor.

Southwestern Barbecued Chicken

SERVES 6

FOR THE SAUCE:
3 slices bacon, cut into ½-inch (12-mm) pieces
¾ cup (3 oz/90 g) chopped yellow onion
2 cloves garlic, minced
1¾ cups (14 fl oz/440 ml) tomato ketchup
¼ cup (2 fl oz/60 ml) pineapple juice
2 tablespoons light corn syrup
1 teaspoon Worcestershire sauce
2 teaspoons chili powder
1 teaspoon ground cumin
¼ teaspoon salt
¼ teaspoon freshly ground pepper

1 chicken, about 3½ lb (1.75 kg), cut into serving pieces

To prepare the sauce, in a saucepan over medium heat, fry the bacon, stirring occasionally, until crisp, about 5 minutes. Using a slotted spoon, transfer the bacon to paper towels to drain and reserve for another use. Add the onion and garlic and sauté over medium heat, stirring occasionally, until tender, about 5 minutes. Add the ketchup, pineapple juice, corn syrup, Worcestershire sauce, chili powder, cumin, salt, and pepper. Bring to a boil, reduce the heat to low, and continue to cook, stirring occasionally, until slightly thickened, 8–10 minutes. Transfer to a bowl and let cool.

Meanwhile, prepare a fire for indirect-heat cooking in a covered grill (see page 11).

Arrange the chicken pieces on the grill rack, cover, open the vents, and grill, turning the pieces every 15 minutes or so, until opaque throughout and the juices run clear, 40–60 minutes. Add more hot coals to the fire if needed to maintain a constant temperature. During the last 15 minutes of grilling, brush the chicken pieces with some of the barbecue sauce.

Transfer to warmed individual plates, brush with the remaining sauce, and serve.

Chicken Breasts with Niçoise Sauce

SERVES 4

White anchovies are a revelation to anyone who thinks anchovies are too strong or too salty. These little fish, which come from Spain and are a popular tapas dish (dressed with lemon juice, garlic, and a drizzle of good olive oil), can be found in specialty-foods stores. White anchovies are plump, juicy, and mild, but still have the briny, quintessentially Mediterranean flavor that lovers of anchovies and other salty foods cherish. Do not make this sauce in a food processor; it will lose its rustic character.

FOR THE NIÇOISE SAUCE:

8 white anchovy fillets, minced
1 tablespoon capers, minced
1 tablespoon minced Niçoise olives,
   (about 4 plump olives, pitted)
1 tablespoon minced shallot
   (about 1 small)
1 teaspoon finely slivered garlic
3½ tablespoons extra-virgin olive oil
2 tablespoons sherry wine vinegar
1 tablespoon finely chopped fresh
   tarragon
¼ teaspoon freshly ground pepper
salt to taste

4 boneless chicken breast halves,
   skinned if desired
salt and freshly ground pepper to taste
lemon wedges (optional)

Prepare a fire in a grill.

To make the sauce, in a bowl, combine the anchovies, capers, olives, shallot, and garlic and mix well. Stir in the olive oil, vinegar, tarragon, and pepper. Taste and, if necessary, season with a little salt.

Season the chicken breasts generously with salt and pepper on both sides. Place on the grill rack and grill, turning once, until opaque throughout and the juices run clear, about 10 minutes total. Transfer to a warmed platter, cover loosely with aluminum foil, and let rest for 3–4 minutes.

Arrange the chicken on warmed individual plates. Mound a spoonful of the sauce on top of each breast and serve with a wedge of lemon.

Chicken Thighs in Yogurt-Curry Marinade

SERVES 4

When peeling fresh ginger for a marinade that will eventually be discarded, there is no need to remove every bit of peel. In this recipe, it is easy to treat the ginger in the same way as the garlic: Cut it into chunks about the size of large garlic cloves and trim off most of the peel, especially the tough ends. Then drop the pieces one at a time, into a food processor with the motor running.

3 cloves garlic
¼ lb (125 g) fresh ginger, peeled
   and cut into chunks
1 cup (8 oz/250 g) plain yogurt
2 teaspoons good-quality curry powder
1 teaspoon ground coriander
8 skinless, boneless chicken thighs
salt and freshly ground pepper to taste
¼ cup (2½ oz/75 g) mango chutney
1 tablespoon finely chopped fresh
   cilantro (fresh coriander)

In a food processor, with the motor running, drop in the garlic cloves and ginger chunks one at a time, processing until finely chopped. Add the yogurt, curry powder, and coriander and process to blend. Scrape the marinade into a baking dish large enough to hold the chicken thighs snugly in a single layer. Add the thighs and turn to coat them with the marinade, rubbing it into all the nooks and crannies. Cover and refrigerate for 24 hours.

Prepare a fire in a covered grill.

Remove the chicken from the marinade, scrape off the excess, and pat completely dry with paper towels. Season with salt and pepper. Place on the grill rack, cover, and grill for 7 minutes. Turn the thighs over, re-cover, and grill until opaque throughout and the juices run clear, about 7 minutes longer. Transfer to a warmed platter, cover loosely with aluminum foil, and let rest for 3–4 minutes.

Arrange 2 thighs on each individual plate and place a dollop of chutney alongside. Dust each serving with the cilantro and serve at once.

Jamaican Jerk Chicken

SERVES 4–6

Jerk is a traditional Jamaican style of cooking that begins by rubbing meat or poultry with a pastelike marinade of chiles, lime juice, herbs, and spices, then grilling it slowly so the marinade forms a coating that seals in the juices. If you like your grilled food spicy, this fiery dish is for you.

8–10 jalapeño chiles, seeded
¼ cup (2 fl oz/60 ml) fresh lime juice
¼ cup (⅓ oz/10 g) chopped fresh rosemary or 1 tablespoon dried rosemary, plus rosemary sprigs for garnish
2 tablespoons chopped fresh thyme or 2 teaspoons dried thyme
2 tablespoons mustard seeds
2 tablespoons Dijon mustard
½ yellow onion, cut into chunks
2 large cloves garlic
1 teaspoon salt
4–5 lb (2–2.5 kg) chicken pieces

In a food processor, combine the chiles, lime juice, rosemary, thyme, mustard seeds, mustard, onion, garlic, and salt. Process until the mixture forms a thick, smooth paste. If time permits, scrape the paste into a small bowl, cover, and refrigerate for about 2 hours or for up to 2 days before using. This allows the paste to firm up a bit and gives the flavors time to blend.

🍗 Pat the chicken dry with paper towels. Rub the chicken pieces with the paste, coating them completely, and place them on a nonaluminum platter or baking sheet. Cover with plastic wrap and refrigerate for at least 2 hours or for up to 24 hours.

🍗 Prepare a fire for indirect-heat cooking in a covered grill (see page 11).

🍗 Place the chicken, skin side down, on the center of the grill rack. Cover and open the vents slightly less than halfway. Cook slowly, turning the chicken every 15 minutes, until opaque throughout and the juices run clear, 60–70 minutes. Add more hot coals to the fire if needed to maintain a constant temperature.

🍗 Transfer the chicken to warmed individual plates, garnish with rosemary sprigs, and serve at once.

Lemon-Rosemary Chicken

SERVES 2–4

Fresh rosemary gives chicken an irresistible flavor, and a few sprigs tossed on the fire during the last few minutes of cooking impart a pleasant smokiness. Rosemary is very easy to grow in your garden.

½ cup (4 fl oz/125 ml) fresh lemon juice
⅓ cup (3 fl oz/80 ml) olive oil
2 tablespoons chopped shallot
2 tablespoons chopped fresh rosemary, plus handful of rosemary sprigs
½ teaspoon salt
½ teaspoon freshly ground pepper
1 frying chicken, about 3½ lb (1.75 kg), quartered

In a small bowl, combine the lemon juice, olive oil, shallot, chopped rosemary, salt, and pepper and mix well. Place the chicken quarters in a large lock-top plastic bag and pour in the marinade. Press out the air and seal the bag tightly. Massage the bag gently to distribute the marinade. Set the bag in a large bowl and refrigerate for at least 2 hours, or all day if more convenient, turning and massaging the bag occasionally.

🍗 Soak the rosemary sprigs in water to cover for about 30 minutes. Prepare a fire in a grill.

🍗 Remove the chicken quarters from the marinade and pat dry with paper towels. Boil the remaining marinade and reserve. Arrange the chicken quarters, skin side down, on the grill rack. Grill, turning frequently, for 30–35 minutes. The last 10 minutes, drop the soaked rosemary sprigs on the fire and brush the chicken two or three times with the reserved marinade. If the chicken starts to get too dark, turn skin side up and move it to a cooler part of the rack, so it isn't directly over the fire, or cool the fire a little by covering the grill and opening the vents halfway.

🍗 Transfer the chicken to warmed individual plates and serve at once.

Lemon Chicken Breasts

SERVES 6

Skinless, boneless chicken breast halves cook quickly and are low in calories.

½ cup (4 fl oz/125 ml) fresh lemon
  juice
½ cup (4 fl oz/125 ml) fresh orange
  juice
2 cloves garlic, minced
1 tablespoon peeled and grated fresh
  ginger
1 tablespoon chopped fresh tarragon
  or 1 teaspoon dried tarragon
½ teaspoon salt
¼ teaspoon freshly ground pepper
6 chicken breast halves, skinned
  and boned

In a small bowl, stir together the lemon juice, orange juice, garlic, ginger, tarragon, salt, and pepper. Arrange the chicken breasts in a shallow non-aluminum container and pour the lemon juice mixture evenly over them. Marinate in the refrigerator for 2–3 hours, turning occasionally.

🌿 Prepare a fire in a grill.

🌿 Remove the chicken from the marinade and pat dry with paper towels. Boil the remaining marinade and reserve. Arrange the chicken on the grill rack. Grill, turning two or three times and brushing with the reserved marinade, until the chicken is opaque throughout and the juices run clear, 15–20 minutes.

🌿 Transfer the chicken to warmed individual plates and serve at once.

Provençal Chicken on Skewers

SERVES 4

These skewers call for some of the classic ingredients of southern France: eggplant, tomatoes, thyme, rosemary, and garlic.

2 cloves garlic, halved
½ cup (4 fl oz/125 ml) olive oil
salt and freshly ground pepper to taste
1 teaspoon dried rosemary
1 teaspoon dried thyme
8 chicken thighs, skinned, boned, and
  trimmed of excess fat
1 eggplant (aubergine), cut into sixteen
  2-inch (5-cm) cubes
8 fresh rosemary sprigs, dipped into
  olive oil
8 plum (Roma) tomatoes, halved

In a large, shallow bowl, combine the garlic, olive oil, salt and pepper, rosemary, and thyme.

🌿 Slit the underside of each chicken thigh, if necessary, so the meat lies flat.

Add the chicken to the oil mixture and coat well. Cover and refrigerate for 1 hour, turning frequently.

🌿 Prepare a fire in a grill.

🌿 Remove the chicken from the marinade. Boil the remaining marinade and reserve. Cut each thigh in half; you should have sixteen 2-inch (5-cm) squares in all. Load each of eight 12-inch (30-cm) skewers in the following manner: 1 eggplant cube, 1 chicken square, 1 rosemary sprig, 1 tomato half, 1 eggplant cube, 1 chicken square, 1 tomato half.

🌿 Arrange the skewers on the grill rack and grill, turning as necessary to brown evenly and basting occasionally with the reserved marinade, until the chicken is opaque throughout and the vegetables are tender, 10–12 minutes. Season with salt and pepper.

🌿 Slip the vegetables and chicken from the skewers onto warmed individual plates. Garnish with the grilled rosemary sprigs and serve at once.

Chicken Liver Brochettes

SERVES 6

Chicken livers should be removed from the grill when still slightly pink inside; overcooking toughens them and ruins their smooth texture. Other poultry livers, such as duck, turkey, and goose, may be cooked in the same way. Grilled Onion Slices (page 200) would complement these brochettes nicely.

8 slices bacon (about 8 oz/250 g), cut into 2-inch (5-cm) lengths
¼ cup (2 fl oz/60 ml) olive oil
1 tablespoon soy sauce
½ cup (1½ oz/45 g) chopped green (spring) onions, including white and green portions, plus 6 extra, white portion only, cut into 2-inch (5-cm) lengths
2 teaspoons chopped fresh thyme or oregano, or ½ teaspoon dried thyme or oregano
½ teaspoon freshly ground pepper
2 lb (1 kg) chicken livers, trimmed and halved

Bring a saucepan filled with water to a boil, add the bacon pieces, and blanch for 3 minutes. Drain well and pat dry with paper towels. Set aside.

❧ Prepare a fire in a grill.

❧ In a large bowl, combine the oil, soy sauce, chopped green onions, thyme or oregano, and pepper. Stir well, then add the chicken livers and toss to coat. The livers may be grilled now, or you may cover the bowl and marinate them in the refrigerator, tossing occasionally, for 1 or 2 hours.

❧ Thread the liver, bacon, and green onion pieces alternately onto 6 skewers. Boil the remaining marinade and reserve. Arrange the skewers on the grill rack and grill, turning occasionally and brushing once or twice with the reserved marinade, until the livers are well browned outside and slightly pink inside, 8–12 minutes. Serve at once.

Grill-Roasted Chicken with Potato Fans

SERVES 4

Baking potatoes and a roasting chicken are good grill partners because both cook in the same amount of time.

FOR THE CHICKEN:

1 roasting chicken, 5–6 lb (2.5–3 kg)
1 lemon, halved
salt and freshly ground pepper to taste
several fresh rosemary, thyme, sage, or parsley sprigs
1–2 tablespoons olive oil or vegetable oil

FOR THE POTATOES:

4 baking potatoes, about ½ lb (250 g) each, peeled
3 tablespoons unsalted butter, melted
1 teaspoon salt
½ teaspoon freshly ground pepper

Prepare a fire for indirect-heat cooking in a covered grill (see page 11).

❧ To prepare the chicken, rinse and then pat dry with paper towels. Rub the chicken inside and out with a cut side of the lemon. Sprinkle inside and out with salt and pepper. Tuck the herb sprigs inside the cavity. Rub the skin with the oil. Truss the chicken: Cross the drumsticks and, using kitchen string, tie the legs together, then tie the legs and wings close to the body. Set the chicken aside.

❧ To prepare the potatoes, slice each one crosswise at ¼-inch (6-mm) intervals, cutting only three-fourths of the way through; the slices must remain attached. In a large bowl, gently turn the potatoes in the melted butter. Sprinkle with the salt and pepper.

❧ Place the chicken, breast side down, on the center of the grill rack. Place the potatoes, cut side up, alongside the bird. Cover and open the vents halfway. After 30 minutes, turn the chicken breast side up and turn the potatoes cut side down. Cook the chicken until the juices run clear when the thigh joint is pierced, or until an instant-read thermometer inserted into the thickest part of the thigh registers 180°F (82°C), about 1 hour total. Add more hot coals to the fire as needed to maintain a constant temperature. The potatoes will be tender in about the same amount of time.

❧ Transfer the chicken to a warmed platter, cover loosely with aluminum foil, and let rest for 10 minutes; keep the potatoes warm on the grill. To serve, snip the strings and carve the chicken. Arrange the potatoes alongside.

Rotisserie Cuban Chicken with Orange, Mint, and Garlic

SERVES 4

1 chicken, 4½–5 lb (2.25–2.5 kg)
salt to taste, plus ½ teaspoon salt
freshly ground pepper to taste,
   plus ¼ teaspoon pepper
½ orange
grated zest of 1 orange
3 cloves garlic, minced
3 tablespoons finely chopped fresh mint
1 tablespoon unsalted butter, at room
   temperature
2 tablespoons olive oil
dash of hot-pepper sauce

Prepare an indirect-heat fire for spit roasting in a covered grill with a rotisserie attachment (see page 9).

🍃 Remove the wishbone from the neck of the chicken, then rinse the chicken and pat dry with paper towels. Sprinkle the cavity with salt and pepper and slip the orange half into it.

🍃 In a bowl, whisk together the orange zest, garlic, mint, butter, olive oil, hot-pepper sauce, ½ teaspoon salt, and ¼ teaspoon pepper. Using your fingertips, gently loosen the skin on the chicken breast and slide some of the seasoning mixture between the skin and flesh. Do the same on the thighs, going slowly and taking care not to tear the skin. Rub the remaining mixture all over the outside of the chicken.

🍃 Using kitchen string, tie the wing tips close to the body, then secure the neck skin onto the back with a small metal skewer. Place one of the holding forks onto the rotisserie spit with the prongs facing inward, then insert the

spit through the chicken cavity and out through the body about 1 inch (2.5 cm) on the breast side of the neck opening, balancing the bird as evenly as possible. Using kitchen string, tie the legs together firmly, tying them to the spit at the same time. Insert the second holding fork securely.

🍃 Attach the spit to the motor, cover the grill, and start the motor. Roast the chicken until the skin is golden and crisp, and the juices run clear when the thigh joint is pierced, or an instant-read thermometer inserted into the thickest part of the thigh registers 180°F (82°C), about 1¼ hours. Transfer to a warmed platter, cover loosely with aluminum foil, and let rest for 5–10 minutes.

🍃 Using poultry shears, cut the chicken into 4 serving pieces. Serve at once.

Chicken Breasts with Double-Garlic Aioli

SERVES 4

FOR THE AIOLI:
20 cloves garlic
1 egg
1 tablespoon red wine vinegar
1 teaspoon Dijon mustard
½ teaspoon salt
½ cup (4 fl oz/125 ml) extra-virgin
   olive oil
½ cup (4 fl oz/125 ml) canola oil
1 tablespoon boiling water
1½ tablespoons fresh lemon juice
¼ teaspoon ground white pepper

4 boneless chicken breast halves,
   skinned if desired
salt and freshly ground black pepper
   to taste
2 tablespoons finely chopped fresh
   flat-leaf (Italian) parsley

To make the aioli, in a small saucepan, combine the garlic with water to cover and bring to a boil. Reduce the heat to medium-low and simmer for 30 seconds. Drain in a sieve, return to the pan, and repeat the simmering and draining two more times. After the third time, let the garlic cool in the sieve for 5 minutes.

🍃 In a food processor, combine the cooled garlic, egg, vinegar, mustard, and salt. Purée until completely smooth, 15–30 seconds, stopping to scrape down the sides of the bowl as necessary. With the motor running, pour in the olive and canola oils in a thin, steady stream, adding them more slowly at first and a little more quickly after the first ½ cup (4 fl oz/125 ml) or so has been emulsified. Add the boiling water, lemon juice, and white pepper and process again. If the aioli is too thick, you can thin it with a teaspoon or two of water.

🍃 Prepare a fire in a grill.

🍃 Place each chicken breast between 2 sheets of plastic wrap. Using a meat pounder, pound lightly to achieve a more even thickness. Season generously on both sides with salt and black pepper.

🍃 Place the chicken breasts on the grill rack and grill, turning once, until browned on both sides and just opaque throughout, about 10 minutes total. Transfer the breasts to a cutting board and let rest for 2 minutes.

🍃 Cut each breast into slices on the diagonal about ½ inch (12 mm) thick. Using tongs, transfer each breast, keeping the slices together in their original shape, to warmed individual plates. Sprinkle with the parsley and serve with a large dollop of the aioli.

Chicken with Sage

SERVES 4–6

½ cup (4 fl oz/125 ml) fresh tangerine
  or orange juice
¼ cup (2 fl oz/60 ml) olive oil
2 teaspoons peeled and grated fresh
  ginger
1 frying chicken, 3½ lb (1.75 kg)
8 fresh sage leaves
3 cloves garlic, crushed
salt and freshly ground pepper to taste

In a large bowl, stir together the tangerine or orange juice, olive oil, and ginger. Add the chicken and turn to coat evenly. Cover and refrigerate for 3 hours.

Prepare a fire for indirect-heat cooking in a covered grill (see page 11).

Remove the chicken from the marinade and place on a work surface. Using your fingers and starting at the cavity, carefully loosen the breast skin from the meat. Do not tear the skin. Gently slip the sage leaves under the skin, distributing them evenly. Rub the chicken with the crushed garlic and season with salt and pepper.

Place the chicken, breast side up, on a small piece of aluminum foil on the grill rack. Cover, open the vents, and grill until the juices run clear when the thigh joint is pierced, or an instant-read thermometer inserted into the thickest part of the thigh registers 180°F (82°C), 50–60 minutes. Add more hot coals to the fire as needed to maintain a constant temperature.

Transfer the chicken to a warmed platter, cover loosely with aluminum foil, and let rest for about 10 minutes. Carve at the table and serve at once.

Tandoori Chicken

SERVES 4

Tandoori refers to foods permeated with a yogurt marinade and then cooked in an Indian earthenware oven called a tandoor. A similar effect is achieved in a covered grill.

FOR THE SAUCE:
1 cucumber
1 cup (8 oz/250 g) plain yogurt
¼ cup (⅓ oz/10 g) chopped fresh
  cilantro (fresh coriander) or mint
½ teaspoon salt
¼ teaspoon freshly ground black pepper

FOR THE CHICKEN:
¾ cup (6 oz/185 g) plain yogurt
3 tablespoons fresh lemon juice
4 tablespoons (2 fl oz/60 ml) peanut oil
  or vegetable oil
1 tablespoon minced garlic
1 tablespoon peeled and grated fresh
  ginger
1 tablespoon curry powder
1 teaspoon ground turmeric
1 teaspoon salt
½ teaspoon cayenne pepper
1 frying chicken, 3½ lb (1.75 kg),
  quartered

To prepare the sauce, peel the cucumber, halve it lengthwise, then scrape out the seeds. Cut the cucumber crosswise into thin slices. In a bowl, stir together the cucumber slices, yogurt, cilantro or mint, salt, and black pepper. Cover and refrigerate until serving.

To prepare the chicken, in a small bowl, stir together the yogurt, lemon juice, 2 tablespoons of the oil, the garlic, ginger, curry powder, turmeric, salt, and cayenne; set aside.

Remove and discard the skin from the chicken. Using a sharp knife, score the chicken meat ½ inch (12 mm) deep at 1-inch (2.5-cm) intervals. Place in a single layer in a shallow nonaluminum dish large enough for the pieces to lie flat. Add the marinade, coating evenly and working it into the cuts. Cover and refrigerate for at least 3 hours or as long as overnight.

Prepare a fire in a covered grill.

Remove the chicken from the marinade. Scrape most of the marinade from the chicken. Boil the remaining marinade and reserve. Rub the chicken with the remaining 2 tablespoons oil. Place on the grill rack and grill, uncovered, for 10 minutes. Turn and brush with some of the reserved marinade. Grill for 10 minutes longer, then again turn and brush with the marinade. Cover the grill, open the vents halfway, and cook until opaque throughout and the juices run clear, about 15 minutes longer.

Transfer to a warmed platter and serve at once. Pass the cucumber-yogurt sauce at the table.

Tropical Chicken Breasts

SERVES 6

A ginger-coconut marinade infuses these chicken breasts with rich flavor and then forms a sweet glaze as the meat cooks on the grill.

1 cup (6 oz/185 g) fresh pineapple chunks or drained, canned unsweetened pineapple chunks

⅔ cup (5 fl oz/160 ml) canned coconut milk

1 piece fresh ginger, 4–5 inches (10–13 cm) long, peeled and thinly sliced

½ teaspoon salt

¼ teaspoon freshly ground pepper

6 skinless, boneless chicken breast halves, 4–6 oz (125–185 g) each

In a blender or food processor, combine the pineapple, coconut milk, ginger, salt, and pepper and process until smooth.

🔥 Arrange the chicken breasts in a single layer in a shallow nonaluminum dish. Pour the pineapple mixture over the chicken and turn to coat evenly. Cover and let marinate in the refrigerator for 2–3 hours.

🔥 Prepare a fire in a grill.

🔥 Remove the chicken breasts from the marinade. Boil the marinade and reserve.

🔥 Arrange the chicken on the grill rack and grill for 5 minutes. Brush with the reserved marinade, turn, and grill for 5 minutes longer. Again brush with the marinade and turn. Continue cooking until the chicken is browned outside, opaque throughout, and the juices run clear, 5–10 minutes longer.

🔥 Transfer to warmed individual plates and serve immediately.

Teriyaki Chicken

SERVES 2–4

A Polynesian favorite, teriyaki was originally brought to the mainland by travelers from Hawaii. The soy-and-ginger marinade, also a favorite for flank steak and lamb kabobs, penetrates the meat with its complex flavors. Serve with the Mixed Vegetable Grill (page 195), if you wish, and rice.

⅓ cup (3 fl oz/80 ml) soy sauce

⅓ cup (3 fl oz/80 ml) dry sherry

¼ cup (2 fl oz/60 ml) vegetable oil

2 tablespoons sugar

2 cloves garlic, minced

1 tablespoon peeled and grated fresh ginger

1 frying chicken, about 3½ lb (1.75 kg), cut into serving pieces

In a small bowl, stir together the soy sauce, sherry, vegetable oil, sugar, garlic, and ginger. Place the chicken in a large lock-top plastic bag and pour in the soy mixture. Press out the air and seal the bag tightly. Massage the bag gently to distribute the marinade. Set the bag in a large bowl and refrigerate for at least 2 hours, or all day if you wish, turning and massaging the bag occasionally.

🔥 Prepare a fire in a grill.

🔥 Remove the chicken pieces from the marinade and pat dry with paper towels. Boil the marinade and reserve. Arrange the chicken pieces, skin side down, on the grill rack. Grill, turning frequently, 30–35 minutes. During the last 15 minutes of cooking, brush the chicken two or three times with the reserved marinade. If the chicken starts to get too dark, turn it skin side up and move it to a cooler part of the grill.

🔥 Transfer to warmed individual plates and serve at once.

Deviled Chicken

SERVES 2–4

Deviled means the chicken is brushed with mustard and sprinkled with bread crumbs to make a spicy, crunchy coating.

1 frying chicken, 3½–4 lb (1.75–2 kg)
Spicy Mop Sauce *(page 293)*
¼ cup (2 oz/60 g) Dijon mustard
2 tablespoons minced shallot or green
   (spring) onion
¼ teaspoon cayenne pepper
1 cup (2 oz/60 g) fresh white bread
   crumbs

First, butterfly the chicken: Place the bird on a work surface, breast side down. Using a sharp knife, cut lengthwise down the backbone, slitting the bird from its neck to its tail. Open the chicken as flat as possible and turn skin side up. Using your fist, firmly strike the breastbone to break the ridge of the bone and flatten the breast.

Place the chicken in a shallow non-aluminum dish large enough for it to lie flat. Pour the mop sauce over the chicken and turn to coat both sides. Cover and refrigerate, turning occasionally, for at least 3 hours or for up to all day.

Prepare a fire for indirect-heat cooking in a covered grill (see page 11).

In a small bowl, stir together the mustard, shallot or green onion, and cayenne; set aside.

Remove the chicken from the marinade and pat dry with paper towels. Place the chicken, skin side down, on the perimeter of the rack, directly over the coals. Grill uncovered, turning frequently, for about 25 minutes. Move the chicken so it is not directly over the fire, turn it skin side up, and brush with the mustard mixture. Sprinkle the bread crumbs over the mustard and pat them in gently. Cover the grill and open the vents halfway. Cook until the crumbs are crisp and very lightly browned and the chicken is opaque throughout and the juices run clear, 10–15 minutes longer.

To serve, cut into pieces and arrange on a warmed platter.

Chicken and Mushroom Kabobs

SERVES 4

A dry marinade of herbs and salt forms a crisp, spicy coating.

1¼ teaspoons salt
1 teaspoon freshly ground black pepper
1 teaspoon dried sage
½ teaspoon dried thyme
½ teaspoon cayenne pepper
1 clove garlic, minced
4 skinless, boneless chicken breast halves
1 tablespoon vegetable oil
12 large fresh mushrooms,
   brushed clean and stems removed
12–16 fresh sage leaves (optional)
2 tablespoons olive oil

In a small bowl, stir together 1 teaspoon of the salt, the black pepper, sage, thyme, cayenne, and garlic; set aside.

Cut the chicken breasts into strips about 3 inches (7.5 cm) long and 1 inch (2.5 cm) wide. Pat them dry with paper towels and place in a large bowl. Add the vegetable oil and toss to coat the chicken strips evenly. Add the herb mixture and toss again to coat completely. Let stand for about 1 hour in the refrigerator.

Prepare a fire in a grill.

Toss the mushroom caps with the sage leaves (if using), olive oil, and the remaining ¼ teaspoon salt. Thread the chicken strips onto skewers alternately with the mushroom caps and sage leaves (if used). Arrange the skewers on the grill rack and grill, turning frequently, until the chicken and mushrooms are lightly browned and the chicken is opaque throughout and the juices run clear, 8–10 minutes.

Transfer to warmed individual plates and serve at once.

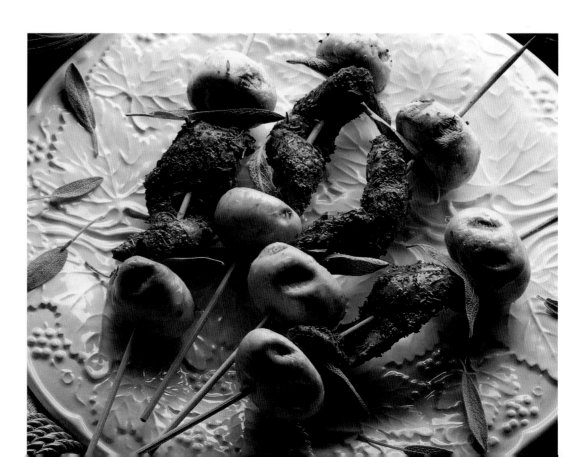

Pacific Rim Chicken with Peanut Sauce

SERVES 6

Serve the chicken strips over noodles and garnish with chopped fresh cilantro (fresh coriander), bean sprouts, shredded coconut, lime wedges, shredded carrots, and chopped peanuts.

6 skinless, boneless chicken breast halves, cut into long strips 1 inch (2.5 cm) wide (12 strips)

1 cup (8 fl oz/250 ml) fresh lime juice

FOR THE SAUCE:

2 tablespoons vegetable oil

3 green (spring) onions, including tender green tops, chopped

1½ cups (12 fl oz/375 ml) coconut milk, or as needed

½ cup (5 oz/155 g) peanut butter

¼ cup (⅓ oz/10 g) chopped fresh cilantro (fresh coriander)

3 tablespoons dark brown sugar

1½ teaspoons ground ginger

½ teaspoon ground cumin

Place the chicken in a shallow non-aluminum dish, pour the lime juice evenly over the top, cover, and refrigerate for 30 minutes.

Prepare a fire in a covered grill.

Meanwhile, prepare the peanut sauce: In a small saucepan over medium heat, warm the vegetable oil. Add the green onions and sauté until tender, about 5 minutes. Stir in the 1½ cups (12 fl oz/ 375 ml) coconut milk, the peanut butter, cilantro, brown sugar, ginger, and cumin. Cook, stirring occasionally, until the sauce thickens slightly, about 5 minutes. If the sauce becomes too thick to pour, add more coconut milk. Pour into a bowl and let cool. (If made ahead, cover and refrigerate until serving.)

Drain the chicken and weave 2 chicken strips onto each of 6 skewers. Place the skewers on the grill rack, cover, open the vents, and grill, turning once, until opaque throughout, about 10 minutes. During the last 5 minutes of grilling, measure out about ¼ cup (2 fl oz/60 ml) of the sauce and brush the chicken lightly with the sauce.

Transfer the skewers to a serving platter and serve at once. Pass the remaining peanut sauce at the table.

Buffalo Chicken Wings

SERVES 6

⅓ cup (3 fl oz/80 ml) vegetable oil

1 small clove garlic, minced

½ teaspoon cayenne pepper

2 tablespoons red wine vinegar

½ teaspoon Tabasco or other hot-pepper sauce, or to taste

24 chicken wings, about 2 lb (1 kg) total weight

FOR THE DRESSING:

1 cup (8 fl oz/250 ml) mayonnaise

½ cup (4 oz/125 g) sour cream

1 small yellow onion, minced

3 cloves garlic, minced

2 tablespoons red wine vinegar

¼ cup (⅓ oz/10 g) minced fresh parsley

½ cup (2½ oz/75 g) crumbled blue cheese

6 large celery stalks, cut into 3-inch (7.5-cm) lengths

Prepare a fire in a grill.

In a bowl, stir together the vegetable oil, garlic, cayenne, vinegar, and hot-pepper sauce. Cut each wing at the joint to make 2 pieces, add to the bowl, and toss gently to coat evenly.

Arrange the wings on a grill screen and place on the grill rack. Grill, turning once, until opaque throughout and the juices run clear, about 12 minutes total.

Meanwhile, prepare the dressing: In a small bowl, stir together the mayonnaise, sour cream, onion, garlic, vinegar, parsley, and blue cheese.

Transfer the wings to serving plates and serve with the celery and the blue cheese dressing.

Flattened Chicken with a Greek Flavor

SERVES 4

Here, a chicken is flattened—or butterflied— to bring more of the bird into direct contact with the heat. This way, it cooks more quickly than a whole chicken, yet retains its juiciness.

1 chicken, 3½–4 lb (1.75–2 kg)
3 tablespoons finely chopped fresh
    oregano or marjoram, plus sprigs
    for garnish (optional)
3 large cloves garlic, finely chopped
grated zest of 1 lemon
¾ teaspoon salt
½ teaspoon coarsely ground pepper
2 tablespoons extra-virgin olive oil
1 lemon, sliced or quartered

Rinse the chicken and pat dry. Remove any excess fat from the chicken cavity, then using a small, sharp knife, remove the wishbone from between the top of the breasts. (This makes the chicken much easier to carve.) Remove the backbone by cutting along either side of it with poultry shears. Place the chicken breast side up and push down on the breast with the palm of your hand to flatten the bird, breaking some of the rib bones.

In a small bowl, combine the chopped oregano or marjoram, garlic, lemon zest, salt, pepper, and olive oil and mix to form a paste. Gently loosen the skin on the breast and thigh to push some of the paste between the skin and flesh, then rub the remaining paste over the rest of the chicken. Place on a platter, cover, and refrigerate for at least 2 hours or for up to 4 hours.

Prepare a fire for indirect-heat cooking in a covered grill (see page 11). Bring the chicken to room temperature.

Place the chicken on the grill rack, cover, and grill until nicely browned, about 20 minutes. Turn the chicken over and continue to grill until the juices run clear when the thigh joint is pierced, or until an instant-read thermometer inserted into the thickest part of the thigh registers 180°F (82°C), 20–25 minutes. Transfer the chicken to a platter, cover loosely with aluminum foil, and let rest for 10 minutes.

Using poultry shears, carve the chicken, cutting between the breasts and along the edges to make 2 breast-wing portions and 2 thigh-drumstick portions. Garnish with the lemon slices or quarters and oregano or marjoram sprigs, if using, and serve.

Hickory-Smoked Chicken

SERVES 4

Dropping aromatic hickory chips on the fire gives this chicken a smoky taste. It is good served hot or cold.

1 roasting chicken, 5–6 lb (2.5–3 kg)
½ lemon
salt and freshly ground pepper to taste
fresh rosemary or parsley sprigs
several fresh ginger slices
1 tablespoon vegetable oil or olive oil

Soak 3 handfuls of hickory chips in water to cover for about 1 hour.

Prepare a fire for indirect-heat cooking in a covered grill (see page 11).

Pat the chicken dry with paper towels. Rub the outside of the chicken with the cut side of the lemon. Sprinkle the bird inside and out with salt and pepper. Tuck rosemary or parsley sprigs and the ginger inside the cavity. Rub the skin with the oil. Truss the bird: Cross the drumsticks and, using kitchen string, tie the legs together, then tie the legs and wings close to the body.

Scoop half of the soaked wood chips out of the water and drop them onto the fire. Place the chicken, breast side down, on the grill rack and cover the grill. After 30 minutes, turn the bird breast side up and sprinkle the remaining wood chips on the fire. Cook the chicken until the juices run clear when the thigh joint is pierced, or until an instant-read thermometer inserted into the thickest part of the thigh registers 180°F (82°C), about 1 hour total. Add more coals to the fire as needed to maintain a constant temperature.

Transfer the chicken to a warmed platter, cover loosely with aluminum foil, and let it rest for 10 minutes. To serve, snip the strings and carve the chicken.

Chicken Kabobs

SERVES 4

Feel free to use your favorite summer vegetables, such as yellow summer squash and bell peppers (capsicums). If you use wooden skewers, soak them well and keep them from direct contact with the flame. Serve the skewers atop a bed of rice pilaf, if you like.

2 skinless, boneless whole chicken
  breasts
1 cup (8 fl oz/250 ml) olive oil
4 cloves garlic, halved
2 tablespoons soy sauce
½ cup (1 oz/30 g) chopped fresh basil
1 lemon, halved
8 large fresh mushrooms, brushed clean
  and thickly sliced
1 red (Spanish) onion, thickly sliced
salt and freshly ground pepper to taste
4 fresh basil or mint sprigs

Prepare a fire in a grill.

Cut the chicken into 2-inch (5-cm) squares; you should have 32 squares in all.

In a large nonaluminum bowl, stir together the olive oil, garlic, soy sauce, chopped basil, and the juice of ½ lemon. Add the chicken, mushrooms, and onion and toss to coat lightly.

Load eight 12-inch (30-cm) skewers with the chicken pieces, mushrooms, and onion. Boil the remaining oil mixture and reserve.

Arrange the skewers on the grill rack and grill, turning to brown all sides and basting occasionally with the reserved oil mixture, until the vegetables are tender and the chicken is opaque throughout and the juices run clear, 10–12 minutes. Season with salt and pepper.

Transfer the skewers to a serving platter and squeeze the juice from the remaining lemon half over them. Garnish with the herb sprigs and serve.

Chicken Breasts with Black Olive Butter

SERVES 6

FOR THE BUTTER:

½ cup (4 oz/125 g) unsalted butter, at room temperature

¼ cup (1¼ oz/37 g) chopped pitted black olives

2 tablespoons chopped fresh parsley or tarragon

1 tablespoon fresh lemon juice

pinch of freshly ground pepper

3 boneless whole chicken breasts with the skin intact, 10–12 oz (315–375 g) each

4 teaspoons vegetable oil

salt and freshly ground pepper to taste

To prepare the butter, in a small bowl, combine the butter, olives, parsley or tarragon, lemon juice, and pepper. Using a fork or wooden spoon, beat vigorously until blended. Transfer half of the butter mixture to a sheet of plastic wrap and shape it into a log about 3 inches (7.5 cm) long and 1 inch (2.5 cm) in diameter. Wrap in the plastic wrap and refrigerate until firm, at least 1 hour. Set the remaining butter mixture aside.

Prepare a fire for indirect-heat cooking in a covered grill (see page 11).

Working with 1 chicken breast at a time, gently slide your fingertips under the skin to make a pocket. Divide the butter mixture in the bowl into 3 equal portions and, using your fingertips, slip a portion under the skin of each breast, distributing it evenly. Tie pieces of kitchen string crosswise around each breast in 2 places, to make a cylindrical roll. Rub the breasts with the vegetable oil, then sprinkle with salt and pepper.

Place the chicken on the center of the grill rack, cover, and open the vents halfway. Cook for 20 minutes. Turn the chicken and continue to cook until browned and opaque throughout and the juices run clear, about 20 minutes longer.

Transfer the breasts to a cutting board, cover loosely with aluminum foil, and let rest for 5 minutes. To serve, snip the strings and cut each breast crosswise into slices ½ inch (12 mm) thick. Arrange on warmed individual plates. Cut the butter log into 6 equal slices and place a slice on top of each serving. Serve at once.

All-American Barbecued Chicken

SERVES 4–6

If your barbecued chicken tends to flare up and get too dark on the grill, the following method of direct- and indirect-heat cooking will give you perfect results. "Frying" chickens, birds weighing 3–4 lb (1.5–2 kg) each, are good for grilling. If you like assorted pieces, use the whole chicken, cut up. Or buy any other chicken parts you like, such as thighs, breasts, or legs. Brush the sauce on for just the last few minutes of cooking, so it doesn't burn. Serve with Corn with Seasoned Butters (page 204) and potato salad or coleslaw.

5–6 lb (2.5–3 kg) chicken pieces

salt and freshly ground pepper to taste

Basic Barbecue Sauce *(page 294)*

Prepare a fire for indirect-heat cooking in a covered grill (see page 11).

Sprinkle the chicken pieces on both sides with salt and pepper. Place them, skin side down, around the edge of the grill rack so they are directly above the hot coals. Grill, uncovered, turning frequently, until well browned, 10–15 minutes. Watch the chicken constantly and have a spray bottle of water handy to douse flare-ups. Move the chicken pieces to the middle of the rack—they may overlap slightly—so that they are no longer directly over the fire.

Cover the grill and open the vents halfway. Cook for 10 minutes. Turn the chicken, brush it with the sauce, re-cover, and cook for 5 minutes more. Brush again with the sauce, then cover and cook until opaque throughout, about 5 minutes longer.

Transfer to warmed individual plates and serve at once. Pass the remaining sauce at the table.

Mustard-Grilled Chicken

SERVES 2–4

Mustard is wonderful with chicken, and in this recipe it does double duty as both a marinade and a basting sauce. The mixture is very spicy. If you desire less heat, reduce the amount of cayenne to 2 teaspoons.

⅔ cup (6 oz/180 g) Dijon mustard
2 tablespoons cayenne pepper
¼ cup (2 fl oz/60 ml) vegetable oil
2 tablespoons white wine vinegar
1 broiler chicken, about 2½ lb
    (1.25 kg), split

In a small bowl, stir together ⅓ cup (3 oz/ 90 g) of the mustard, 1 tablespoon of the cayenne, the vegetable oil, and the vinegar. Place the chicken in a large lock-top plastic bag and pour in the mustard mixture. Press out the air and seal the bag tightly. Massage gently to distribute the marinade. Set in a large bowl and refrigerate for at least 2 hours, turning and rubbing the bag occasionally.

Prepare a fire for indirect-heat cooking in a covered grill (see page 11).

Combine the remaining ⅓ cup (3 oz/ 90 g) mustard with the remaining 1 tablespoon cayenne. Remove the chicken from the marinade, allowing as much marinade as possible to cling to the surface. Place the chicken, skin side down, in the center of the grill rack. Grill, turning frequently, for about 25 minutes; do not worry if some of the marinade sticks to the grill. Turn the chicken skin side up and brush it with the mustard-cayenne mixture. Cover the grill, open the vents halfway, and cook until opaque throughout and the juices run clear, about 10 minutes longer.

If necessary, cut the chicken into smaller portions, then transfer to warmed individual plates and serve.

Chicken Paillards with Grilled Tangerines and Green Onion Oil

SERVES 4

Grilled tangerines are delicious and provide a lovely sour-sweet complement to these lean chicken paillards. The green onion oil is easy to make and packed with flavor.

FOR THE GREEN ONION OIL:

2 green (spring) onions, including
    tender green tops, minced
1 cup (8 fl oz/250 ml) canola oil

4 skinless, boneless chicken breast
    halves
1½ tablespoons olive oil
½ teaspoon minced anchovy fillet,
    anchovy paste, or salt
½ teaspoon chopped fresh oregano
1 tablespoon white wine vinegar
⅛ teaspoon freshly ground pepper

4 tangerine or orange slices, each
    ⅜ inch (1 cm) thick
olive oil
salt and freshly ground pepper to taste

Two hours before serving time, make the green onion oil: Combine the green onions and canola oil in a jar, cap tightly, and shake vigorously. Refrigerate until ready to serve. (Any leftover oil will keep, refrigerated, for up to 10 days.)

Place each chicken breast between 2 sheets of plastic wrap. Using a meat pounder, pound lightly to an even thickness of no less than ⅜ inch (1 cm) thick.

In a shallow nonaluminum dish, combine the olive oil, anchovy or salt, oregano, vinegar, and pepper. Add the chicken breasts and brush all sides with the mixture. Cover and refrigerate for 30 minutes.

Meanwhile, prepare a fire in a grill.

Bring a small saucepan three-fourths full of water to a boil. Add the citrus slices, blanch for 2 minutes, and drain. Pat dry.

Brush the citrus slices with olive oil and season with salt and pepper. Place on the grill rack and grill, turning once, until lightly charred, 2–3 minutes on each side. Transfer to a plate. Place the chicken breasts on the grill rack and grill, turning once, until opaque throughout and the juices run clear, about 1½ minutes on each side. Using a spatula, rotate each breast halfway through the cooking time on each side to achieve a crosshatch pattern.

Transfer the chicken breasts to warmed individual plates. Top each with a citrus slice and drizzle a scant tablespoon of the green onion oil over the top.

Other Birds

Any bird, from a tiny squab to a big turkey, benefits from exposure to the smoke and searing heat of an open fire. Butterflying, or flattening, poultry helps to bring more of the bird into contact with the hot grill, yielding plenty of crisp, crusty skin. Brining is a recently rediscovered method for ensuring moist meat and is especially suited to some of the leaner types of poultry. For those with a rotisserie, no better way exists to present a perfectly cooked bird: crisp on the outside, moist on the inside.

Duck with Orange and Vermouth

SERVES 2

The easiest cut of duck to grill is a bone-in breast because it isn't as fat laden as other parts of the bird. This orange-infused duck breast makes an elegant meal for two. Serve with puréed parsnips or celeriac (celery root) and a green vegetable.

1 cup (8 fl oz/250 ml) fresh orange juice
½ cup (4 fl oz/125 ml) dry white vermouth
¼ cup (2½ oz/75 g) orange marmalade
1 tablespoon chopped fresh thyme or 1 teaspoon dried thyme
½ teaspoon salt
1 bone-in whole duck breast, 1¼–1½ lb (625–750 g)

In a small bowl, whisk together the orange juice, vermouth, marmalade, thyme, and salt. Using a sharp knife, score the duck skin with several crisscross diagonal cuts about ¼ inch (6 mm)

deep. Place the duck breast in a shallow nonaluminum dish large enough for it to lie flat. Pour the marinade over the breast and turn to coat both sides. Cover and refrigerate, turning occasionally, for at least 1 hour or for up to all day.

▶ Prepare a fire in a grill.

▶ Remove the duck from the marinade and pat dry with paper towels. Boil the remaining marinade and reserve.

▶ Place the duck on the grill rack. Grill, turning frequently and brushing three or four times with the reserved marinade, until the skin is well browned and the meat is still slightly pink at the bone, 18–20 minutes. For medium to well done, grill an additional 5–7 minutes.

▶ Remove the duck from the grill, cover loosely with aluminum foil, and let rest for 5 minutes. Cut the meat from the bone into thin slices and arrange on warmed individual plates. If you wish, remove the crispy skin, cut into thin strips and serve with the meat.

Cornish Hens with Ginger Butter

SERVES 4

Cornish hens can easily dry out on the grill, but a garlic-ginger butter rubbed under the skin tempers that tendency and makes these birds juicy and flavorful.

2 shallots or green (spring) onions, finely chopped
3 large cloves garlic, chopped
¼ cup (2 oz/60 g) unsalted butter, at room temperature
2 tablespoons peeled and grated fresh ginger
2 tablespoons chopped fresh parsley
½ teaspoon salt, plus salt to taste
¼ teaspoon freshly ground pepper, plus pepper to taste
4 Cornish hens, about 1½ lb (750 g) each

Prepare a fire in a covered grill.

In a bowl, combine the shallots or green onions, garlic, butter, ginger, parsley, ½ teaspoon salt, and ¼ teaspoon pepper. Beat with a wooden spoon until blended.

Starting at the neck end of each bird, gently slide your fingers under the skin covering the breast, gradually working them between the flesh and skin down toward the thighs. Proceed slowly so you do not tear the skin.

Divide the butter mixture into 4 fairly equal-sized portions and slip a portion under the skin of each bird. With your fingertips, work the ginger butter under the skin, covering all of the breast meat and easing it toward the thighs as best you can. Sprinkle each body cavity with salt and pepper. Truss each bird with kitchen string, securing the legs and wings close to the body.

Place the hens, breast side up, on the grill rack. Grill for about 20 minutes. Turn them breast down and cover the grill, opening the vents halfway. Cook until the juices run clear when a thigh joint is pierced, 20–25 minutes longer.

Remove from the grill, let rest for 5 minutes, then serve at once.

Herbed Butterflied Squab

SERVES 4

Small birds such as squab and quail cook quickly on the grill and are good for a festive dinner. Your butcher can butterfly them for you.

1½ teaspoons salt
1 teaspoon freshly ground pepper
2 tablespoons chopped fresh thyme or 2 teaspoons dried thyme
1 teaspoon crushed bay leaf
2 teaspoons crushed juniper berries
4 squabs (young pigeons), about 1 lb (500 g) each, butterflied
olive oil
handful of fresh thyme sprigs (optional)

In a small bowl, stir together the salt, pepper, thyme, bay leaf, and juniper berries. Rub each squab lightly with olive oil, then sprinkle each bird with one-fourth of the herb mixture and rub it gently into the skin. Place the birds on a large platter or in an enameled baking pan, laying them flat, and cover with plastic wrap. Marinate in the refrigerator for at least 2 hours or, preferably, for up to overnight.

If using the thyme sprigs, soak in water to cover for about 30 minutes. Prepare a fire in a grill.

Arrange the squabs, breast side down, on the grill rack. Grill for 15–20 minutes, turning them two or three times and brushing once or twice with oil. The squabs are done when the skin is well browned and the meat is slightly pink when slashed to the bone in the thickest part. During the last few minutes of cooking, place a damp sprig of thyme under each bird. The sprigs will smoke gently, giving off a pleasant aroma and flavor.

Transfer to warmed individual plates and serve at once.

Grill-Roasted Turkey

SERVES 10–12

This turkey comes out juicy, with a smoky flavor and dark brown skin. A roasting chicken may be done the same way: For a 5–6-lb (2.5–3-kg) bird, halve all the ingredients and cook for about 1½ hours total, or to the suggested temperature on an instant-read thermometer.

1 turkey, 10–12 lb (5–6 kg)

2 tablespoons olive oil

2 tablespoons chopped fresh rosemary
   or 2 teaspoons dried rosemary

salt and freshly ground pepper to taste

2 lemons, quartered

large handful of fresh sage, tarragon,
   or parsley sprigs

½ cup (4 oz/125 g) unsalted butter,
   melted

2 tablespoons fresh lemon juice

Soak 3 handfuls hickory chips in water to cover for about 1 hour. Prepare a fire for indirect-heat cooking in a covered grill (see page 11).

 Pat the turkey dry with paper towels and rub with the olive oil and rosemary. Sprinkle inside and out with salt and pepper. Tuck the lemon quarters and herb sprigs inside the cavity. Truss the bird with kitchen string, securing the legs and wings close to the body. Scoop half of the wood chips out of the water and drop them onto the fire. Place the turkey, breast side up, in the center of the grill rack. Cover and cook for 1 hour.

 In a small bowl, stir together the melted butter and lemon juice. Drop the remaining wood chips on the fire. Brush the turkey with half of the butter mixture, then cover and cook for 45 minutes longer, adding more coals if necessary to maintain a constant temperature. Brush with the remaining butter mixture, then cook, covered, for 30–45 minutes longer, or until the juices run clear when a thigh joint is pierced, or an instant-read thermometer inserted into the thickest part of the thigh registers 180°F (82°C). Total cooking time is about 2½ hours.

 Transfer the turkey to a warmed platter, cover loosely with aluminum foil, and let rest for 15–20 minutes. Snip the string, carve, and arrange on the platter. Serve at once.

Thyme and Mustard Quail

SERVES 4

Cooks who never hesitate to barbecue chicken and turkey are often apprehensive about grilling quail because they are less common. Do not be shy about these single-serving birds. Their succulent dark meat is moist and delicious.

⅓ cup (4 oz/125 g) Dijon mustard
½ cup (4 fl oz/125 ml) dry white
　or red wine
⅓ cup (3 fl oz/80 ml) olive oil
1 tablespoon chopped fresh thyme
　or 1 teaspoon dried thyme
8 quail, about 5 oz (155 g) each
salt and freshly ground pepper to taste

Prepare a fire in a grill.

🔥 In a small bowl, stir together the mustard, wine, 3 tablespoons of the oil, and the thyme; set aside. Pat the quail dry with paper towels. Rub them with the remaining oil and sprinkle lightly with salt and pepper.

🔥 Place the quail, breast side down, on the grill rack. Grill for about 8 minutes, turning them frequently to brown evenly. Brush the mustard mixture on the quail and cook for about 5 minutes longer, turning them once. Boil the mustard mixture and brush on quail again. Do not overcook the birds; the meat should remain slightly pink at the bone.

🔥 Transfer to a warmed platter and serve at once.

Hickory-Smoked Turkey Thighs

SERVES 8

Dropping damp hickory chips onto the fire gives turkey a subtle, smoky taste. The dry rub forms a spicy coating and helps bring out the turkey's natural flavor. Large turkey thighs are easy to cook, and each one makes two generous helpings, so this is a good recipe to double for a crowd. Serve with cranberry sauce and potato salad or coleslaw.

FOR THE RUB:
1½ teaspoons salt
1 teaspoon freshly ground pepper
1 teaspoon dried sage
1 teaspoon dried thyme
grated zest of 1 lemon

4 turkey thighs, about 1½ lb (750 g)
　each
4 teaspoons vegetable oil

Soak a handful of hickory chips in water to cover for at least 1 hour.

🔥 To prepare the rub, in a small bowl, stir together the salt, pepper, sage, thyme, and lemon zest. Pat the turkey thighs dry with paper towels. Rub them with the vegetable oil, and then rub each one with the herb marinade. Cover and refrigerate for 1 hour or up to several hours.

🔥 Prepare a fire for indirect-heat cooking in a covered grill (see page 11). Scoop the hickory chips out of the water and drop them onto the fire.

🔥 Place the turkey thighs, skin side down, on the center of the grill rack. Cover and open the vents halfway. Cook, turning two or three times, until well browned, opaque throughout, and the juices run clear, 50–60 minutes.

🔥 Transfer the thighs to a cutting board, cut each one in half along one side of the bone, and arrange on warmed individual plates. Serve immediately.

Bacon-Wrapped Cornish Hens

SERVES 4

Cornish hens tend to be dry, but a couple of slices of blanched bacon tied around each bird help to keep it moist and succulent. This recipe is delicious served with Ratatouille from the Grill (page 184).

8 slices bacon, about ½ lb (250 g) total
4 Cornish hens, about 1¼ lb (625 g) each
salt and freshly ground pepper to taste
4–8 fresh parsley sprigs
4–8 fresh thyme sprigs

Prepare a fire for indirect-heat cooking in a covered grill (see page 11).

Fill a large saucepan two-thirds full with water and bring to a boil over high heat. Add the bacon and blanch for 3 minutes. Drain, then rinse the bacon with cold water and pat dry with paper towels. Set aside.

Pat the hens dry with paper towels. Sprinkle them inside and out with salt and pepper to taste. Tuck a sprig or two of parsley and thyme into each body cavity. Crisscross 2 slices of bacon across the breast of each hen. Using kitchen string, tie the bacon securely to the birds.

Place the hens, breast side up, on the center of the grill rack. Cover and open the vents halfway. Cook for 30 minutes, then turn breast side down. Continue cooking, covered, until the birds are well browned, opaque throughout and the juices run clear, 20–25 minutes longer.

Transfer the birds to a warmed platter or individual plates. Snip the strings and arrange the bacon alongside.

Turkey Kabobs with Peanut Dipping Sauce

SERVES 4–6

Skewers of turkey breast meat are easy to cook even on a small grill. Serve over steamed or fried rice and accompany with the peanut dipping sauce.

1 skinless, boneless turkey breast, 2 lb (1 kg)
½ cup (4 fl oz/125 ml) dry white wine
¼ cup (2 fl oz/60 ml) soy sauce
¼ cup (2 fl oz/60 ml) vegetable oil or olive oil
1 tablespoon sugar
1 large clove garlic, minced
½ teaspoon freshly ground pepper

Peanut Dipping Sauce *(page 294)*

Cut the turkey breast into 1½-inch (4-cm) cubes. In a large bowl, whisk together the wine, soy sauce, oil, sugar, garlic, and pepper. Add the turkey and toss to coat evenly. Cover and refrigerate, tossing occasionally, for at least 3 hours or for up to all day.

Prepare a fire in a grill.

Remove the turkey from the marinade and pat dry with paper towels. Boil the remaining marinade and reserve. Thread the turkey onto 4 or 6 skewers.

Arrange the skewers on the grill rack. Grill, turning frequently and brushing occasionally with the reserved marinade, until the turkey is opaque throughout, about 20 minutes.

Transfer the skewers to warmed individual plates and serve immediately with the peanut sauce.

Guava-Glazed Duck

SERVES 4

Twice-cooked duck sounds like an item from a Chinese menu, but here it is used as a technique for ridding the duck of much of its fat without incinerating the bird. Duck and fruit are often paired, and this recipe is no exception, with its rich guava glaze flavored with sherry. Since duck wings are small, they should be seen as snacks for the chef rather than servings on their own.

FOR THE GLAZE:

½ cup (5 oz/155 g) guava marmalade
  or jelly
3 tablespoons dry sherry
3 tablespoons sherry vinegar
1 tablespoon tomato paste
1 tablespoon dark corn syrup
1 tablespoon dark molasses
1 tablespoon Dijon mustard
1 tablespoon minced yellow onion
1 large clove garlic, minced
½ teaspoon ground cumin

1 duck, cut into serving pieces
  (2 leg-thigh combinations, 2 breasts,
  and 2 wings) *(see note)*
salt and freshly ground pepper to taste
fresh cilantro (fresh coriander) sprigs
  (optional)

To prepare the glaze, in a saucepan, combine the marmalade or jelly, sherry, vinegar, tomato paste, corn syrup, molasses, mustard, onion, garlic, and cumin. Stir to mix well and place over medium-low heat. Bring to a slow simmer, cover partially, and cook until very thick, stirring occasionally, about 10 minutes. Set aside to cool.

Place the duck pieces in a steamer rack over boiling water, cover the steamer, and steam until the skin on the drumsticks begins to pull back, about 40 minutes.

Meanwhile, prepare a fire for indirect-heat cooking in a covered grill (see page 11).

Remove the duck pieces from the steamer and, when cool enough to handle, cut several small slits on each piece, slicing through the skin but not into the meat. Season generously with salt and pepper and rub some of the glaze into the cuts.

Place the duck legs, skin side down, over the drip pan and cover the grill. Grill for 20 minutes. Add the breasts and wings, skin side down, and continue grilling for 5 minutes. Turn all the pieces over and grill until the skin begins to crisp, about 15 minutes longer. Brush all the pieces generously with the guava glaze and continue grilling, turning and basting often on all sides with the glaze, until a deep, dark brown, 5–6 minutes longer. If the glaze is in danger of burning, move the duck pieces to a cooler part of the grill or remove the cover.

Transfer to a serving platter and tuck a few cilantro sprigs around the edges, if you like. Serve at once.

Brined Turkey

SERVES 8

Brining a turkey takes little effort and greatly enhances the juiciness of the meat, but you need to start the process at least 12 hours before the bird goes on the grill. Serve with garlic mashed potatoes and cranberry sauce for a festive holiday meal.

FOR THE BRINE:

1 cup (8 oz/250 g) kosher salt
½ cup (3½ oz/105 g) firmly packed
  dark brown sugar
1 qt (1 l) warm water
3 qt (3 l) cold water

1 turkey, 10–12 lb (5–6 kg)
vegetable oil

In a nonaluminum container large enough to hold the turkey and the brine, prepare the brine: Combine the kosher salt, brown sugar, and warm water, stirring to dissolve the salt and sugar. Add the cold water and stir well.

Remove any giblets from the cavity of the turkey and save for another use. Trim off the tail and the wing tips. Rinse the turkey with cold running water, then immerse it in the brine. (If the brine does not cover the turkey completely, mix up an additional half recipe, or as needed, to cover.) Cover the container and refrigerate for at least 12 hours or for up to 24 hours. Drain, rinse with cold running water, and pat dry with paper towels.

Prepare a fire for indirect-heat cooking in a covered grill (see page 11).

Rub the outside of the turkey with vegetable oil. Place the turkey, breast side up, on the grill rack. Cover, close the vents halfway, and grill until juices run clear when a thigh joint is pierced or an instant-read thermometer inserted into the thigh at the thickest part registers 180°F (82°C), 3½–4½ hours. Add more hot coals to the fire as needed to maintain a constant temperature.

Transfer the turkey to a cutting board and let rest for 10 minutes. Carve into slices and arrange on a platter. Serve hot or warm.

Turkey Sausages with Chutney Mustard

SERVES 4–6

It is important to cook sausages fully. If you like, prick the sausages several times with a fork, then blanch them in simmering water for about 5 minutes before grilling.

½ cup (4 oz/125 g) whole-grain mustard
¼ cup (2½ oz/75 g) mango chutney
¼ cup (⅓ oz/10 g) chopped fresh
   cilantro (fresh coriander)
2 lb (1 kg) turkey sausages

Prepare a fire in a grill.

In a small bowl, stir together the mustard, chutney, and cilantro. Cover and refrigerate until serving.

Arrange the sausages on the grill rack. Grill, turning every 2 minutes, until the sausages are well browned on the outside and no longer pink in the center, about 15 minutes.

Transfer the sausages to a warmed platter. Pass the chutney mustard at the table.

Turkey Breast with Ancho Rub

SERVES 6

Serve the sliced turkey with warm corn bread and mashed sweet potatoes garnished with dried cranberries.

FOR THE RUB:

3 ancho chiles, seeded
4 cloves garlic, mashed
2 tablespoons chili powder
2 tablespoons paprika
1 tablespoon grated lemon zest
½ teaspoon ground cinnamon

1 boneless turkey breast, about
   1½ lb (750 g)
vegetable oil

To prepare the rub, tear the chiles into small pieces. Transfer to a spice grinder and grind into a powder. In a small bowl, combine the ground chiles, garlic, chili powder, paprika, lemon zest, and cinnamon.

Brush the turkey breast with the vegetable oil, then spread the chili mixture evenly over the entire surface. Place in a nonaluminum dish, cover, and refrigerate for at least 6 hours or for up to 24 hours.

Prepare a fire for indirect-heat cooking in a covered grill (see page 11).

Place the turkey breast on the grill rack, cover, partially close the vents, and grill until opaque throughout and juices run clear, about 1 hour and 20 minutes. Add more hot coals to the fire as needed to maintain a constant temperature.

Transfer the turkey breast to a cutting board, cover loosely with aluminum foil, and let rest for 5–10 minutes. Thinly slice the breast and arrange on warmed individual plates. Serve hot or warm.

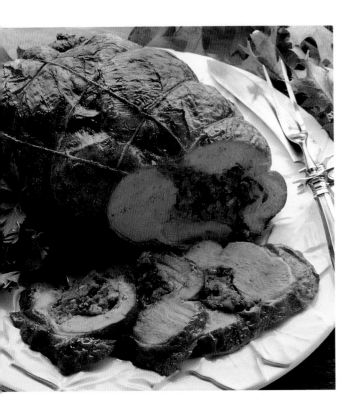

Stuffed Turkey Breast

SERVES 8–10

A boned and butterflied turkey breast cooks quickly and is easy to carve. Your butcher will butterfly it for you.

½ cup (4 oz/125 g) unsalted butter

½ cup (2½ oz/75 g) finely chopped celery

½ cup (2½ oz/75 g) finely chopped yellow onion

3 cups (6 oz/185 g) fresh white bread crumbs

1 teaspoon dried thyme

1 teaspoon dried sage

⅓ cup (2 oz/60 g) raisins

⅓ cup (1½ oz/45 g) chopped walnuts

salt and freshly ground pepper to taste

¼ cup (2 fl oz/60 ml) chicken stock or turkey stock, if needed

1 turkey breast, 6–8 lb (3–4 kg), boned and butterflied, with skin intact

vegetable oil

In a frying pan over medium heat, melt the butter. Add the celery and onion and sauté until soft, about 5 minutes. Transfer to a large bowl. Add the bread crumbs, thyme, sage, raisins, and walnuts and mix well. Season with salt and pepper. The mixture should be moist but not wet. If too dry, add the stock.

Soak 3 handfuls of hickory chips or oak chips in water to cover for about 1 hour. Place the turkey breast, skin side down, on a work surface; you will have 2 large flaps of meat. Sprinkle with salt and pepper. Spread the stuffing over 1 flap of meat and down the center of the breast, then fold the other flap over it. With kitchen string, tie the breast together in four or five places to make a tight, cylindrical roll. Rub with vegetable oil and sprinkle with salt and pepper.

Prepare a fire for indirect-heat cooking in a covered grill (see page 11). Drop half of the wood chips on the fire. Place the rolled breast in the center of the grill rack, cover, and open the vents halfway. Cook for about 1 hour, turning twice. Sprinkle the remaining chips on the fire and add more coals if necessary to maintain a constant temperature. Cook for 45–60 minutes longer. It is done when juices run clear and an instant-read thermometer inserted into the thickest part registers 170°F (77°C).

Transfer the turkey breast to a warmed platter, cover loosely with aluminum foil, and let rest for 10 minutes. Snip the strings, then slice and serve.

Turkey Burgers with Apple-Mint Relish

SERVES 6

FOR THE RELISH:

2 apples, preferably Golden Delicious

¼ cup (2 fl oz/60 ml) cider vinegar

2 tablespoons chopped fresh mint or 1 teaspoon dried mint

1 tablespoon sugar

1 tablespoon vegetable oil

½ teaspoon celery seeds

½ teaspoon mustard seeds

⅛ teaspoon salt

FOR THE BURGERS:

2 lb (1 kg) ground (minced) turkey

1 cup (4 oz/125 g) shredded cheddar cheese

¼ cup (1 oz/30 g) chopped shallot

1 clove garlic, minced

1½ teaspoons salt

½ teaspoon freshly ground pepper

To prepare the relish, peel, halve, and core the apples. Chop them finely or, using the large holes of a handheld grater/shredder, shred them. Transfer to a large bowl and add the vinegar, mint, sugar, oil, celery seeds, mustard seeds, and salt. Stir and toss to combine, then cover and refrigerate for at least 2 hours before serving to blend the flavors.

Prepare a fire in a grill.

To prepare the turkey burgers, in a large bowl, combine the turkey, cheese, shallot, garlic, salt, and pepper. Using a fork, mix gently to combine. Shape into 6 patties, each about 3 inches (7.5 cm) in diameter and 1 inch (2.5 cm) thick.

Place the patties on the grill rack. Grill, turning two or three times, until the burgers are well browned on both sides and no longer pink in the center, 16–20 minutes.

Serve at once on individual plates. Pass the relish at the table.

Beef, Pork & Lamb

Beef

Nothing epitomizes the joy of outdoor cooking like the sight of a steak sizzling over a bed of glowing coals. In fact, many knowledgeable cooks insist there is no better way to cook most cuts of beef than over a crackling fire. Flank, skirt, and short ribs are all less traditional cuts for the grill, but all yield delicious, smoky results and happily pair with Asian and Latin flavors. And, of course, no grilling repertoire would be complete without a few superb hamburger recipes.

Beef Top Round with Jalapeño Marinade

SERVES 6

Top round, sometimes labeled London broil, is a tasty cut, but you must be careful not to overcook it, or its flavor will be lost and its texture will toughen. Accompany the thinly sliced beef with Fennel and Endive with Olive Vinaigrette (page 221).

3 jalapeño chiles
⅔ cup (5 fl oz/160 ml) dry red wine
⅓ cup (3 fl oz/80 ml) olive oil
2 large cloves garlic
handful of fresh flat-leaf (Italian)
   parsley sprigs
1 teaspoon salt
½ teaspoon freshly ground pepper
1 top round beef steak, about
   2½ lb (1.25 kg)

Halve the chiles and remove their stems, seeds, and ribs. In a blender or food processor, combine the jalapeños, wine, olive oil, garlic, parsley, salt, and pepper. Process until smooth.

Using a sharp knife, score the surface of the steak with crisscross cuts about ⅛ inch (3 mm) deep and 2 inches (5 cm) apart. Place in a large lock-top plastic bag and pour in the jalapeño mixture. Press out the air and seal the bag tightly. Place in a large bowl and refrigerate, turning and massaging the bag occasionally, for at least 6 hours or for up to 2 days.

Prepare a fire in a grill.

Remove the steak from the marinade and pat it dry with paper towels. Boil the remaining marinade and reserve.

Place the steak on the grill rack. Grill, turning and brushing with the reserved marinade three or four times, until done to your liking, 14–16 minutes for rare or 18–20 minutes for medium.

Carve into thin slices on the diagonal and across the grain. Arrange on a warmed platter and serve at once.

Steak Fajitas

SERVES 6

A casual meal from the grill, fajitas are traditionally made from skirt steak, but flank steak can also be used. If you use skirt steak, be sure to have your butcher skin it for you. Tuck the flavorful meat strips into tortillas warmed on the grill.

⅓ cup (3 fl oz/80 ml) tequila
¼ cup (2 fl oz/60 ml) fresh lime juice
2 tablespoons vegetable oil
2 cloves garlic, minced
½ teaspoon salt, plus salt to taste
½ teaspoon red pepper flakes
2 lb (1 kg) skirt steak
2 red (Spanish) or yellow onions,
   cut crosswise into slices
   ½ inch (12 mm) thick
3 red or green bell peppers (capsicums),
   seeded and cut crosswise into rings
   ½ inch (12 mm) thick
olive oil or vegetable oil for brushing
12 or more flour tortillas, each
   8–10 inches (20–25 cm) in
   diameter, warmed
tomato salsa (optional)
guacamole (optional)
sour cream (optional)

In a small bowl, whisk together the tequila, lime juice, vegetable oil, garlic, the ½ teaspoon salt, and the red pepper flakes. Place the meat in a shallow non-aluminum dish large enough for it to lie flat. Pour the tequila mixture over the steak and turn to coat both sides. Cover and refrigerate, turning occasionally, for at least 3 hours or for up to all day.

🔥 Prepare a fire in a grill.

🔥 Remove the meat from the marinade and pat it dry with paper towels. Boil the remaining marinade and reserve.

🔥 Arrange the onion slices and bell pepper rings on the grill rack. Brush them with the olive oil or vegetable oil and sprinkle with salt to taste. Grill for 3 minutes, then turn and again brush with oil. Grill until lightly browned, about 3 minutes longer. Transfer to a platter, separating the onion slices into rings; set aside while you cook the meat.

🔥 Place the steak on the grill rack. Grill, turning and brushing with the reserved marinade every 2 minutes, until done to your liking, about 8 minutes total for rare or 10 minutes for medium.

🔥 Cut the steak into thin slices on the diagonal and across the grain. Mound the steak slices on the platter with the onions and bell peppers. At the table, place the sliced steak on warm tortillas. Top with salsa, guacamole, and/or sour cream, if desired, then roll up or fold and eat out of hand.

Hamburgers with Grilled Tomatoes

SERVES 6

To ensure the juiciest burgers, handle the meat as little as possible when shaping the patties. For cheeseburgers, place a slice of Swiss or cheddar cheese on each patty about 1 minute before removing it from the grill. If you like, serve on toasted sour-dough, onion, or Kaiser rolls.

⅔ cup (5 fl oz/160 ml) mayonnaise
1 tablespoon prepared horseradish
2 lb (1 kg) lean ground (minced) beef
2 tablespoons Dijon mustard
2 tablespoons Worcestershire sauce
1 teaspoon salt, plus salt to taste
½ teaspoon freshly ground pepper
3 firm but ripe tomatoes, cut into slices
   ½–¾ inch (12 mm–2 cm) thick
3–4 tablespoons olive oil

Prepare a fire in a grill.

🔥 In a small bowl, stir together the mayonnaise and horseradish. Cover and refrigerate until serving.

🔥 In a large bowl, combine the beef, mustard, Worcestershire sauce, 1 teaspoon salt, and pepper. Using a fork, stir to combine the ingredients. Divide the meat into 6 equal portions and gently pat and press each portion into a patty about 3 inches (7.5 cm) in diameter and 1 inch (2.5 cm) thick.

🔥 Place the patties on the grill rack. Grill, turning every 2 minutes, until done to your liking, about 8 minutes total for rare, 10 minutes for medium, or 12 minutes for well done. About 4 minutes before the burgers are done, arrange the tomatoes on the rack, sprinkle them with salt to taste and brush with some of the olive oil. Grill for about 2 minutes, then turn and again brush with olive oil. Grill until the tomatoes are very lightly browned on both sides, about 2 minutes longer.

🔥 Transfer the burgers to a warmed platter and place the tomato slices atop and around them. Pass the horseradish mayonnaise at the table.

Old-Fashioned Rib Roast

SERVES 6

If you like beef prepared simply, this dish is for you. Before cooking, tie the roast at 1-inch (2.5-cm) intervals for roasting, or have the butcher do it for you. Serve it with baking potatoes, if you like: Place them on the grill rack around the roast for the last hour or so of cooking.

4 teaspoons coarse or kosher salt
3 tablespoons chopped fresh thyme
  or 2 teaspoons dried thyme
1½ teaspoons freshly ground pepper
2 large cloves garlic, minced
finely grated zest of 1 lemon or lime
1 beef rib roast, 6–7 lb (3–3.5 kg),
  trimmed of excess fat and tied for
  roasting *(see note)*
2 tablespoons vegetable oil

Prepare a fire for indirect-heat cooking in a covered grill (see page 11).

In a small bowl, stir together the salt, thyme, pepper, garlic, and lemon or lime zest; set aside.

Pat the roast dry with paper towels. Rub with the vegetable oil, then rub the salt mixture over the entire surface of the meat.

Place the roast, rib side down, on the center of the grill rack. Cover and open the vents halfway. Cook for 45 minutes. Turn the roast rib side up and cook until done to your liking, about 45 minutes longer for rare or 55–60 minutes longer for medium, or until an instant-read thermometer inserted into the thickest portion of the roast away from the bone registers 130°F (54°C) for medium-rare and 140°F (60°C) for medium. Add more coals to the fire as necessary to maintain a constant temperature.

Transfer the roast to a cutting board, cover loosely with aluminum foil, and let rest for 10 minutes. To serve, snip and discard the strings. Carve the meat across the grain into slices ¾–1 inch (2–2.5 cm) thick and arrange on a warmed platter.

Skirt Steak with Cumin and Sweet Onion Salsa

SERVES 4

Flank steak has gained popularity because of its dual benefits: great flavor and lack of fat. Skirt steak is less familiar to many and, except for its role in fajitas, is largely ignored by home cooks. But skirt steak has every advantage of flank steak and is arguably the more tender of the two cuts. These cuts should not be cooked beyond medium-rare, or they will become tough due to their lean nature. Sweet onions have a short season, but there are several varieties from which to choose: Maui, Walla Walla, Vidalia, and Texas 1015 are all good choices. They are much more perishable than the normal onion, so they must be refrigerated and used within a day or two of purchase.

3 tablespoons cumin seeds
½ cup (4 fl oz/125 ml) olive oil
¼ cup (2 fl oz/60 ml) fresh lime juice
  (about 3 limes)
1 small jalapeño chile, or to taste,
  seeded and sliced
2 large cloves garlic, sliced
¾ cup (1 oz/30 g) coarsely chopped
  fresh cilantro (fresh coriander)
1 tablespoon coarsely cracked pepper,
  plus pepper to taste
1 teaspoon salt, plus salt to taste
2 lb (1 kg) skirt steak, in 1 or more
  pieces
¾ cup (3 oz/90 g) chopped sweet
  onion *(see note)*
3 ripe plum (Roma) tomatoes, seeded
  and cut into ¼-inch (6-mm) dice

In a small, dry frying pan over low heat, toast the cumin seeds just until they are fragrant, about 5 minutes, watching carefully to prevent burning. Transfer to a blender and add the ½ cup (4 fl oz/125 ml) olive oil, the ¼ cup (2 fl oz/60 ml) lime juice, jalapeño, garlic, cilantro, the 1 tablespoon pepper, and the 1 teaspoon salt. Process to form a purée that is thick and almost smooth, about 1 minute.

Pour half of the purée into a large, shallow nonaluminum dish and add the steak. Cover and refrigerate the remaining purée to use as a base for the salsa. Generously brush the meat all over with the purée. Cover and refrigerate for 24 hours, turning once.

Prepare a fire in a grill.

Remove the meat from the refrigerator and transfer to a platter, scraping away and discarding the marinade. Bring the meat to room temperature.

In a serving bowl, combine the reserved purée, the onion, and the tomatoes and mix well. Taste and adjust the seasonings.

Place the steak on the grill rack and grill, turning once, for 3 minutes on each side, for medium-rare. Transfer to a cutting board, cover loosely with aluminum foil, and let rest for 3–4 minutes.

To serve, slice the steak across the grain into diagonal strips. Transfer to warmed individual plates. Top with a large spoonful of the salsa. Serve at once.

Far Eastern Steak Salad

SERVES 4

Sometimes it pays to cook steak just to have leftovers for salads and sandwiches. Here is a delicious example with a Far Eastern accent.

FOR THE VINAIGRETTE:

2 tablespoons Dijon mustard
3 tablespoons peeled and grated
   fresh ginger
3 tablespoons red wine vinegar
2 tablespoons soy sauce
1 cup (8 fl oz/250 ml) olive oil
2 teaspoons brown sugar
salt and freshly ground pepper to taste

1 lb (500 g) flank steak or sirloin steak
salt and freshly ground pepper to taste
½ lb (250 g) green beans, snow peas
   (mangetouts), or snap peas, trimmed
3 bunches watercress or 4 cups (4–5 oz/
   125–155 g) young, tender spinach,
   tough stems removed
2 cucumbers, peeled, cut in half lengthwise, seeded, and cut crosswise into
   slices ⅛ inch (3 mm) thick
2 red bell peppers (capsicums), seeded
   and cut into long, narrow strips

To prepare the vinaigrette, in a small bowl, combine the mustard, ginger, vinegar, soy sauce, olive oil, brown sugar, salt, and pepper. Place the steak in a shallow dish. Pour ⅓ cup (3 fl oz/80 ml) of the vinaigrette over the steak and let stand at room temperature for 1 hour.

🍢 Prepare a fire in a grill.

🍢 Remove the steak from the vinaigrette, discarding the vinaigrette. Pat the steak dry with paper towels, and sprinkle with salt and pepper. Place on the grill rack and grill, turning once, for 3 minutes on each side for rare, or until done to your liking. Transfer to a plate and let cool until it can be handled.

🍢 Bring a saucepan filled with salted water to a boil. Add the green beans and boil for 4–5 minutes or the peas and boil for 2 minutes. Drain immediately and immerse in ice water until cool. Drain again; pat dry with paper towels.

🍢 Place the watercress or spinach in a bowl, add ¼ cup (2 fl oz/60 ml) of the reserved vinaigrette, and toss well. Divide the greens among 4 salad plates. In the same bowl combine the cucumbers, bell peppers, green beans or peas, and ⅓ cup (3 fl oz/80 ml) of the remaining vinaigrette. Toss well and divide among the plates. Cut the steak into slices about ¼ inch (6 mm) thick. Place atop the vegetables. Drizzle the remaining vinaigrette over the steak.

Gingered Skirt Steak

SERVES 6

Skirt steak is the diaphragm muscle, and it has a rich, beefy flavor. Although it is relatively inexpensive, skirt steak is sometimes hard to find, so you might have to special-order it. Be sure to have the butcher skin it for you. Served with grilled onions on a crusty French roll, it makes a great steak sandwich.

1 lime
½ cup (4 fl oz/125 ml) dry red wine
⅓ cup (3 fl oz/80 ml) soy sauce
2 tablespoons grated fresh ginger
2 cloves garlic, minced
1 tablespoon sugar
dash of Tabasco or other hot-pepper
    sauce
3 lb (1.5 kg) skirt steak

Grate the zest from the lime, then juice it. In a small bowl, stir together the lime zest and juice, wine, soy sauce, ginger, garlic, sugar, and hot-pepper sauce. Place the meat in a nonaluminum container large enough to accommodate it flat. Pour the marinade evenly over the steak and then turn the meat to coat both sides. Cover and refrigerate for at least 3 hours or for up to all day, turning the meat occasionally.

Prepare a fire in a grill.

Remove the meat from the marinade and pat the meat dry with paper towels and place on the grill rack. Boil the remaining marinade and reserve. Grill for 6–8 minutes, turning every minute or so and brushing two or three times with the reserved marinade. Skirt steak is best served rare and will toughen if overcooked. Cut into serving pieces and arrange on individual plates.

Marinated Beef Tenderloin with Tarragon Butter

SERVES 6–8

Tenderloin is costly, but it's the most succulent cut of beef, with no waste. Have the butcher trim it for you, and plan ahead so you can marinate it for at least a day.

1 beef tenderloin, about 4 lb (2 kg)
   after trimming
Red Wine Marinade *(page 292)*
½ cup (4 oz/125 g) unsalted butter,
   at room temperature
2 tablespoons chopped fresh tarragon
   or 2 teaspoons dried tarragon
2 tablespoons chopped fresh parsley
1 tablespoon fresh lemon juice
½ teaspoon salt
½ teaspoon freshly ground pepper

Place the beef in a lock-top plastic bag and pour in the marinade. Press out the air and seal the bag tightly. Refrigerate for at least several hours or for up to all day, turning the bag occasionally.

Meanwhile, in a bowl, combine the butter, tarragon, parsley, lemon juice, salt, and pepper and beat with a wooden spoon. Transfer to a sheet of plastic wrap and shape into a rough log about 4 inches (10 cm) long and 1 inch (2.5 cm) wide. Wrap in the plastic wrap and chill until firm.

Prepare a fire in a covered grill.

Remove the meat from the marinade and pat dry with paper towels. Place the meat on the grill rack and grill, turning it frequently to brown all sides, for about 20 minutes. Cover the grill, open the vents halfway, and cook until an instant-read thermometer inserted into the meat registers 130°F (54°C) for medium-rare or 140°F (60°C) for medium.

Transfer the meat to a warmed platter, cover loosely with aluminum foil, and let rest for 10 minutes. Carve across the grain into slices ¾–1 inch (2–2.5 cm) thick. Top each serving with a pat of tarragon butter.

Beef Kabobs with Pineapple Relish

SERVES 4

The marinade used for these kabobs recalls the one used for satay. You can also substitute 3–4 raw mangoes, peeled, pitted, and cut into ½-inch (12-mm) cubes, for the pineapple.

1½ lb (750 g) beef fillet or sirloin, cut
   into 1-inch (2.5-cm) cubes
¼ cup (2 oz/60 g) grated yellow onion
1 tablespoon finely minced garlic
2 tablespoons ground coriander
1 tablespoon ground caraway
2 teaspoons curry powder
2 tablespoons soy sauce
½ cup (4 fl oz/125 ml) coconut milk
2 tablespoons fresh lemon juice

FOR THE PINEAPPLE RELISH:

1 tablespoon peanut oil or vegetable oil
1 yellow onion, thinly sliced
2 fresh red chiles, seeded, if desired, and
   chopped
1 small pineapple, peeled and cut into
   1-inch (2.5-cm) cubes
1 teaspoon ground cinnamon
¼ cup (2 oz/60 g) firmly packed
   brown sugar
grated or shredded zest of 1 lemon
   or lime
juice of 1 lemon or 2 limes

Place the beef in a shallow dish. In a small bowl, stir together the onion, garlic, coriander, caraway, curry powder, soy sauce, coconut milk, and lemon juice. Pour over the beef and toss well. Let stand at room temperature for 1–2 hours.

Meanwhile, prepare the relish: Heat the oil in a sauté pan over low heat. Add the onion and chiles and sauté until the onion softens, about 5 minutes. Add all the remaining ingredients and cook over medium heat until the pineapple is tender, about 10 minutes. Remove from the heat, let cool, then refrigerate.

Prepare a fire in a grill.

Thread the beef onto skewers and place the skewers on the grill rack. Grill, turning to cook evenly on all sides, 7–8 minutes for medium-rare, or until done to your liking.

Serve the kabobs with the relish on the side.

Cumin Steak with Spicy Salsa

SERVES 4

This simple onion and citrus marinade accents the beefiness of the steak. Serve with black beans and tortillas, corn on the cob, or roasted potatoes topped with sour cream and chopped roasted chiles, tomatoes, and green (spring) onions.

2 lb (1 kg) flank steak or 4 rib-eye
   steaks, about ½ lb (250 g) each
1 yellow onion, coarsely chopped
2 cloves garlic, finely minced
2 teaspoons ground cumin
2 teaspoons freshly ground pepper
½ cup (4 fl oz/125 ml) fresh
   lemon juice

FOR THE SALSA:

2 avocados, pitted, peeled, and cut into
   ½-inch (12-mm) chunks
4 plum (Roma) tomatoes, peeled,
   seeded, and cut into ½-inch (12 mm)
   chunks
1 teaspoon finely minced jalapeño chile
1 teaspoon finely minced garlic
¼ cup (2 oz/60 g) finely minced
   green bell pepper (capsicum)
3 tablespoons finely minced red
   (Spanish) onion

2 tablespoons red wine vinegar or
   fresh lemon juice
2 tablespoons minced fresh cilantro
   (fresh coriander)
½ cup (4 fl oz/125 ml) olive oil
salt and freshly ground pepper to taste

olive oil
salt to taste

Place the steak(s) in a shallow dish. In a food processor or blender, combine the onion, garlic, cumin, pepper, and lemon juice and pulse a few times to combine. Pour over the steak(s), cover, and let stand for 1 hour at room temperature or cover and refrigerate for 2 hours.

Meanwhile, prepare the salsa: Combine the avocados, tomatoes, chile, garlic, bell pepper, onion, wine vinegar or lemon juice, cilantro, olive oil, salt, and pepper in a bowl and mix well. Set aside at room temperature.

Prepare a fire in a grill.

Remove the steak(s) from the marinade. Brush lightly with olive oil and sprinkle with salt. Place on the grill rack and grill, turning once, for 3 minutes on each side for rare, or until done to your liking.

Slice across the grain. Spoon the salsa over the steak(s) and serve.

Kansas City Beef Brisket

SERVES 8

Brisket of beef, a flavorful but none-too-tender cut, is a perfect choice for slow roasting on a covered grill. Here it's prepared as it is in the BBQ restaurants of Kansas City, Missouri—with plenty of spices and barbecue sauce.

2 teaspoons paprika
1½ teaspoons salt
½ teaspoon freshly ground black pepper
½ teaspoon cayenne pepper
1 beef brisket, 4–5 lb (2–2.5 kg), trimmed of excess fat
2 tablespoons vegetable oil
double recipe Midwestern Barbecue Sauce *(page 294)*

Soak 3 handfuls of hickory chips in water to cover for about 1 hour.

Prepare a fire for indirect-heat cooking in a covered grill (see page 11).

In a small cup or bowl, stir together the paprika, salt, black pepper, and cayenne. Pat the brisket dry with paper towels. Rub the entire surface of the brisket with the vegetable oil, then rub the paprika mixture over the meat.

Scoop half of the soaked wood chips out of the water and drop them onto the fire. Place the brisket on the center of the grill rack, cover, and open the vents slightly less than halfway, or enough to maintain a slow, steady heat. Cook for 1 hour. Turn the brisket, scoop the remaining wood chips from the water, and drop them onto the fire. Cook for 1 hour longer. Brush lightly with the sauce, then turn the brisket and cook, turning two or three times and brushing lightly with the sauce, until the brisket is well browned and has formed a crust on the outside, about 3½ hours total. Add more coals to the fire every hour or so as necessary to maintain a constant temperature.

Transfer the brisket to a cutting board and let rest for 10 minutes, then carve into thin slices across the grain; the slices will likely crumble a little.

Alternatively, pull the meat apart with 2 forks. Arrange the meat on a warmed platter or individual plates. Boil the remaining sauce and spoon it over the top of the brisket. Pass the remaining sauce at the table.

Steak Sandwiches with Chive Butter

SERVES 4

These delectable open-faced sandwiches are topped with a pat of chive butter that melts slowly over the steak, forming an instant herb sauce.

FOR THE CHIVE BUTTER:

¼ cup (2 oz/60 g) unsalted butter, at room temperature

2 tablespoons chopped fresh chives or 2 teaspoons dried chives

2 teaspoons fresh lemon juice

½ teaspoon salt

¼ teaspoon freshly ground pepper

FOR THE STEAKS:

4 beef tenderloin steaks, about 6 oz (185 g) each

salt and freshly ground pepper to taste

4 slices firm-textured white sandwich bread

1–1½ cups (1–1½ oz/30–45 g) watercress sprigs, tough stems removed

To prepare the chive butter, in a small bowl, combine the butter, chives, lemon juice, salt, and pepper. Using a fork, beat vigorously until blended. Transfer to a sheet of plastic wrap and shape into a log about 2 inches (5 cm) long and 1 inch (2.5 cm) in diameter. Wrap in the plastic wrap and chill until firm.

Prepare a fire in a grill.

To prepare the steaks, sprinkle them lightly with salt and pepper, and place them on the grill rack. Grill, turning every 2 minutes, for about 8 minutes total for rare or 10 minutes for medium, or until done to your liking. About 4 minutes before the steaks are done, arrange the bread slices on the rack and grill, turning once, until lightly browned, about 4 minutes total.

Transfer the bread to individual plates. Place a small handful of watercress on each bread slice and place a steak on the watercress. Cut the chive butter into 4 equal slices and place a slice on each steak. Serve at once.

Peppery Flank Steak

SERVES 4

Because a flank steak is a thin piece of meat, the flavor of a marinade penetrates it completely. Serve this peppery beef rare, with grilled green (spring) onions and tomatoes and skewered or baked potatoes.

2 tablespoons fresh lime juice
grated zest of 1 lime
2 cloves garlic, minced
½ teaspoon hot chile oil
¼ cup (2 fl oz/60 ml) vegetable oil
1 teaspoon red pepper flakes
½ cup (4 fl oz/125 ml) dry red wine
1 tablespoon sugar
2 tablespoons soy sauce
1½ lb (750 g) flank steak

In a small bowl, stir together the lime juice, lime zest, garlic, chile oil, vegetable oil, red pepper flakes, wine, sugar, and soy sauce. Place the meat in a nonaluminum container. Pour the mixture over the steak, cover with plastic wrap, and refrigerate for at least 2 hours or, preferably, all day, turning the meat occasionally and basting with the marinade.

🔖 Prepare a fire in a grill.

🔖 Remove the steak from the marinade and pat it dry with paper towels. Boil the remaining marinade and reserve. Place the steak on the grill rack and grill, turning once and brushing two or three times with the marinade, for 10–12 minutes. The meat tastes best when rare.

🔖 To serve, carve on the diagonal into thin slices.

Hamburgers with Grilled Mushrooms and Jalapeño Ketchup

SERVES 6

Few meals are more appealing to the entire family than old-fashioned hamburgers topped with mushrooms. If you don't have time to make the jalapeño-spiked ketchup, look for one at a specialty-foods store.

FOR THE JALAPEÑO KETCHUP:
2 lb (1 kg) ripe tomatoes
1 yellow onion, minced
¼ cup (2 fl oz/60 ml) cider vinegar
¼ cup (2 oz/60 g) firmly packed
  dark brown sugar
¼ teaspoon ground cinnamon
¼ teaspoon salt
¼ teaspoon freshly ground pepper
2 jalapeño chiles, seeded and chopped,
  or to taste

2 lb (1 kg) ground (minced) sirloin,
  top round, or chuck
1 small yellow onion, chopped
salt and freshly ground pepper to taste
1 lb (500 g) fresh white mushrooms,
  brushed clean and sliced
vegetable oil
6 hamburger buns, split
6 lettuce leaves

The day before serving, prepare the ketchup: In a food processor or blender, working in batches, purée the tomatoes. Pass through a sieve placed over a bowl; discard the contents of the sieve. Transfer to a saucepan and add the onion, vinegar, brown sugar, cinnamon, salt, pepper, and jalapeño chiles. Bring to a boil over medium-high heat, reduce the heat to low, and continue to cook, uncovered, until the mixture reduces to a thick ketchuplike consistency, 20–30 minutes. Remove from the heat, let cool, and pour into a jar. Cover and refrigerate overnight to blend the flavors. Stir well and bring to room temperature before serving.

🔖 Prepare a fire in a grill.

🔖 In a bowl, combine the meat with the onion, salt, and pepper. Mix well. Divide the mixture into 6 equal portions, and shape each portion into a patty about 1 inch (2.5 cm) thick. Brush the mushrooms with vegetable oil and place on an oiled grill screen.

🔖 Place the patties and the grill screen on the grill rack and grill, turning once, until the mushrooms are tender and browned and the burgers are done to your liking, about 10 minutes for medium. About 2 minutes before the burgers are ready, place the buns, cut sides down, on the grill rack to toast lightly.

🔖 Transfer the buns to individual plates and top each bottom with a lettuce leaf and a burger. Divide the mushrooms evenly among the burgers. Pass the ketchup at the table. Serve hot.

Steak with Balsamic Vinegar and Black Pepper

SERVES 4

Flank steak can stand in for sirloin steak, if you like. Serve this simple, tasty dish with potatoes and grilled mushrooms or radicchio basted with some of the remaining marinade that has been boiled.

1 sirloin steak, 1½ lb (750 g)
⅓ cup (3 fl oz/80 ml) balsamic vinegar
2 tablespoons olive oil
2 tablespoons honey
1 tablespoon freshly ground pepper
salt to taste

Place the steak in a shallow dish. In a small bowl, stir together the vinegar, oil, honey, and pepper. Pour over the steak, cover, and let stand at room temperature for 1 hour or cover and refrigerate for 2 hours.

Prepare a fire in a grill.

Remove the steak from the marinade and pat dry with paper towels. Sprinkle lightly with salt. Place the steak on the grill rack and grill, turning once, for 6 minutes total for rare, or until done to your liking.

Transfer to a platter, thinly slice, and serve at once.

All-American Beef Short Ribs

SERVES 4

Short ribs benefit from long, slow cooking, so that the meat practically falls off the bone.

1 cup (8 fl oz/250 ml) unsweetened
   pineapple juice
¼ cup (2 fl oz/60 ml) vegetable oil
¼ cup (2 fl oz/60 ml) soy sauce
¼ cup (2 oz/60 g) firmly packed light
   brown sugar
1 tablespoon chili powder
4 lb (2 kg) beef short ribs, trimmed
   of excess fat
Midwestern Barbecue Sauce *(page 294)*

In a small bowl, whisk together the pineapple juice, vegetable oil, soy sauce, brown sugar, and chili powder. Place the ribs in a large lock-top plastic bag and pour in the pineapple mixture. Press out the air and seal the bag tightly. Massage the bag gently to distribute the marinade evenly. Refrigerate for at least 4 hours or for up to 2 days, turning occasionally.

Prepare a fire for indirect-heat cooking in a covered grill (see page 11).

Remove the ribs from the marinade and pat them dry with paper towels. Boil the remaining marinade and reserve.

Place the ribs on the center of the grill rack, cover, and open the vents

halfway. Cook for 1 hour, then turn and brush with the reserved marinade. Add coals to the fire as necessary to maintain a constant temperature. Continue to cook, brushing with the marinade and turning every 20–30 minutes, until the meat is well browned and begins to shrink from the bone, 1½–2 hours longer.

To serve, transfer the ribs to warmed individual plates. Pass the barbecue sauce at the table.

Charred Rib-eye Steak with Salsa Verde

SERVES 4

Garlicky and redolent of capers and parsley, the Italian green sauce that accompanies this steak is its natural partner. Some backyard cooks contend that salting a steak before cooking draws out precious juices, so this recipe calls for salting only when the steak is turned on the grill. The best solution is to try it both ways and make your own decision. Either way, use good-quality sea salt.

FOR THE SAUCE:

2½ cups (2½ oz/75 g) packed fresh
   flat-leaf (Italian) parsley leaves
½ cup (½ oz/15 g) packed fresh mint
   leaves
2 cloves garlic, minced
2 tablespoons capers, rinsed and drained
1 tablespoon Dijon mustard
1 tablespoon red wine vinegar
⅔ cup (5 fl oz/160 ml) extra-virgin
   olive oil

4 well-marbled rib-eye steaks, each
   10–12 oz (315–375 g) and 1 inch
   (2.5 cm) thick
freshly ground pepper and sea salt to taste
1 lemon, quartered

To prepare the sauce, in a food processor, combine the parsley, mint, garlic, capers, mustard, and vinegar. Pulse until well combined. With the motor running, drizzle in the olive oil in a slow, steady stream and continue to process until smooth. Transfer to a bowl, cover, and refrigerate for at least 1 hour or for up to 4 hours for the flavors to marry. (The sauce may be refrigerated for up to 24 hours before serving, but it is best served within 3–4 hours while it is still a bright, vibrant green.)

Prepare a fire in a grill.

Season the steaks with pepper and place over the hottest part of the fire for 2 minutes. Turn the steaks, salt the cooked side, and cook for another 2 minutes. Move the steaks to a cooler part of the grill. Continue to grill, turning once, for a total of 3 minutes longer for medium-rare, or until done to your liking.

Transfer the steaks to a warmed platter, cover loosely with aluminum foil, and let rest for 3–4 minutes. Transfer to warmed individual plates and serve with a dollop of the sauce and a wedge of lemon.

Veal Chops, Valdostana Style

SERVES 6

This recipe comes from Val d'Aosta, a mountainous area in the Piedmont region of northern Italy known for its production of fontina cheese and for its rustic cuisine. The veal chops can be stuffed and refrigerated for 6–8 hours before cooking.

6 large veal chops, each about
   ¾ lb (375 g) with bone in and
   1 inch (2.5 cm) thick
6 thin slices prosciutto
6 thin slices fontina cheese
12 fresh sage leaves
olive oil for brushing
salt and freshly ground pepper to taste
2 cups (16 fl oz/500 ml) tomato sauce,
   heated

Cut a horizontal pocket in each veal chop. Insert 1 prosciutto slice, 1 cheese slice, and 2 sage leaves into each pocket. Alternatively, coarsely chop the prosciutto, cheese, and sage; mix together, and then spread evenly inside each chop pocket.

🍃 Prepare a fire in a grill.

🍃 Brush the chops lightly with olive oil and sprinkle with salt and pepper. Place the chops on the grill rack and grill, turning once, about 4 minutes on each side for rare, or until done to your liking.

🍃 Transfer to warmed individual plates and spoon the hot tomato sauce over the top. Serve at once.

Mexican-Style Skirt Steak

SERVES 4

If you want to temper the fire of this spicy dish, seed the jalapeño chiles. Serve the steak with rice, beans, and warm corn tortillas.

1½–2 lb (750 g–1 kg) skirt steak

FOR THE MARINADE:
2 tablespoons ground cumin
1 tablespoon dried oregano
1 tablespoon chili powder
2 teaspoons minced garlic
⅓ cup (3 fl oz/80 ml) beer or red wine
   vinegar

FOR THE SAUCE:
3 tablespoons olive oil
2 large yellow onions, cut into slices
   ¼ inch (6 mm) thick
2 green bell peppers (capsicums),
   seeded and cut into slices
   ½ inch (12 mm) thick
2 red bell peppers (capsicums),
   seeded and cut into slices
   ½ inch (12 mm) thick
jalapeño chiles, seeded, if desired,
   and minced
1 tablespoon minced garlic
1 tablespoon dried oregano
3 cups (18 oz/560 g) peeled, seeded,
   and diced tomatoes (optional)
¼ cup (2 fl oz/60 ml) fresh lemon juice
¼ cup (⅓ oz/10 g) chopped fresh
   cilantro (fresh coriander)
salt and freshly ground pepper to taste

Remove the skin from the skirt steak (or ask your butcher to do it) and cut the steak into 4 uniform portions. Place in a shallow dish. (Some parts may be thin and some thick, so select the thicker portions for this dish and save the rest for another use.)

🍃 In a small bowl, combine all the marinade ingredients and pour over the meat. Cover and refrigerate for 1–2 hours or up to 4–6 hours.

🍃 Meanwhile, prepare the sauce: Heat the oil in a large sauté pan over medium heat. Add the onions and sauté until softened, 5–7 minutes. Add the green and red bell peppers and cook for 5–7 minutes longer. Stir in the jalapeños, garlic, oregano, and tomatoes (if using), and cook, stirring, for a few minutes. Add the lemon juice and cilantro; simmer for 1–2 minutes. Taste and adjust the seasoning. Keep warm.

🍃 Prepare a fire in a grill.

🍃 Remove the steaks from the marinade, discarding the marinade. Place the steaks on the grill rack and grill, turning once, 6 minutes total for rare, or until done to your liking.

🍃 Transfer the steaks to warmed individual plates, spoon on the sauce, and serve at once.

Steak with Sauce Poivrade

SERVES 4

The traditional French sauce can be prepared a day or so ahead of time, up to the point where the butter is added. Accompany with fried potatoes or potato gratin and some sautéed spinach.

1 yellow onion, finely chopped
1 carrot, peeled and finely chopped
2 cloves garlic, finely minced
½ cup (4 fl oz/125 ml) red wine vinegar
½ cup (4 fl oz/125 ml) beef stock
1 cup (8 fl oz/250 ml) dry red wine
¼ teaspoon ground mace or nutmeg
1 teaspoon chopped fresh thyme
  or ½ teaspoon dried thyme
1 tablespoon coarsely ground pepper
salt to taste
4 rib-eye steaks, New York strip
  steaks, or beef fillet steaks, about
  ½ lb (250 g) each
olive oil
freshly ground pepper to taste
6 tablespoons (3 oz/90 g) unsalted
  butter
chopped fresh flat-leaf (Italian) parsley

In a saucepan over high heat, combine the onion, carrot, garlic, and vinegar and reduce the liquid by half, just a few minutes. Add the stock, wine, mace or nutmeg, and thyme; boil again until reduced by half. Add the coarse pepper and salt and set aside.

🍂 Prepare a fire in a grill.

🍂 Brush the steaks with olive oil and sprinkle lightly with salt and pepper. Place the steaks on the grill rack and grill, turning once, for 6 minutes total for rare, or until done to your liking. Transfer to warmed individual plates.

🍂 Bring the sauce to a boil, reduce the heat, and swirl in the butter. Spoon the sauce over the steaks and top with parsley.

Sesame Flank Steak

SERVES 4

Because flank steaks are thin, the flavor of the sesame marinade will permeate them thoroughly, producing a wonderfully aromatic result. This steak cooks quickly and is easy to do on a small grill or hibachi. Grilled baby bok choy and yellow bell peppers (capsicums) are good accompaniments.

FOR THE MARINADE:
¼ cup (2 fl oz/60 ml) vegetable oil
¼ cup (2 fl oz/60 ml) Asian sesame oil
¼ cup (2 fl oz/60 ml) soy sauce
2 tablespoons fresh lemon juice
2 tablespoons peeled and grated fresh
  ginger

1 flank steak, about 1½ lb (750 g)

To prepare the marinade, in a small bowl, whisk together the vegetable oil, sesame oil, soy sauce, lemon juice, and ginger. Place the steak in a shallow nonaluminum dish large enough to accommodate it flat. Pour the marinade over the steak and turn to coat evenly. Cover and refrigerate for at least 3 hours or for up to a day, turning the meat occasionally.

🍂 Prepare a fire in a grill.

🍂 Remove the steak from the marinade and pat it dry with paper towels. Boil the remaining marinade and reserve. Place the steak on the grill rack and grill, turning two or three times and brushing with the reserved marinade, until done to your liking, about 10 minutes total for rare, or 12–14 minutes for medium.

🍂 Transfer the steak to a cutting board. Let rest for 3 minutes; cut into thin slices on the diagonal. Arrange the slices on a platter and serve.

Veal Loin Chops with Tarragon, Mushrooms, and Cream

SERVES 6

This rich mushroom-laden tarragon sauce complements the delicate flavor of veal.

FOR THE SAUCE:

6 tablespoons (3 oz/90 g) unsalted
   butter
6–8 shallots, chopped
¾ lb (375 g) fresh white mushrooms,
   brushed clean and sliced ¼ inch
   (6 mm) thick
2 tablespoons minced fresh tarragon
   or 1 tablespoon dried tarragon
½ cup (4 fl oz/125 ml) dry white wine
1 cup (8 fl oz/250 ml) heavy (double)
   cream
salt and freshly ground pepper to taste

6 veal loin chops, each about
   ¾ lb (375 g) with bone in

olive oil
salt and freshly ground pepper to taste

Prepare a fire in a grill.

To prepare the sauce, melt the butter in a sauté pan over medium heat. Add the shallots and sauté until soft, about 5 minutes. Raise the heat, add the mushrooms, and sauté, stirring often, until the mushrooms are tender and give off a little liquid, 1–2 minutes. Add the tarragon, wine, and cream and cook until slightly reduced. Season with salt and pepper. Keep warm.

Brush the veal chops lightly with olive oil and sprinkle with salt and pepper. Place on the grill rack and grill, turning once, for 4 minutes on each side for medium-rare, or until done to your liking.

Transfer the chops to warmed individual plates and spoon the sauce over the top. Serve at once.

Bourbon-Marinated Chuck Roast

SERVES 6–8

Marinating the meat in bourbon and spices yields a roast that is flavorful, if a bit nontraditional. Serve with Roasted Autumn Vegetables (page 208).

⅔ cup (5 fl oz/160 ml) bourbon
   whiskey
⅓ cup (3 fl oz/80 ml) vegetable oil
⅓ cup (3 fl oz/80 ml) cider vinegar
1 tablespoon Dijon mustard
1 teaspoon salt
½ teaspoon freshly ground pepper
1 boneless beef chuck roast,
   3–3½ lb (1.5–1.75 kg)

In a small bowl, whisk together the bourbon, vegetable oil, vinegar, mustard, salt, and pepper. Place the beef in a large lock-top plastic bag and pour in the bourbon mixture. Press out the air and seal the bag tightly. Refrigerate for at least 1 day or for up to 3 days, turning the bag occasionally.

Prepare a fire for indirect-heat cooking in a covered grill (see page 11).

Remove the meat from the marinade and pat it dry with paper towels. Boil the remaining marinade and reserve.

Place the meat on the center of the grill rack, cover, and open the vents halfway. Cook, turning three or four times and brushing with the reserved marinade, until the roast is well browned and an instant-read thermometer inserted into the thickest part registers 130°F (54°C) for medium-rare or 140°F (60°C) for medium, 45–60 minutes.

Transfer the chuck roast to a cutting board. Cover loosely with aluminum foil and let rest for 10 minutes. To serve, carve into thin slices across the grain and arrange on warmed individual plates.

Korean Short Ribs

SERVES 4 OR 5

While most short ribs are braised or roasted, Korean cooks have an ingenious method of tenderizing the meat before grilling to a crusty turn. They rub the ribs with sugar to soften the meat and then marinate the ribs in a rich sesame, soy, and ginger paste. Steamed rice and garlic-laced spinach are excellent accompaniments.

4 lb (2 kg) short ribs

⅓ cup (3 oz/90 g) sugar

½ cup (2 oz/60 g) sesame seeds

¼ cup (2 fl oz/60 ml) Asian sesame oil

½ cup (4 fl oz/125 ml), plus
  2 tablespoons soy sauce

3 cloves garlic, finely minced

2 teaspoons red pepper flakes

1 tablespoon peeled and grated
  fresh ginger

3 tablespoons all-purpose (plain) flour

Make deep cuts through the meat on the ribs at regular intervals. Rub the sugar into the meat and let stand at room temperature for 30 minutes.

Place the sesame seeds in a small, dry frying pan over medium-low heat and toast, stirring frequently, until golden, about 3 minutes. Let cool, then pulverize using a mortar and pestle.

In a small bowl, stir together the ground sesame seeds, sesame oil, soy sauce, garlic, red pepper flakes, ginger, and flour. Coat the ribs with the mixture and let stand for about 1 hour longer in the refrigerator.

Prepare a fire in a grill.

Place the ribs on the grill rack and grill, turning once, until well browned on the outside but still somewhat rare in the center, about 5 minutes per side, or until done to your liking.

Transfer the ribs to a warmed platter and serve.

Tenderloin Pepper Steaks

SERVES 4

*If you like black pepper, you know how
good this dish is. Any tender steak, such as
a T-bone or New York, may be prepared
the same way. To crush peppercorns coarsely,
smash them with the bottom of a heavy
saucepan.*

4 beef tenderloin steaks, 6–8 oz
   (185–250 g) each
salt to taste
4 tablespoons (1 oz/30 g) coarsely
   crushed peppercorns
½ recipe Italian Herb Butter *(page 204)*

Sprinkle each steak lightly with salt,
then rub about ½ tablespoon of the
peppercorns into each side, pressing
the pepper firmly into the meat.

🍃 Prepare a fire in a grill.

🍃 Arrange the steaks on the grill rack
and grill, turning them every 1 or
2 minutes, about 8 minutes total for rare
or about 10 minutes total for medium.
Transfer to individual plates and top
each steak with a slice of the flavored
butter. Serve at once.

Rotisserie Rib Eye with Crispy Crust

SERVES 4

This is one of the easiest and most impressive cuts for spit roasting, especially for a smaller group. Its symmetrical shape makes it easy to balance on the rotisserie spit, and although it may seem like a lot of meat, the roast will shrink considerably. In addition, the meat is so succulent, the exterior so crisp and delectably crunchy, that diners may want more than their usual portions, so don't plan on serving an extra guest. If you like, top each serving with a dollop of Niçoise Sauce (page 72) in place of the lemon wedges.

1 boneless rib-eye roast, 4½–5 lb
　(2.25–2.5 kg)
6 anchovy fillets, soaked in warm water
　for 10 minutes, drained, and patted dry
4 large cloves garlic, halved lengthwise,
　then each half cut into 6 slivers
½ cup (4 oz/125 g) butter, melted
1 tablespoon all-purpose (plain) flour,
　sifted
lemon wedges

Bring the roast to room temperature, about 30 minutes. Make 48 deep gashes over the surface, spacing them at 1-inch (2.5-cm) intervals. Cut each anchovy fillet crosswise into 8 pieces. Poke a sliver of garlic and a little piece of anchovy into each slit.

While the roast comes to room temperature, prepare an indirect-heat fire for spit roasting in a covered grill with a rotisserie attachment (see page 9).

Place 1 holding fork on the rotisserie spit with the prongs facing inward. Mount the beef through the cut side at a slight diagonal (that is, the spit should enter near the lower edge and exit closer to the fat side). Secure the beef in the center of the spit by attaching

the second holding fork and screwing both forks into place.

Attach the spit to the motor and start the motor. Baste the roast with melted butter, cover, and roast, basting 3 more times, until an instant-read thermometer inserted into the thickest part of the roast registers 125°F (52°C) for rare, about 1 hour. About 15 minutes before you think the roast will be done, sprinkle it lightly and evenly with the flour. When the meat is done, transfer to a platter, cover loosely with aluminum foil, and let rest for 8–10 minutes.

Carve the roast and arrange the slices on a warmed platter. Serve immediately with the lemon wedges.

Star Anise and Pomegranate Flank Steak

SERVES 4

Look for the pomegranate syrup in Middle Eastern markets and specialty-food stores. Flank steak should not be cooked beyond medium-rare, or it will become tough due to its lean nature.

FOR THE MARINADE:

½ cup (4 fl oz/125 ml) low-sodium
　soy sauce
½ cup (4 fl oz/125 ml) pomegranate
　syrup
1 tablespoon Worcestershire sauce
1 tablespoon Asian sesame oil
juice of 1 lime
½ small yellow onion, sliced
3 cloves garlic, sliced
1-inch (2.5-cm) piece fresh ginger,
　peeled and grated
2 tablespoons dry mustard
10 star anise
¼ teaspoon freshly ground pepper

1 flank steak, about 2 lb (1 kg) and
　1 inch (2.5 cm) thick

To make the marinade, in a saucepan stir together the soy sauce, pomegranate syrup, Worcestershire sauce, sesame oil, lime juice, onion, garlic, ginger, mustard, anise, and pepper. Place over high heat and bring to a boil. Remove from the heat, pour into a shallow nonaluminum dish or pan large enough to lay the steak flat, and let cool.

Add the steak to the cooled marinade and turn to coat well on both sides. Cover and refrigerate for 24 hours, turning about 4 times during this period.

Prepare a fire in a grill.

Remove the flank steak from the marinade, scraping off any clinging ingredients. Pat the steak dry with paper towels and place on the grill rack. Grill, turning once, for 4 minutes on each side for medium-rare or until done to taste. Turn the steak 90 degrees halfway through the cooking time on each side to create crosshatch grill marks, if desired. Transfer to a warmed platter, cover loosely with aluminum foil, and let rest for 10 minutes.

Slice the steak across the grain about ⅜ inch (1 cm) thick and transfer to warmed individual plates. Drizzle with some of the juices that accumulated on the platter during the resting time, then serve at once.

Pork

Around the world, pork turns up in countless guises on the grill. Grilled sausages with a side of sauerkraut remind us of the prominent role pork plays in German cuisine, while Hoisin Pork Loin shows off China's centuries-old culinary contribution. Mexico, Southeast Asia, and, of course, America all boast a vast treasury of grilling recipes for this versatile meat as well.

Grilled Pork Chops with Fried Sage

SERVES 4

There is something almost primal about cooking up nice, thick chops, and the added flavor and texture that come from the crisp-fried sage leaves included here are a revelation.

⅓ cup (3 fl oz/80 ml) fresh lemon juice
2 tablespoons fruity extra-virgin
   olive oil
2 small cloves garlic, finely chopped
½ teaspoon salt
½ teaspoon freshly ground pepper
4 pork chops, each about 10 oz (315 g)
   and 1 inch (2.5 cm) thick
20–40 fresh sage leaves
½ cup (4 fl oz/125 ml) olive oil

In a shallow nonaluminum dish or pan large enough to hold all the chops in a single layer, whisk together the lemon juice, extra-virgin olive oil, garlic, salt, and pepper. Trim off the excess fat from the edges of the chops, leaving a thin layer to help baste the chops as they cook. Place in the marinade and turn to coat evenly. Cover and refrigerate for at least 1 hour or for up to 3 hours, turning occasionally.

Prepare a fire in a grill. Remove the chops from the marinade and pat dry with paper towels. Bring the chops to room temperature. Meanwhile, combine the sage and olive oil in a small saucepan and set aside while you grill the chops.

Place the chops on the grill rack and grill, turning once, until browned and almost firm to the touch, about 8 minutes total. They should be pale pink when cut into at the center. Transfer to a warmed platter, cover loosely with aluminum foil, and let rest for 3–4 minutes.

While the chops are resting, place the pan holding the sage leaves over high heat and fry until bubbling, crisp, and golden brown, about 4 minutes. Using a slotted spoon, lift the leaves out of the oil, allowing the excess oil to drop back into the pan.

Place 5–10 sage leaves on top of each chop and serve at once.

Hickory-Smoked Fresh Ham

SERVES 10–14

A fresh ham is often called leg of pork, and it is large enough to feed a crowd. Have your butcher trim the ham of excess fat and tie it for roasting. Serve with scalloped or mashed potatoes and corn bread.

2 tablespoons coarse or kosher salt
2 teaspoons freshly ground pepper
2 teaspoons dried thyme
2 teaspoons dried sage
3 cloves garlic, minced
½ teaspoon ground allspice or cloves
1 shank-end partial leg of pork, about 10½ lb (5.25 kg), trimmed of excess fat and tied for roasting *(see note)*
2 tablespoons vegetable oil or olive oil

Soak 3 handfuls of hickory chips in water to cover for about 1 hour.

Prepare a fire for indirect-heat cooking in a covered grill (see page 11).

In a small bowl, stir together the salt, pepper, thyme, sage, garlic, and allspice or cloves. Pat the meat dry with paper towels. Rub the entire surface of the meat with the oil, then rub the meat with the herb mixture.

Scoop half of the soaked wood chips out of the water and drop them onto the fire. Place the pork on the center of the grill rack, cover, and open the vents halfway. Cook for about 1 hour. Turn over the roast and add a few more coals to the fire if necessary to maintain a constant temperature. Scoop the remaining wood chips from the water and drop them onto the fire. Continue to cook until the pork is well browned all over and the herb rub has formed a dry, crispy crust, or until an instant-read thermometer inserted into the thickest part of the pork away from the bone registers 160°F (71°C), about 2 hours longer; add a few more coals to the fire as necessary to maintain a constant temperature.

Remove from the grill and transfer to a cutting board. Cover loosely with aluminum foil and let rest for 15 minutes.

To serve, snip the strings, carve the meat across the grain into slices about ¼ inch (6 mm) thick, and arrange on a warmed platter.

Mustard-Glazed Ribs

SERVES 4–6

The amount of mustard-honey basting sauce is generous because you'll want plenty to pass at the table. For a smoky flavor, toss a couple handfuls of damp hickory chips onto the fire. You may, if you wish, substitute 2 slabs of regular spareribs for the baby back ribs.

2 tablespoons vegetable oil
1 small yellow onion, chopped
1 cup (12 oz/375 g) honey
1 cup (8 oz/250 g) Dijon mustard
½ cup (4 fl oz/125 ml) cider vinegar
½ teaspoon salt, plus salt to taste
1 teaspoon ground cloves
about 6 lb (3 kg) baby back ribs,
  in slabs
freshly ground pepper to taste

In a saucepan over medium heat, warm the vegetable oil. Add the onion and sauté until soft, about 5 minutes. Add the honey, mustard, vinegar, the ½ teaspoon salt, and cloves. Stir well and bring to a boil. Reduce the heat to low and simmer for about 5 minutes, stirring occasionally. Remove from the heat and set aside.

🔥 Prepare a fire for indirect-heat cooking in a covered grill (see page 11).

🔥 Generously salt and pepper the ribs on both sides. Place on the grill rack, cover, and open the vents halfway. Cook for 40 minutes, turning the ribs once. Add more coals to the fire if necessary to maintain a constant temperature.

🔥 Brush the tops of the ribs with some of the sauce, then cover and cook for 10 minutes longer. Turn the ribs, brush with a little more sauce, cover, and cook for another 10 minutes. Total cooking time is about 1 hour.

🔥 Remove from the grill and cut into single-rib pieces. Mound on a warmed platter. Boil the remaining sauce and pass at the table.

Pork Tenderloin with Dried-Fruit Chutney

SERVES 6

Chutney and pork are natural partners. For this recipe, try using dried apples, cherries, or figs for any of the dried fruits. For variation, try lapsang souchong tea instead of orange spice to give the chutney a smoky flavor that pairs well with the grilled pork. Serve this dish with steamed rice and grilled vegetables or simply garnish with thin strips of orange peel and a fresh herb sprig.

FOR THE DRIED-FRUIT CHUTNEY:

6 tablespoons (3 fl oz/90 ml) balsamic vinegar

½ cup (3½ oz/105 g) firmly packed brown sugar

¼ lb (125 g) dried apricots

¼ lb (125 g) dried pitted prunes

¼ lb (125 g) dried cranberries

1 teaspoon grated orange zest

juice of 1 orange

½ cup (4 fl oz/125 ml) brewed orange spice tea

¼ teaspoon ground cinnamon

¼ teaspoon ground allspice

3 pork tenderloins, about ¾ lb (375 g) each, trimmed of excess fat

2 tablespoons vegetable oil

salt and freshly ground pepper to taste

To prepare the chutney, in a saucepan, combine the vinegar, brown sugar, apricots, prunes, cranberries, orange zest and juice, tea, cinnamon, and allspice. Bring to a boil over medium heat, stirring occasionally, then reduce the heat to low. Simmer gently, uncovered, until thick, 1–2 hours, adding water as necessary to prevent sticking. Let cool to room temperature.

Prepare a fire in a grill.

Brush the pork tenderloins with the vegetable oil and season with salt and pepper. Place on the grill rack and grill, turning occasionally, until golden brown on all sides, firm to the touch, and pale pink when cut in the thickest portion, about 12 minutes.

Transfer the tenderloins to a cutting board and cover loosely with aluminum foil. Let rest for 2–3 minutes before carving. Cut crosswise into slices ½ inch (12 mm) thick. Place 4 or 5 slices on each plate along with a spoonful of chutney. Serve immediately.

Pork Tenderloins with Guacamole

SERVES 4–6

Pork is quite lean, which means it can be dry. The key is not to overcook it.

½ cup (4 fl oz/125 ml) dry red or
   white wine
2 tablespoons balsamic vinegar or red
   or white wine vinegar
2 tablespoons olive oil or vegetable oil
2 teaspoons chopped fresh thyme
   or ½ teaspoon dried thyme
½ teaspoon salt, plus salt to taste
¼ teaspoon freshly ground pepper, plus
   pepper to taste
2 pork tenderloins, about 1 lb (500 g)
   each, trimmed of visible fat
2 or 3 large, ripe avocados
1 large ripe tomato, peeled, seeded,
   and chopped
1 clove garlic, minced
2 tablespoons chopped fresh cilantro
   (fresh coriander)
2 tablespoons fresh lime juice
¼ teaspoon Tabasco or other
   hot-pepper sauce, or to taste
1 teaspoon minced fresh jalapeño
   chile (optional)
flour or corn tortillas, warmed

In a small bowl, stir together the wine, vinegar, oil, thyme, ½ teaspoon salt, and ¼ teaspoon pepper. Place the tenderloins in a nonaluminum container just large enough to hold them in a single layer. Pour the wine mixture evenly over the pork. Cover and refrigerate for at least 2 hours, turning occasionally.

Pit and peel the avocados, place in a bowl, and mash coarsely with a fork, leaving a few small lumps. Mix in the tomato, garlic, and cilantro, then mix in the lime juice, hot-pepper sauce, and jalapeño (if using), and season with salt and pepper. Press a piece of plastic wrap directly onto the surface of the guacamole and refrigerate until serving.

Prepare a fire in a grill.

Remove the tenderloins from the marinade and pat them dry with paper towels. Boil the remaining marinade and reserve. Place the tenderloins on the grill rack and grill, brushing the meat occasionally with the reserved marinade and turning occasionally to brown evenly, until firm to the touch and pale pink when cut in the thickest portion, 15–18 minutes.

Transfer to a cutting board and let rest for 5 minutes. Cut on the diagonal into thin slices. Serve with the guacamole and tortillas.

Pork Loin with Madeira

SERVES 8

This flavorful loin is good with apple or pear halves prepared as directed in Mixed Fruit Grill (page 254) but without the sweet sauce.

1½ cups (12 fl oz/375 ml) Madeira
   wine
¼ cup (2 fl oz/60 ml) vegetable oil or
   olive oil
¼ cup (2 fl oz/60 ml) red or white
   wine vinegar

1 teaspoon salt
1 teaspoon ground allspice
½ teaspoon ground cloves
½ teaspoon freshly ground pepper
1 boneless pork loin, 3½–4 lb
   (1.75–2 kg), trimmed of excess fat
   and tied for roasting

In a small bowl, whisk together the wine, oil, vinegar, salt, allspice, cloves, and pepper. Place the pork in a large lock-top plastic bag and pour in the wine mixture. Press out the air and seal the bag tightly. Massage the bag gently to distribute the marinade evenly. Refrigerate for at least 6 hours or for up to 2 days, turning the bag occasionally.

Prepare a fire for indirect-heat cooking in a covered grill (see page 11).

Remove the pork from the marinade and pat it dry with paper towels. Place on the grill rack, cover, and open the vents halfway. Cook for 45 minutes, then turn the roast. Add more coals to the fire if necessary to maintain a constant temperature. Continue to cook, turning once more, until an instant-read thermometer inserted into the thickest part registers 150°F (65°C), 50–60 minutes longer.

Transfer to a cutting board, cover loosely with aluminum foil, and let rest for 10 minutes. To serve, snip the strings, carve into thin slices across the grain, and arrange on a warmed platter.

Salt-Brined Pork Loin

SERVES 4

This recipe can be made with a boneless pork loin, but the meat is much juicier and tastier when roasted on the bone. If you have never tried brining pork before, this dish will come as a revelation, as the use of a brine yields an incredibly moist and juicy result. If using the bone-in loin, ask your butcher to chine (cut through) the base of the bones, making the meat easy to carve.

2½ qt (2.5 l) water

¾ cup (6 oz/185 g) sugar

½ cup (4 oz/125 g) kosher salt

3 cloves garlic

2 bay leaves

2 tablespoons juniper berries

1 tablespoon dried thyme

1½ teaspoons peppercorns

5 allspice berries or ⅛ teaspoon ground allspice

1 bone-in pork loin, 3–4 lb (1.5–2 kg), fat trimmed to a layer ⅛ inch (3 mm) thick

5 oz (155 g) apple-smoked bacon, thinly sliced (about 4 slices)

Select a tall, narrow nonaluminum container large enough to hold the pork loin and the brine (about 4 qt/4 l capacity) and add 2 qt (2 l) of the water. In a small saucepan over low heat, combine the remaining 2 cups (16 fl oz/500 ml) water, the sugar, and the salt. Heat, stirring, just until the salt and sugar dissolve, then remove from the heat and let cool slightly. Add to the cold water.

In a mortar with a pestle or in a bowl with the back of a fork or spoon, lightly crush together the garlic cloves, bay leaves, juniper berries, thyme, peppercorns, and allspice. Stir into the brine mixture and add the pork. If necessary, slip a plate into the container to keep the meat completely submerged. Refrigerate for 48 hours.

Remove the pork from the brine and pat dry with paper towels. Discard the brine. Place the pork on a platter, cover loosely with a kitchen towel, and let come to room temperature. Wrap the bacon slices around the fat side of the meat and secure with kitchen twine.

Prepare an indirect-heat fire for spit roasting in a covered grill with a rotisserie attachment (see page 9).

Slide a holding fork onto the spit with the prongs pointing inward. Mount the pork loin onto the spit, placing the spit as close to the center of gravity as possible (remember that the bone side will weigh more than the meat side). Secure with the second holding fork. Most rotisserie attachments include a counterweight system, and this can be attached to control the balance more accurately.

Attach the spit to the motor, start the motor, cover the grill, and roast the loin until an instant-read thermometer inserted into the thickest point of the loin away from the bone and the spit registers 150°F (65°C), 50–65 minutes. Remove the loin from the spit, place it on a platter, cover loosely with aluminum foil, and let rest for 15–20 minutes.

To serve, discard the twine and bacon and carve the roast. Some portions will have a bone in them and some won't, depending on how thick you carve the slices and how many you will be serving.

Simple Spareribs

SERVES 4–6

This preparation was inspired by the late James Beard, who liked ribs seasoned with just salt and pepper and roasted at a high temperature. Grilled corn on the cob makes a nice accompaniment.

about 6 lb (3 kg) pork spareribs, in slabs

2 tablespoons vegetable oil

coarse or kosher salt

freshly ground coarse pepper

Prepare a fire for indirect-heat cooking in a covered grill (see page 11).

Pat the ribs dry with paper towels. Rub them with the vegetable oil, then sprinkle liberally with salt and pepper.

Place the ribs on the center of the grill rack, cover, and open the vents halfway. Cook for 30 minutes, then turn the ribs and cook until well browned on the outside and no longer pink when cut at the bone, 30–40 minutes longer. Add more coals to the fire if necessary to maintain a constant temperature.

To serve, cut the slabs into single-rib pieces and mound on a warmed platter.

Prosciutto-Wrapped Figs Stuffed with Smoked Mozzarella

SERVES 4

Here, the prosciutto acts as a shield for the delicate figs and becomes lusciously browned in the process. These morsels make lovely appetizers to be eaten out of hand while the rest of the meal is being grilled.

4 fresh figs, or 4 large dried figs soaked
   in sherry to cover for 30 minutes
   and drained
1 oz (30 g) smoked mozzarella cheese,
   cut into 4 equal pieces
pinch of ground nutmeg
4 large, medium-thick slices prosciutto
olive oil
freshly ground pepper to taste
lemon wedges
coarse country bread wedges

Prepare a fire in a grill.

🗲 Slice off the stem end of each fresh or dried fig just below the neck, where it starts to widen. Cut a slit in the side of each fig and open the fig out like a book. Lightly sprinkle the mozzarella pieces with nutmeg. Push a piece of cheese inside each fig and squeeze the opening closed as fully as possible. Lay each fig crosswise on a short side of a prosciutto slice and roll up loosely. Secure it in place with a toothpick.

🗲 Brush the prosciutto packages lightly with olive oil and season with pepper. Place them along the cooler edge of the grill rack and grill, turning occasionally and moving them around to keep them from charring, about 5 minutes. They are ready when the prosciutto is crispy and the cheese has just melted.

🗲 Remove the toothpicks and place the figs on small plates. Squeeze lemon juice on top and serve with bread wedges.

Whole Leg of Pork over Pecan Wood

SERVES 15-20

In England, the skin, or crackling, of pork is considered a delicacy. Spit-roasting a leg of pork (sometimes called a fresh ham) with some, if not all, of the skin still in place produces a pleasantly salty, toothsome result. The key to success is to keep the skin dry and rub it with oil and salt just before starting the rotisserie motor. Basting is unnecessary, as the roast has enough of its own fat to stay moist without it. Be sure to ask your butcher to remove the aitchbone. You will need 30–40 pounds (15–20 kg) of pecan wood chunks.

1 leg of pork, 15–20 lb (7.5–10 kg),
   with skin intact and aitchbone
   removed *(see note)*
olive oil
about 3 tablespoons kosher salt

Bring the pork leg to room temperature. Using a sharp, sturdy knife, score the skin in long lines about ¾ inch (2 cm) apart, cutting into the skin and some of the fat but not all the way through to the meat. To achieve a good center of balance on the spit for this slightly unwieldy cut, visualize the bone that is remaining in the leg. It is off to one side, so that a larger percentage of meat falls on one side of the bone than the other. Insert the spit so that it runs parallel to the bone on the heavier side, thus making the weight on either side of the spit roughly equal. Most rotisserie attachments include a counterweight system, and this can be attached to control the balance more accurately. Mount the roast onto the spit, securing it firmly between the two holding forks, as described above. If any pieces are hanging down, wrap with stainless-steel wire, starting on one of the holding forks and winding the wire around to make a compact barrel shape before securing the wire on the far holding fork. Rub the outside surfaces of the roast with olive oil and salt, working some of the salt into the cuts.

🗲 While the leg is coming to room temperature, prepare an indirect-heat fire of pecan wood for spit roasting in a covered grill with a rotisserie attachment (see page 9).

🗲 Attach the spit to the motor, start the motor, and cover the grill. Roast the pork, making sure that the drippings are going into the drip pan, as a tremendous amount of fat will be rendered out during the cooking. Count on 3½–4½ hours of cooking time, replenishing the wood as needed, but make your doneness decision based purely on the internal temperature, tested with an instant-read thermometer, making sure the thermometer is not touching the bone or the spit itself. A large roast like this will gain an additional 10°–15°F (4°–6°C) during its resting period, so it is advisable to remove the roast from the heat when the internal temperature reaches 140°–145°F (60–63°C). Too much hotter and the pork will be dry. Let the leg rest for 30 minutes.

🗲 To serve, carve the meat, snipping the cracklings into bite-sized pieces with kitchen shears. Serve the meat and the cracklings warm.

Hickory-Smoked Ribs

SERVES 4–6

4–5 lb (2–2.5 kg) baby back ribs, in
  slabs
1½ cups (12 fl oz/375 ml) beer or water

FOR THE MOP SAUCE:
¼ cup (2 fl oz/60 ml) vegetable oil
1 yellow onion, minced
2 cloves garlic, minced
1 can (15 oz/470 g) tomato sauce
¼ cup (2 fl oz/60 ml) tomato ketchup
¼ cup (2 fl oz/60 ml) cider vinegar
¼ cup (2 fl oz/60 ml) fresh orange juice
¼ cup (2 oz/60 g) firmly packed dark
  brown sugar

2 tablespoons Dijon mustard
1 teaspoon Worcestershire sauce
salt and freshly ground pepper to taste

Prepare a fire for indirect-heat cooking
in a covered grill (see page 11). At the
same time, put 3 handfuls of hickory
chips in water to cover to soak.

🍃 Place each rib rack on a piece of
heavy-duty aluminum foil. Sprinkle
each rack with 3–4 tablespoons of the
beer or water. Wrap tightly and place
on the grill rack. Cover, open the vents,
and cook for 35 minutes.

🍃 Meanwhile, prepare the sauce: In a
saucepan over medium heat, warm the
oil. Add the onion and garlic and sauté

until tender, about 5 minutes. Stir in the
tomato sauce, ketchup, vinegar, orange
juice, brown sugar, mustard, Worcestershire sauce, salt, and pepper. Bring to a
boil, reduce the heat to low, and cook
until thick, about 15 minutes.

🍃 Scoop the wood chips out of the
water and sprinkle over the hot coals.
Unwrap the ribs, place on the grill
rack, cover, partially close the vents,
and grill until tender, 20–30 minutes.
During the last 10 minutes of grilling,
brush the ribs with some of the sauce.

🍃 Transfer the ribs to a work surface,
cut the racks in half, and mop with
more sauce. Pass the remaining sauce
at the table.

Hoisin Pork Loin

SERVES 6–8

FOR THE SAUCE:

1 cup (8 fl oz/250 ml) hoisin sauce

3 tablespoons honey

2 tablespoons dry sherry

1 teaspoon Asian sesame oil

1 boneless pork loin, 3 lb (1.5 kg), tied
for roasting

1 lb (500 g) baby bok choy

1 lb (500 g) baby carrots, peeled

vegetable oil

To prepare the sauce, in a small saucepan over medium heat, combine the hoisin sauce, honey, sherry, and sesame oil. Bring to a boil, stirring constantly.

Reduce the heat to low and cook until slightly thickened, 2–3 minutes. Remove from the heat and let cool.

🔥 Place the pork in a nonaluminum dish and brush it with about one-third of the sauce. Cover and refrigerate for 4–6 hours.

🔥 Bring a saucepan three-fourths full of lightly salted water to a boil. Add the bok choy and parboil for 5 minutes. Using a slotted spoon, transfer to a plate. Add the carrots to the same boiling water and parboil for 5 minutes, drain, and set aside with the bok choy.

🔥 Prepare a fire for indirect-heat cooking in a covered grill (see page 11).

🔥 Place the pork on the grill rack, cover, partially close the vents, and grill,

turning once, until an instant-read thermometer inserted into the roast at the thickest part registers 150°F (65°C), 40–50 minutes. About 10 minutes before the pork is done, brush the bok choy and carrots with vegetable oil, place on a grill screen, and grill, turning as necessary, until the vegetables are lightly browned and tender when pierced, 10–15 minutes.

🔥 Transfer the pork to a cutting board and let rest for 5 minutes. Remove the vegetables from the screen and keep warm. Slice the pork thinly against the grain. Boil the remaining sauce and brush it on the pork slices. Surround with the grilled vegetables and serve hot.

Curried Pork Satay

SERVES 6

Satay is strips or pieces of meat that are soaked in a spicy marinade—the more red pepper flakes you use, the spicier they will be. Like all skewered meats, they cook quickly and are easy to do even on a small grill. Serve on a bed of rice, along with chutney or a tart fruit relish. Tender lamb may be prepared in the same way, although it will need to cook for only 8–10 minutes.

¼ cup (2 fl oz/60 ml) soy sauce

¼ cup (2 fl oz/60 ml) vegetable oil

¼ cup (2 fl oz/60 ml) dry red or white wine

1 tablespoon sugar

2 teaspoons curry powder

½–1 teaspoon red pepper flakes

2½ lb (1.25 kg) lean, boneless pork, cut into 1½-inch (4-cm) cubes

In a large bowl, stir together the soy sauce, oil, wine, sugar, curry powder, and red pepper flakes. Add the pork and toss to coat well. Cover and refrigerate for at least 2 hours, tossing occasionally.

Prepare a fire in a grill.

Remove the pork from the marinade and pat dry with paper towels. Boil the remaining marinade and reserve. Thread the pork onto skewers. Arrange the skewers on the grill rack. Grill, turning frequently and brushing occasionally with the reserved marinade, until cooked through, about 20 minutes.

Transfer to warmed individual plates and serve.

Orange-and-Ginger-Glazed Pork Roast

SERVES 8

The optional dry marinade helps bring out the natural flavor of pork, and the orange-ginger mixture gives the meat a dark, spicy glaze. Since boneless pork loin is so easy to carve and serve, this is a good recipe to double for a crowd. Accompany it with grilled apple rings or applesauce.

2 tablespoons vegetable oil, if needed

1 boneless pork loin, 3½–4 lb (1.75–2 kg), tied for roasting

Dry Marinade for Pork *(page 293)* (optional)

½ cup (5 oz/155 g) orange marmalade

⅓ cup (3 oz/90 g) Dijon mustard

1 tablespoon peeled and grated fresh ginger

1 tablespoon Worcestershire sauce

¼–½ teaspoon salt

¼–½ teaspoon freshly ground pepper

If you are using the marinade, rub the oil over the pork, then coat it evenly with the dry marinade. Cover and refrigerate for several hours.

Meanwhile, in a small bowl, stir together the marmalade, mustard, ginger, Worcestershire sauce, salt, and pepper.

Prepare a fire for indirect-heat cooking in a covered grill (see page 11).

Place the pork on the grill rack so it is not directly over the fire, cover, and open the vents halfway. Cook for 45 minutes, then turn the roast. Add more coals if necessary to maintain a constant temperature. Cook, brushing with the marmalade mixture every 10 minutes and turning once or twice, until an instant-read thermometer registers 160°F (70°C), 40–50 minutes longer.

Transfer to a cutting board, cover loosely with aluminum foil, and let rest for 10 minutes. Snip the strings, cut into thin slices, arrange on a warmed platter, and serve.

Country Bread and Pork Tenderloin Skewers

SERVES 4

It is crucial to the success of this dish that the bread cubes be slightly smaller (about one-fourth smaller) than the pork cubes, otherwise the bread will come into contact with the grill and char. The correct result is crisp bread croutons alternating with chunks of juicy pork, all basted by the melting, salty bacon. Serve the skewers over a simple green salad to catch the juices.

1¼ lb (625 g) pork tenderloin, cut into
   1-inch (2.5-cm) cubes (20 cubes)
20 cubes coarse country bread *(see note)*
16 pieces unsmoked bacon, each ¾ inch
   (2 cm) square
3 tablespoons olive oil
¾ teaspoon salt
¼ teaspoon freshly ground pepper
generous ¼ teaspoon chili powder
1 teaspoon chopped fresh sage
2 lemons, cut into wedges

Prepare a fire in a grill.

In a bowl, combine the pork cubes, bread cubes, bacon, and olive oil. Toss to combine. Add the salt, pepper, chili powder, and sage and toss gently to coat evenly. Let stand for 5 minutes.

Thread the ingredients onto skewers in the following order: pork, bread, and bacon. Each skewer should have 5 pieces of pork, 5 pieces of bread, and 4 pieces of bacon. Place on the grill rack and grill for 3–4 minutes on each of all 4 sides, watching carefully that the bread does not burn. The bread should be golden brown and crisp, and the pork should be firm and just lightly golden.

Transfer to individual plates and squeeze a little lemon juice over each skewer. Serve at once.

Spareribs, Vietnamese Style

SERVES 4

This is a nontraditional take on spareribs, which are usually slathered with a thick sauce. Here, they are only lightly swabbed and then cooked on a rotisserie, which ensures a crisp, mahogany brown exterior and a meltingly tender center that is subtly perfumed with lemongrass. Sweet soy sauce, called kecap manis, *is a popular ingredient in Indonesia. Look for it, along with the fish sauce and lemongrass, in Southeast Asian stores.*

2 fat lemongrass stalks
1 tablespoon minced garlic
3 tablespoons honey
2 tablespoons sweet soy sauce
1 tablespoon fish sauce
2½ tablespoons fresh lime juice (about
   1 large lime), plus 1 lime, quartered
1 teaspoon freshly ground pepper
1 rack spareribs, 2½–3 lb (1.25–1.5 kg)
2 tablespoons chopped fresh basil,
   preferably Thai basil

Trim away the root end and the fibrous tops from the lemongrass stalks. Peel away and discard the tough outer layers from the remaining bulbous bottom portion of each stalk, then chop coarsely and place in a nonaluminum baking dish large enough to hold the rack of ribs flat. Add the garlic, honey, sweet soy sauce, fish sauce, lime juice, and pepper and whisk thoroughly. Place the rack of ribs in the dish, turning to coat and brushing the marinade onto both sides. Cover with a kitchen towel and let stand for about 1 hour at room temperature or for up to 2 hours in the refrigerator. (If refrigerated, bring back to room temperature before grilling.)

Prepare an indirect-heat fire for spit roasting in a covered grill with a rotisserie attachment (see page 9).

Slide a holding fork onto the spit with the prongs pointing inward. Remove the rack of ribs from the marinade. Boil the remaining marinade and reserve. Place the rack, bony side up, on a work surface. Starting at the thinner, narrower end of the rack, push the spit into the meat between the first and second ribs. Continue threading the spit over and under alternate pairs of ribs and out at the wider end of the rack. Slide the second holding fork onto the spit, and push both forks together, centering the rack. Tighten the holding forks.

Attach the spit to the motor, cover the grill, start the motor and roast the ribs for 20 minutes without basting (this will develop a nice crisp crust). Do not replenish the coals during this time, but let them die down naturally to provide a gentler heat after the initial searing. (On a gas grill, reduce the heat after the first 25 minutes.) Baste once after 20 minutes and then again every 10 minutes until the ribs are deep brown, the juices run clear when the ribs are pierced with a knife, and the fat has stopped dripping off, 20–30 minutes longer. Transfer the ribs to a platter, cover loosely with aluminum foil, and let rest for 5 minutes.

To serve, carve into individual ribs or divide the rack into quarters. Serve with the lime wedges and a scattering of basil.

Salad of Pork, Pears, and Toasted Pecans

SERVES 6

Apples and walnuts can be substituted for the pears and pecans in this early fall salad. Accompany with your favorite bread.

½ cup (2 oz/60 g) pecans
1 tablespoon peanut oil
salt and freshly ground pepper to taste
pinch of sugar
2 pork tenderloins, about ¾ lb (375 g)
   each, trimmed of excess fat
1 tablespoon olive oil

FOR THE DRESSING:
6 tablespoons olive oil
2 tablespoons sherry vinegar
1 tablespoon hazelnut (filbert) oil
salt and freshly ground pepper to taste

2 firm but ripe pears, preferably Bosc,
   halved, cored, and thinly sliced
   lengthwise
3–4 large handfuls assorted greens such
   as red-leaf or butter lettuce and/or
   bitter greens such as frisée, radicchio,
   arugula (rocket), and/or mizuna
   (6–8 cups/6–8 oz/185–250 g)

Prepare a fire in a grill. Preheat an oven to 350°F (180°C).

🌿 In a bowl, combine the pecans, peanut oil, salt, pepper, and sugar and toss well to coat the nuts. Spread the pecans on a baking sheet and bake until lightly golden, 5–7 minutes. Let cool.

🌿 Brush the pork tenderloins with the olive oil and season with salt and pepper. Place on the grill rack and grill, turning occasionally to brown evenly, until firm to the touch and pale pink when cut in the thickest portion, about 12 minutes.

🌿 Transfer to a cutting board, cover loosely with aluminum foil, and let rest for 2–3 minutes before carving.

Cut crosswise into slices about ¼ inch (6 mm) thick.

🌿 To make the dressing, in a small bowl, whisk together the olive oil, sherry vinegar, hazelnut oil, salt, and pepper.

🌿 In a large bowl, combine the pear slices, greens, warm pork, pecans, and dressing and toss to mix well. Transfer to individual plates and serve immediately.

Mustard-Glazed Sausages with Sauerkraut Relish

SERVES 4–6

For this recipe, use any type of fresh sausages made from pork, beef, or lamb, or a combination. Whichever type you choose, it is important that you cook them fully. You can remove some of the fat, and reduce the tendency toward flare-ups on the fire, by first pricking the sausages several times with a fork, then blanching them in simmering water for about 5 minutes before grilling.

FOR THE SAUERKRAUT RELISH:

3 cups (1–1¼ lb/500–625 g) sauerkraut (fresh or canned)

¼ cup (⅓ oz/10 g) chopped fresh flat-leaf (Italian) parsley

¼ cup (2 fl oz/60 ml) cider vinegar

3 tablespoons olive oil

4 teaspoons sugar

¼ teaspoon freshly ground pepper

FOR THE SAUSAGES:

½ cup (4 oz/125 g) Dijon mustard

¼ cup (3 oz/90 g) honey

2 tablespoons white wine vinegar or cider vinegar

2 lb (1 kg) fresh sausages, one kind or a combination, 1–1¼ inches (2.5–3 cm) in diameter

To prepare the relish, place the sauerkraut in a colander and rinse under cold running water. Drain well, then squeeze with your hands to remove the excess water. In a large bowl, combine the sauerkraut, parsley, vinegar, olive oil, sugar, and pepper. Stir and toss with a fork to mix. Cover and refrigerate for at least 2 hours or for up to 3 days, to blend the flavors.

🖌 Prepare a fire in a grill.

🖌 To prepare the sausages, in a small bowl, whisk together the mustard, honey, and vinegar; set aside.

🖌 Arrange the sausages on the grill rack. Grill, turning frequently, until well browned and fully cooked, 15–18 minutes. During the last 6–8 minutes of grilling, brush the sausages two or three times with the mustard mixture.

🖌 To serve, spread the sauerkraut relish on warmed individual plates and arrange the sausages on top.

Lamb

The aroma of smoke seems to marry particularly well with the assertive, slightly gamy character of good lamb. Those who love to grill this flavorful meat can easily make it a year-round activity. Rosemary-Smoked Lamb Chops fill the spring air with an herbal aroma, while nothing says summer like Grilled Lamb Burgers with Mint, Tomatoes, and Garlic, especially when an icy glass of lemonade is on hand to keep the chef cool. In wintertime, in temperate climates, Lamb and Potato Skewers are perfect, as they require only quick dashes outdoors for brief tending on the grill.

Herbed Rack of Lamb

SERVES 2 OR 3

Depending upon the rest of your menu— and the appetites of your guests—one rack of lamb will serve two or three people. Round out the meal with such dishes as grilled eggplant (aubergine), potatoes, and polenta.

1 rack of lamb, about 2 lb (1 kg), with 8 ribs
1 clove garlic, cut into slivers
vegetable oil or olive oil
2 tablespoons Dry Marinade for Lamb (page 293)

Prepare a fire in a grill.

🔖 Trim off the outside fat from the rack of lamb; do not worry about removing every single bit. For a special-occasion dinner, you may want to trim the meat from the last 2 or 3 inches (5 or 7.5 cm) of each rib bone, then scrape the bones clean with a knife.

🔖 Make a small slit between each rib and insert a sliver of garlic. Rub the meat with oil, then rub with the dry marinade. If you have scraped the bones, cover each of the tips with a piece of aluminum foil.

🔖 Place the lamb on the grill rack and grill, turning several times, until an instant-read thermometer registers 130°F (54°C) for medium-rare or 140°F (60°C) for medium, 20–25 minutes. Remove the pieces of aluminum foil and cut the ribs into individual chops to serve.

Wine-Scented Leg of Lamb

SERVES 6–8

A butterflied leg of lamb is one that is boned and spread out flat; as a result it cooks more evenly and is easier to carve than a bone-in leg. Ask your butcher to prepare it for you. This is a natural with Grill-Roasted Garlic (page 216) and pilaf or mashed potatoes.

⅔ cup (5 fl oz/160 ml) dry red or
  white wine
¼ cup (2 fl oz/60 ml) olive oil
3 tablespoons soy sauce
2 tablespoons chopped fresh thyme or
  rosemary, or 2 teaspoons dried thyme
  or rosemary
2 teaspoons grated lemon zest
2 cloves garlic, minced
½ teaspoon salt
½ teaspoon freshly ground pepper
1 leg of lamb, 6–7 lb (3–3.5 kg),
  trimmed of excess fat, boned, and
  butterflied

In a bowl, whisk together the wine, olive oil, soy sauce, thyme or rosemary, lemon zest, garlic, salt, and pepper.

 Place the lamb in a large lock-top plastic bag and pour in the wine mixture. Press out the air and seal the bag tightly. Refrigerate for at least 3 hours or for up to all day, turning the bag occasionally.

 Prepare a fire in a grill.

 Remove the lamb from the marinade and pat it dry with paper towels. Boil the remaining marinade and reserve.

 Place the lamb on the grill rack and grill, turning several times and brushing with the reserved marinade, until done to your liking when cut into with a knife, or until an instant-read thermometer inserted into the thickest part of the leg registers 130°F (54°C)

for medium-rare and 140°F (60°C) for medium, 35–45 minutes.

 Transfer the lamb to a cutting board, cover loosely with aluminum foil, and let rest for 5 minutes. To serve, carve into thin slices and arrange on a warmed platter or individual plates.

Saffron Lamb Kabobs

SERVES 4–6

Tender cubes of lamb cut from the leg work well for kabobs. Serve on a bed of rice pilaf. Although saffron is expensive, its special flavor is worth the cost. You will extract more essence from a small amount if you first steep it in hot water or stock.

½ teaspoon saffron threads
½ cup (4 fl oz/125 ml) beef stock,
  boiling
½ cup (4 fl oz/125 ml) dry red or
  white wine
2 tablespoons vegetable oil
½ teaspoon ground cardamom
½ teaspoon salt
¼ teaspoon freshly ground pepper
2 lb (1 kg) lean, boneless lamb, cut
  into 1½-inch (4-cm) cubes

In a large bowl, stir together the saffron and beef stock and let stand for at least 30 minutes. Add the wine, oil, cardamom, salt, and pepper. Add the lamb cubes and toss to combine. Cover and refrigerate for at least 3 hours, tossing occasionally.

 Prepare a fire in a grill.

 Remove the lamb from the marinade and pat the meat dry with paper towels, then thread it onto skewers. Boil the remaining marinade and reserve. Arrange the skewers on the grill rack and grill, turning frequently and brushing occasionally with the reserved marinade, until browned but still pink in the center, about 8 minutes. Transfer to individual plates and serve.

1 large eggplant (aubergine),
   3–4 inches (7.5–10 cm) in diameter
   and 6–7 inches (15–18 cm) long
salt for sprinkling, plus 1½ teaspoons salt
2 lb (1 kg) ground (minced) lamb
½ teaspoon freshly ground pepper
2 cloves garlic, minced
½ cup (4 fl oz/125 ml) olive oil

Cover a baking sheet with paper towels.
Trim the eggplant and then cut crosswise into slices about ½ inch (12 mm)
thick. You should have 12 good-sized
slices in all. Sprinkle both sides of each
slice lightly with salt. Spread the slices
out on the prepared baking sheet and
cover with more paper towels. Let stand
for about 1 hour.

🔥 Prepare a fire in a grill.

🔥 Rinse the eggplant slices and pat
them dry with paper towels. Set aside.

🔥 In a large bowl, combine the lamb,
1½ teaspoons salt, pepper, and garlic. Mix
gently to combine, handling the meat as
lightly as possible. Shape the mixture into
6 patties, each about 3½ inches (9 cm)
in diameter and 1 inch (2.5 cm) thick.

🔥 Arrange the eggplant slices and the
lamb patties on the grill rack. Grill,
turning both the burgers and the eggplant slices every 2–3 minutes and
brushing the eggplant slices with the
olive oil each time you turn them. Grill
the eggplant until lightly browned on
both sides, about 8 minutes total. Grill
the lamb until done to your liking, about
8 minutes total for rare, 10 minutes for
medium, or 12 minutes for well done.

🔥 To serve, slip each lamb burger
between 2 eggplant slices and place on
warmed individual plates. Serve at once.

Rosemary-Smoked Lamb Chops

SERVES 4

*Loin or rib lamb chops about 1 inch
(2.5 cm) thick are the best type for grilling
because they brown well outside and
remain pink in the center.*

6–8 fresh rosemary sprigs, plus
  2 tablespoons chopped
¼ cup (2 fl oz/60 ml) olive oil
½ teaspoon salt
¼ teaspoon freshly ground pepper
8 rib or loin lamb chops, about 1 inch
  (2.5 cm) thick, trimmed of excess fat

Prepare a fire in a grill.

🔥 Soak the rosemary sprigs in water
to cover for about 30 minutes before
beginning to grill.

🔥 In a small bowl, whisk together the
oil, chopped rosemary, salt, and pepper.
Rub a small amount of this mixture

over the surface of each chop. Reserve
the remainder to brush on the chops
as they cook.

🔥 Drop a few damp rosemary sprigs on
the fire. Arrange the chops on the grill
rack. Grill, turning two or three times
and brushing lightly with the remaining
rosemary mixture, until browned but
still pink in the center, about 8 minutes.

🔥 Drop the remaining rosemary
sprigs on the fire midway through the
cooking.

🔥 Transfer to individual plates to serve.

Lamb and Eggplant Burgers

SERVES 6

*Eggplant slices replace the buns on these
burgers, easily eaten with a knife and fork.
Lettuce leaves, tomato slices, raw or grilled
onion slices, and mayonnaise flavored with
minced garlic are good condiments.*

Fillet of Lamb with Roasted Peppers and Onions

SERVES 6

To make this recipe, the fillet must first be removed from each lamb rack. You can bone the rack yourself by carefully cutting around the fillet with a long, sharp boning knife, or ask your butcher to do it.

¼ cup (2 fl oz/60 ml) olive oil
1 tablespoon minced fresh rosemary
salt and freshly ground pepper to taste
3 racks of lamb, 1½–2 lb (750 g–1 kg)
    each, boned and trimmed of excess fat
2 red bell peppers (capsicums),
    quartered lengthwise and seeded
2 yellow bell peppers (capsicums),
    quartered lengthwise and seeded
3 large red (Spanish) onions, cut into
    slices ¾ inch (2 cm) thick

FOR THE DRESSING:
¼ cup (2 fl oz/60 ml) extra-virgin
    olive oil
1 tablespoon red wine vinegar
2 teaspoons minced mixed fresh herbs
    such as rosemary, oregano, mint,
    chives, and/or thyme, in any
    combination
salt and freshly ground pepper to taste

fresh rosemary sprigs

In a bowl, whisk together the olive oil, rosemary, and a pinch each of salt and pepper. Add the lamb fillets and turn to coat completely. Marinate for 1 hour in the refrigerator.

Meanwhile, prepare a fire in a grill.

When the lamb has marinated for 1 hour, add the bell peppers and coat completely with the marinade. Arrange the onion slices on a plate and brush with any marinade remaining in the bottom of the bowl.

To prepare the dressing, in a bowl, whisk together the olive oil, vinegar, and mixed herbs. Season with salt and pepper. Set aside.

Place the lamb fillets on the grill rack and grill, turning every 5 minutes, until well browned on the outside and pink when cut in the thickest portion, 20–25 minutes total. When the lamb has been on the grill 10 minutes, place the onion slices on the grill and cook until they soften on one side, 5–7 minutes. Turn the onions and place the bell peppers, skin side down, on the rack. Cook the onions and peppers, turning the peppers once, until soft, 5–10 minutes longer.

Transfer the lamb and vegetables to a warmed platter. Quickly whisk the dressing and drizzle evenly over the top. Garnish with the rosemary sprigs and serve at once.

Butterflied Leg of Lamb with Mediterranean Rub

SERVES 6–8

This recipe calls for a boned and butterflied—or flattened—leg of lamb. Ask your butcher to prepare it for you. Serve the grilled lamb with warm pita bread and Couscous Salad with Cucumber, Peppers, and Tomatoes (page 228).

FOR THE MEDITERRANEAN RUB:
¼ cup (1½ oz/45 g) dried rosemary
¼ cup (2 oz/60 g) firmly packed
    dark brown sugar
2 tablespoons dried oregano
4 cloves garlic, minced
salt and freshly ground pepper to taste

1 leg of lamb, 7–8 lb (3.5–4 kg), trimmed
    of excess fat, boned, and butterflied

To prepare the rub, in a food processor or a mortar, combine the rosemary, brown sugar, oregano, garlic, salt, and pepper. Process, or grind with a pestle, until fine. (The rub can be made up to 24 hours in advance and refrigerated in a lock-top plastic bag.) Rub the mixture all over the lamb, pressing it into the meat so that it adheres to the surface. Place in a nonaluminum dish, cover, and refrigerate overnight.

Prepare a fire for indirect-heat cooking in a covered grill (see page 11).

Place the lamb on the grill rack so it is directly over the fire and sear, turning once, 3–4 minutes on each side. Transfer the lamb to the center of the grill rack, cover, open the vents, and grill, turning once, until an instant-read thermometer inserted into the thickest part registers 130°F (54°C) for medium-rare or 140°F (60°C) for medium, 35–45 minutes.

Transfer to a cutting board and let rest for 5 minutes. Cut across the grain into thin slices, arrange them on a platter, and serve warm.

Lamb and Eggplant Brochettes with Provençal Dressing

SERVES 6

When making lamb brochettes, use a good cut, such as leg, or the meat may be tough. Other vegetables can be used in place of or in addition to the eggplant—zucchini (courgettes); red, yellow, or green bell pepper (capsicum) chunks; yellow or red cherry tomatoes; or blanched pearl onions. Steamed couscous or rice makes a good accompaniment. Garnish the dish with sprigs of thyme or oregano, if you like.

1½ lb (750 g) boneless leg of lamb, trimmed of excess fat and cut into 1–1½-inch (2.5–4-cm) cubes

8 Asian (slender) eggplants (aubergines), unpeeled, cut into 1-inch (2.5-cm) pieces
3 tablespoons olive oil
salt and freshly ground pepper to taste

FOR THE PROVENÇAL DRESSING:

6 tablespoons (3 fl oz/90 ml) extra-virgin olive oil
2 tablespoons red wine vinegar
1 tablespoon tomato paste
1 clove garlic, minced
¼ teaspoon chopped fresh rosemary
¼ teaspoon chopped fresh thyme
¼ teaspoon chopped fresh oregano
salt and freshly ground pepper to taste

Place the lamb and eggplant pieces in a bowl. Add the olive oil, salt, and pepper and toss well. Refrigerate until ready to cook.

🔥 To make the dressing, in a small bowl, whisk together the extra-virgin olive oil, vinegar, tomato paste, garlic, rosemary, thyme, oregano, salt, and pepper. Set aside.

🔥 Prepare a fire in a grill.

🔥 Thread equal amounts of lamb and eggplant onto 12 skewers, alternating the lamb and eggplant pieces. Place the skewers on the grill rack and grill, turning occasionally, until the lamb is still pink at the center and the eggplant is golden and cooked through, 10–12 minutes total.

🔥 Transfer the skewers to warmed individual plates. Quickly whisk the dressing and drizzle it over the skewers. Serve at once.

Salad of Grilled Lamb, Potatoes, and Garlic Mayonnaise

SERVES 6

2 lb (1 kg) small red potatoes, unpeeled
  and well scrubbed
2 tablespoons olive oil
salt and freshly ground pepper to taste

FOR THE GARLIC MAYONNAISE:

1 egg yolk
1 teaspoon Dijon mustard
⅓ cup (3 fl oz/80 ml) olive oil
⅓ cup (3 fl oz/80 ml) vegetable oil
juice of ½ lemon
2 or 3 cloves garlic, minced
salt and freshly ground pepper to taste
2 tablespoons warm water

1 leg of lamb, 3–3¼ lb (1.5–1.65 kg),
  trimmed of excess fat, boned, and
  butterflied
2 tablespoons olive oil
salt and freshly ground pepper to taste
3 red bell peppers (capsicums), roasted
  and cut lengthwise into strips 1 inch
  (2.5 cm) wide (optional)
fresh flat-leaf (Italian) parsley leaves

Preheat an oven to 375°F (190°C).
Prepare a fire in a grill.

🌿 Place the potatoes in a single layer
in a baking dish. Add the oil, salt, and
pepper and turn the potatoes to coat
them evenly. Cover with aluminum foil
and bake until tender, 40–50 minutes.
Remove from the oven and uncover.

🌿 Meanwhile, prepare the garlic mayonnaise: In a bowl, whisk together the egg
yolk, mustard, and 1 tablespoon of the
olive oil until an emulsion forms. In a
cup, combine the remaining olive oil
and the vegetable oil. Whisking constantly, gradually add the oils until the
emulsion thickens. Add the lemon juice,

garlic, salt, and pepper. Whisk in the
warm water to make the mayonnaise
barely fluid. Cover and refrigerate.

🌿 Rub the lamb with the olive oil, salt,
and pepper. About 10 minutes after
placing the potatoes in the oven, place
the lamb on the grill rack and grill until
the first side is golden brown, about 15
minutes. Turn and continue to cook until
an instant-read thermometer inserted
into the thickest part registers 130°F
(54°C) for medium-rare, about 15 minutes longer, or until done to your liking.

🌿 Transfer to a cutting board, cover
loosely with aluminum foil, and let rest
for 10 minutes before carving.

🌿 Meanwhile, place the potatoes on
the grill rack and grill, turning occasionally, until hot and well marked,
about 10 minutes.

🌿 Cut the lamb across the grain into
thin slices and arrange on individual
plates with the potatoes and the roasted
bell peppers, if using. Garnish with
parsley and pass the garlic mayonnaise
at the table.

Lamb Tikka

SERVES 6

These Indian kabobs are a variation on the well-known tandoori cooking. Lamb, used here, is a favorite; chunks of skinless, boneless chicken breast are also good. Serve with crisp vegetables such as chunks of cucumber, radishes, or hearts of lettuce.

1½–2 lb (750 g–1 kg) meat from lamb
   leg, cut into 1-inch (2.5-cm) cubes
1 clove garlic, quartered lengthwise
1 yellow onion, quartered
1 tablespoon peeled and grated fresh
   ginger
½ cup (4 oz/125 g) plain yogurt
3 tablespoons fresh lemon juice
1 tablespoon minced fresh mint
1 tablespoon minced fresh cilantro
   (fresh coriander)
1 tablespoon garam masala
1 teaspoon ground cumin
1 teaspoon ground turmeric
1 teaspoon salt

Place the lamb in a bowl. Put the garlic, onion, ginger, yogurt, lemon juice, mint, cilantro, garam masala, cumin, turmeric, and salt into a blender and whirl until smooth. Pour the yogurt mixture over the lamb and mix thoroughly so that each piece of meat is evenly coated. Cover and refrigerate for 6–8 hours.

🌿 Prepare a fire in a grill.

🌿 Remove the lamb from the marinade and pat it dry with paper towels. Thread 3 lamb cubes onto each skewer and place on the grill rack. Grill, turning once, until tender but still pink at the center, about 5 minutes on each side.

🌿 Transfer the skewers to a warmed platter or individual plates and serve at once.

Lamb Shoulder Chops with Sweet Ginger, Soy, and Shallot Glaze

SERVES 4

Shoulder chops are a less expensive option to costly lamb rib chops, but many cooks do not try them for fear that the meat will be tough. But there is a simple key to the successful grilling of shoulder chops: lots of flavor, little time. Slightly pink is the best way to serve them, and this is easily achieved on an outdoor grill. The sweet ginger preserves lend a wonderful flavor to the meat.

⅓ cup (3½ oz/105 g) ginger preserves
¼ cup (1½ oz/45 g) minced shallot
¼ cup (2 fl oz/60 ml) fresh lemon juice
3 tablespoons olive oil
3 tablespoons low-sodium soy sauce
4 lamb shoulder chops, each about
   ½ inch (12 mm) thick
8 green (spring) onions, tough green
   ends trimmed

In a bowl, whisk together the ginger preserves, shallot, lemon juice, olive oil, and soy sauce. Transfer about half of the mixture to a shallow nonaluminum dish. Reserve the remaining ginger mixture for serving. Place the chops and the green onions in the dish and brush generously with the ginger mixture. Set aside at room temperature until ready to grill. (If desired, cover and refrigerate the chops and onions for up to 6 hours. Bring to room temperature before proceeding.)

🌿 Prepare a fire in a grill.

🌿 Place the chops on the grill rack and grill, turning once, until light pink at the center, about 2½ minutes on each side. Watch carefully and move the chops to a cooler area of the grill if they begin to char.

🌿 Grill the green onions on a grill screen. They are ready when they are slightly charred and limp, about 4 minutes total.

🌿 Transfer the chops to warmed individual plates and accompany each chop with 2 green onions. Drizzle the chops and onions with the reserved ginger mixture and serve at once.

Lamb and Potato Skewers

SERVES 4–6

Meat and potatoes can share the same skewer as long as they will cook in about the same amount of time. Cubes of tender beef may also be skewered this way. If you have them, sturdy branches of fresh rosemary, about 8 inches (20 cm) long and soaked in water to cover for about 30 minutes, make aromatic and unusual skewers.

12 small boiling potatoes
2 lb (1 kg) lean, boneless lamb, cut into
  1½-inch (4-cm) cubes
½ cup (4 fl oz/125 ml) olive oil
1 tablespoon chopped fresh rosemary
1 tablespoon fresh lemon juice
¼ teaspoon salt
¼ teaspoon freshly ground pepper

Prepare a fire in a grill.

Cook the potatoes in boiling salted water to cover until they are barely tender when pierced, about 10 minutes. Drain well and cover with cold water. Let stand for about 2 minutes, then drain again and pat dry with paper towels. Thread the potatoes alternately with the lamb onto skewers.

In a small bowl, whisk together the oil, rosemary, lemon juice, salt, and pepper until blended.

Arrange the skewers on the grill rack. Grill, turning two or three times and brushing with the olive oil mixture, until the lamb is tender but still pink at the center, 6–8 minutes.

Transfer the skewers to a warmed platter or individual plates and serve at once.

Grilled Butterflied Leg of Lamb with Mint Mustard

SERVES 6–8

Grilled butterflied leg of lamb can be served with a variety of other sauces, such as mint jelly or a fruit chutney.

¼ cup (2 fl oz/60 ml) olive oil
3 cloves garlic, minced
salt and freshly ground pepper
1 leg of lamb, 5–6 lb (2.5–3 kg),
  trimmed of excess fat, boned, and
  butterflied

FOR THE MINT MUSTARD:

6 tablespoons chopped fresh mint, plus
  fresh mint sprigs for garnish (optional)
3 tablespoons mayonnaise
¾ cup (6 oz/185 g) Dijon mustard
1 clove garlic, minced
1 teaspoon fresh lemon juice

In a bowl, whisk together the olive oil, garlic, salt, and pepper. Place the lamb in a shallow dish and rub the mixture over the entire surface of the meat. Cover and refrigerate overnight.

Prepare a fire in a grill.

To prepare the mint mustard, in a small bowl, stir together the chopped mint, mayonnaise, mustard, garlic, and lemon juice. Set aside.

Place the lamb on the grill rack and grill until the first side is golden, about 15 minutes. Turn and continue to cook until golden on the second side and an instant-read thermometer inserted into the thickest part registers 130°F (54°C) for medium-rare, about 15 minutes longer, or until done to your liking.

Transfer to a cutting board, cover loosely with aluminum foil, and let rest for 10 minutes before carving.

Cut the lamb across the grain into thin slices and arrange on a warmed platter. Garnish with the mint sprigs, if using, and pass the mint mustard at the table. Serve immediately.

4 tomatoes, peeled, seeded, and chopped
6 slices coarse country bread

In a bowl, combine the lamb, onion, minced garlic, 2 tablespoons of the chopped mint, cumin, 1 teaspoon salt, and ½ teaspoon pepper. Mix well and form into 6 patties each about ½ inch (12 mm) thick. Cover and refrigerate for 1 hour.

🔥 Prepare a fire in a grill.

🔥 Bring a small saucepan three-fourths full of water to a boil. Add the whole garlic cloves and simmer, uncovered, until just soft, 10–15 minutes. Drain.

🔥 In a frying pan over medium heat, warm 2 tablespoons of the olive oil. Add the tomatoes, remaining 4 table-spoons chopped mint, and the garlic cloves and season with salt and pepper. Simmer until the juices evaporate and the sauce thickens slightly, 5–10 min-utes. Remove from the heat, cover, and keep warm.

🔥 Brush the bread slices with the remaining 2 tablespoons olive oil and place on the grill rack. Grill, turning once, until golden, about 10 minutes total. Grill the lamb burgers at the same time, turning once, until pink when cut at the thickest part, 8–10 min-utes total.

🔥 Place 1 slice of grilled bread on each plate and top with a lamb burger. Spoon the warm sauce on top, garnish with the mint sprigs, and serve.

Grilled Lamb Burgers with Mint, Tomatoes, and Garlic

SERVES 6

This is a terrific dish for lamb and garlic lovers. Serve it during the summer when the tomatoes and mint are at their best and the temperatures are perfect for outdoor grilling.

2 lb (1 kg) ground (minced) lamb
¼ cup (1½ oz/45 g) minced red (Spanish) onion
2 cloves garlic, minced, plus 24 whole cloves garlic
6 tablespoons (½ oz/15 g) chopped fresh mint, plus sprigs for garnish
½ teaspoon ground cumin
1 teaspoon salt, plus salt to taste
½ teaspoon coarsely ground pepper, plus pepper to taste
4 tablespoons (2 fl oz/60 ml) extra-virgin olive oil

Lamb Sandwich with Feta and Cucumber Salad

SERVES 6

For added color and flavor, tuck a few tomato slices, lettuce leaves, or pitted Kalamata olives into this delicious sandwich.

FOR THE SALAD:
6 oz (185 g) feta cheese, crumbled
2 tablespoons extra-virgin olive oil
2 tablespoons fresh lemon juice
salt and freshly ground pepper to taste
1 cucumber, peeled, halved lengthwise, seeded, and cut into ½-inch (12-mm) dice
½ small red (Spanish) onion, cut into ¼-inch (6-mm) dice
1 tablespoon chopped fresh mint
1 tablespoon chopped fresh parsley, preferably flat-leaf (Italian)
1 tablespoon chopped fresh dill

1 piece boneless leg of lamb, 1½–2 lb (750 g–1 kg), trimmed of excess fat and butterflied
1 tablespoon extra-virgin olive oil
6 pita breads, each 6 inches (15 cm) in diameter, halved and heated

Prepare a fire in a grill.

🔥 To prepare the salad, in a bowl, com-bine the feta, olive oil, lemon juice, salt, and pepper and mash together with a fork. Stir in the cucumber, onion, mint, parsley, and dill. Set aside.

🔥 Brush the lamb with the 1 table-spoon olive oil. Place on a grill rack and grill, turning once, until golden brown and an instant-read thermometer inserted into the thickest part registers 130°–135°F (54°–57°C) for medium-rare, about 30 minutes total.

🔥 Transfer the lamb to a cutting board, cover loosely with aluminum foil, and let rest for 10 minutes before carving. Slice the meat across the grain and distribute the lamb and the salad evenly among the pita halves. Serve immediately.

Vegetables, Sides & Salads

On the Grill

From corn to asparagus, radicchio to sweet potatoes, vegetables are right at home over a bed of hot coals. Pastas and breads take beautifully to the grill, too, benefiting from the unique flavor and texture that grilling provides. Many of the recipes in this chapter, such as Mixed Vegetable Pasta and Stuffed Acorn Squash, make wonderful vegetarian main courses. Dishes such as Spicy Eggplant and Portobello Mushrooms on Salad Greens work well as side or main dishes, depending on how they are paired with other selections.

Ratatouille from the Grill

SERVES 6

Grilled vegetables are combined to make a backyard version of Provence's famed ratatouille.

1 large eggplant (aubergine)
salt for sprinkling, plus 1 teaspoon salt
1 large yellow onion
2 zucchini (courgettes) or yellow crookneck squashes
2 red or green bell peppers (capsicums)
8–10 large fresh mushrooms, brushed clean
¾ cup (6 fl oz/180 ml) olive oil
1 large tomato, peeled, seeded, and chopped
3 tablespoons white wine vinegar
2 cloves garlic, minced
½ teaspoon freshly ground pepper
½ cup (¾ oz/20 g) chopped fresh basil or parsley

Prepare a fire in a grill.

Trim the eggplant and then cut crosswise into slices about ½ inch (12 mm) thick. Place in a colander and salt liberally to draw out the moisture. Let stand for 30 minutes.

Rinse the eggplant slices and pat them dry with paper towels. Set aside.

Prepare the remaining vegetables as follows: Cut the onion into slices ½ inch (12 mm) thick. Halve the squashes lengthwise. Cut the bell peppers into rings 1 inch (2.5 cm) thick, removing seeds and ribs. Trim the stem ends of the mushrooms.

Arrange the vegetables on a grill screen and grill, turning two or three times and brushing them with ½ cup (4 fl oz/120 ml) of the olive oil, until tender-crisp when pierced, 10–12 minutes. Remove from the grill and let cool. Cut into bite-sized pieces.

Meanwhile, in a large serving bowl, stir or whisk together the remaining ¼ cup (2 fl oz/60 ml) olive oil, the tomato, vinegar, garlic, the 1 teaspoon salt, the pepper, and the basil or parsley. Add the vegetables to the tomato mixture and toss gently to combine. Serve at room temperature.

Crisp Tofu with Oyster Sauce

SERVES 6

Oyster sauce, a thick, concentrated paste made from oysters, brine, and soy sauce, is available in well-stocked food stores and in Asian markets. Serve the tofu and vegetables over brown or white rice and sprinkle with pickled ginger.

1 package (12 oz/375 g) firm tofu, drained and cut into slices ¾ inch (2 cm) thick

3 tablespoons oyster sauce

6 green (spring) onions, trimmed but left whole

¼ lb (125 g) snow peas (mangetouts), trimmed

2 green bell peppers (capsicums), seeded and cut lengthwise into strips ½ inch (12 mm) wide

vegetable oil or canola oil for brushing

Prepare a fire in a grill.

🌿 Brush the tofu slices on both sides with the oyster sauce. Brush the green onions, snow peas, and bell peppers with the oil. Place the tofu and vegetables on an oiled grill screen and grill, turning the tofu once and the vegetables as necessary, until the tofu is crisp and heated through and the bell peppers, onions, and snow peas are tender and slightly charred, about 6 minutes for the vegetables and about 10 minutes for the tofu slices.

🌿 Transfer to a warmed platter and serve hot.

Stuffed Acorn Squash

SERVES 4

This savory stuffing is infused with the sweetness of prunes. For a heartier dish, add some cooked ground (minced) beef or sausage to the mixture.

¼ cup (2 oz/60 g) unsalted butter

½ cup (2½ oz/75 g) finely chopped yellow onion

½ cup (2½ oz/75 g) finely chopped celery

2 cups (4 oz/125 g) fresh white bread crumbs

1 teaspoon dried sage

½ teaspoon salt, plus salt to taste

¼ teaspoon freshly ground pepper, plus pepper to taste

½ cup (3 oz/90 g) chopped prunes

¼ cup (1 oz/30 g) chopped walnuts

3 tablespoons water

2 acorn squashes

Prepare a fire for indirect-heat cooking in a covered grill (see page 11).

🌿 In a frying pan over medium heat, melt the butter. When hot, add the onion and celery and cook, stirring frequently, until softened and wilted slightly, about 5 minutes. Scrape into a large bowl and add the bread crumbs, sage, the ½ teaspoon salt, the ¼ teaspoon pepper, prunes, and walnuts. Sprinkle the water over the top. Stir and toss with a fork to distribute the ingredients evenly. Set aside.

🌿 Cut out four 6-inch (15-cm) squares of aluminum foil; set aside. Using a large, sharp knife, cut each squash in half through the stem end. Using a spoon, scrape out the seeds and any fibers, and discard. Season the cut sides generously with salt and pepper. Divide the bread crumb mixture evenly among the squash cavities, pressing it down lightly. To prevent the stuffing from drying out, cover each squash with a square of foil, folding it down over the sides.

🌿 Place the stuffed squashes, foil side up, on the center of the grill rack, cover, and open the vents halfway. Cook for 45 minutes. Remove the foil and continue cooking in the covered grill until the squash is tender when pierced and the stuffing is lightly browned, about 15 minutes longer.

🌿 Transfer to a warmed platter and serve at once.

Pizza with Pears, Pancetta, and Wilted Arugula

MAKES 2 PIZZAS; SERVES 4

Given the decades-old fascination with both grilling and pizza, grilled pizza is an inevitable result. You will need to work quickly when cooking pizza on the grill. In this recipe, you top the crust after the pizza has been flipped, so have all the topping ingredients assembled within reach. This pizza is cooked directly on the grill rack, resulting in a crisp crust with appealing grill marks. Consider hosting a top-your-own party, and let your guests select from various toppings to customize their own pizzas.

FOR THE PIZZA DOUGH:

3½ cups (17½ oz/545 g) all-purpose (plain) flour

2½ teaspoons (1 envelope) quick-rise yeast

1 tablespoon sugar

1 tablespoon salt

1 teaspoon dried oregano, or scant 2 teaspoons chopped fresh oregano

1¼ cups (10 fl oz/310 ml) warm water

2 tablespoons olive oil

FOR THE TOPPING:

4 ripe pears, peeled, cored, and chopped

freshly ground pepper to taste

½ cup (2½ oz/75 g) pine nuts

¼ lb (125 g) baby arugula (rocket) leaves

olive oil

6 oz (185 g) thinly sliced pancetta, coarsely chopped

To prepare the dough, in a food processor, combine the flour, yeast, sugar, salt, and oregano and pulse briefly to mix. With the motor running, add the warm water and the olive oil in a slow, steady stream and process until the dough comes together in a rough mass. Process for about 40 seconds longer, then transfer to a lightly floured work surface and knead until smooth and elastic. Form the dough into a ball, place in an oiled bowl, and turn the ball to coat it with oil. Cover the bowl with plastic wrap and set in a warm place until the dough is doubled in bulk, about 1½ hours. (If desired, you can punch down the dough at this point and refrigerate it for up to 3 hours before rolling it out. Bring it to room temperature.)

🌿 Prepare a fire for indirect-heat cooking in a covered grill (see page 11).

🌿 To prepare the topping, place the pears in a bowl and season generously with pepper. In a small, dry frying pan over medium heat, toast the pine nuts, shaking the pan often, until golden, about 3 minutes. Pour into a small bowl. Place the arugula in another bowl, drizzle with a little olive oil, and toss to coat lightly and evenly. Place the pears, pine nuts, arugula, and pancetta alongside the grill.

🌿 Punch down the dough and transfer to a lightly floured work surface. Divide in half and roll each half into a smooth ball. Cover with a kitchen towel and let rest for 10 minutes. On the floured surface, roll out the halves, one at a time, into large, rough ovals a little less than ¼ inch (6 mm) thick. (If the dough is resisting your efforts to roll it out nice and large, cover it with the towel and let rest for 3–4 minutes, then roll again and it will comply. Also, if you are not ready to grill immediately, the ovals can be covered with the towel for up to 20 minutes.)

🌿 Place a dough oval on the cool part of the grill rack and cover the grill. Cook until the surface of the dough bubbles and the bottom is marked from the grate, about 3 minutes. Punch down the bubbles with a wooden spatula and, using 2 wooden spatulas or a pizza peel, flip the crust over. Immediately scatter half each of the pears, pancetta, and pine nuts over the crust, leaving a ¼-inch (6-mm) border uncovered. (Work very quickly at this point, so you can close the grill as soon as possible.) Cover the grill and grill until the pears and pancetta look cooked, about 8 minutes. Uncover, scatter half of the arugula over the top, again leaving the border. Re-cover and grill for 1 minute longer to wilt the arugula. The edges should be crisp and the underside should be nicely marked but not charred. Do not overcook, or the dough will become brittle.

🌿 Slide the pizza onto a plate and repeat with the other dough oval. Cut the pizzas into quarters and serve at once.

Portobello Mushrooms on Salad Greens

SERVES 6

FOR THE RED WINE MARINADE:
½ cup (4 fl oz/125 ml) dry red wine
½ cup (4 fl oz/125 ml) vegetable oil
½ cup (4 fl oz/125 ml) fresh orange juice
1 tablespoon chopped fresh basil

6 large fresh portobello mushrooms,
  brushed clean and stems removed

FOR THE MUSTARD VINAIGRETTE:
1 tablespoon Dijon mustard
3 tablespoons red wine vinegar
½ teaspoon salt
¼ teaspoon freshly ground pepper
½ cup (4 fl oz/125 ml) extra-virgin
  olive oil

8 cups (8 oz/250 g) torn assorted
  salad greens

To prepare the marinade, in a small bowl, stir together the wine, oil, orange juice, and basil. Divide between 2 large lock-top plastic bags. Put 3 mushrooms in each bag, seal, and turn several times to coat evenly. Let stand at room temperature for 1 hour.

To prepare the vinaigrette, in a large bowl, whisk together the mustard, vinegar, salt, and pepper. Slowly whisk in the olive oil. Set aside.

Prepare a fire in a covered grill.

Place the mushrooms on the grill rack, cover, open the vents, and grill, turning once, until moist on the underside and just firm to the touch on the top, 3–4 minutes on each side. Remove from the grill.

Add the greens to the bowl with the vinaigrette and toss well. Divide among individual plates. Cut the mushrooms into slices about ¼ inch (6 mm) thick, divide among the salads, and serve.

Mixed Vegetable Pasta

SERVES 6

Try rosemary branches, soaked and stripped of leaves, for skewers.

FOR THE DRESSING:

⅓ cup (3 fl oz/80 ml) olive oil

⅓ cup (3 fl oz/80 ml) rice vinegar

2 cloves garlic, minced

1 tablespoon peeled and grated fresh ginger

freshly ground pepper to taste

3 carrots, peeled and sliced ¼ inch (6 mm) thick

2 Asian (slender) eggplants (aubergines), trimmed and cut on the diagonal into slices ½ inch (12 mm) thick

1 red bell pepper (capsicum), seeded and cut crosswise into slices ½ inch (12 mm) thick

2 yellow summer squashes, sliced ½ inch (12 mm) thick

olive oil

¾ lb (375 g) penne

Prepare a fire in a grill.

🍃 To prepare the dressing, in a large bowl, whisk together the olive oil, vinegar, garlic, ginger, and pepper. Set aside.

🍃 Bring a saucepan three-fourths full of salted water to a boil. Add the carrots and parboil for 5 minutes. Drain and pat dry. Thread the carrots, eggplant, bell pepper, and squash slices onto 6 skewers, dividing evenly. Brush with the oil. Grill, turning as necessary, until tender, about 15 minutes.

🍃 Meanwhile, bring a large saucepan three-fourths full of salted water to a boil. Add the penne, stir well, and cook until firm yet tender to the bite, about 10 minutes or according to the package directions. Drain, transfer to the bowl with the dressing, and toss to coat.

🍃 Serve in warmed bowls, topped with the grilled vegetable skewers.

Ratatouille Pizza

SERVES 6

FOR THE PIZZA DOUGH:

1 teaspoon sugar

1 scant cup (8 fl oz/250 ml) warm water

2½ teaspoons (1 envelope) active dry yeast

2¾ cups (14 oz/440 g) all-purpose (plain) flour

½ teaspoon salt

2 tablespoons olive oil

FOR THE TOPPING:

1 large eggplant (aubergine), peeled and cut into slices ½ inch (12 mm) thick

1 zucchini (courgette), cut into slices ½ inch (12 mm) thick

1 large yellow onion, cut into slices ½ inch (12 mm) thick

2 large tomatoes, cut into slices ½ inch (12 mm) thick

olive oil for brushing and drizzling

2 tablespoons chopped fresh oregano

½ teaspoon salt

¼ teaspoon freshly ground pepper

¼ cup (1 oz/30 g) grated Parmesan or pecorino romano cheese

To prepare the dough, in a small bowl, dissolve the sugar in the warm water. Sprinkle the yeast over the top and let stand until foamy, about 5 minutes.

In a food processor, combine the flour and salt and pulse briefly to combine. Add the olive oil and the yeast mixture and process until a soft, slightly sticky dough forms, about 10 seconds. (Alternatively, combine the ingredients in a bowl and stir with a wooden spoon until combined.)

Turn out the dough onto a lightly floured work surface and knead until smooth, about 5 minutes. If the dough is too sticky, work in more flour, a tablespoon at a time, until smooth. Form the dough into a ball, place in a bowl, cover with a kitchen towel, and let rise in a warm place until the dough is doubled in bulk, 45–60 minutes.

Meanwhile, prepare a fire in a covered grill. Place a pizza stone on the grill rack.

To prepare the topping, brush the eggplant, zucchini, onion, and tomato slices generously with oil, set on a grill screen, and place the screen on the grill rack. Grill, turning once, until tender, about 2 minutes on each side for the tomatoes, about 4 minutes on each side for the zucchini, about 5 minutes on each side for the onion, and up to 7 minutes on each side for the eggplant. Transfer the vegetables to a platter. Separate the onion slices into rings.

Punch down the dough and let stand for 5 minutes. Turn out onto the floured work surface and knead for a few minutes until smooth. Roll out the dough into a round about 12 inches (30 cm) in diameter.

Brush the top surface of the dough with olive oil and place directly on the hot pizza stone. Arrange the eggplant slices over the dough and top with the zucchini, onion, and tomatoes. Sprinkle with the oregano, salt, and pepper, and drizzle lightly with olive oil.

Cover, open the vents, and grill, rotating once, until the crust is golden, 8–10 minutes. Watch carefully, as the crust may burn if the coals are too hot.

Transfer the pizza to a serving platter, sprinkle with the cheese, and cut into serving pieces. Serve hot.

Stuffed Mushrooms and Summer Squashes

SERVES 3 AS A MAIN COURSE OR 4–6 AS AN ACCOMPANIMENT

These stuffed vegetables are a fine main course for a vegetarian meal or a good accompaniment to grilled fish.

12 large fresh white mushrooms, brushed clean

4 zucchini (courgettes) or yellow crookneck squashes

4 tablespoons (2 fl oz/60 ml) olive oil

1 small yellow onion, chopped

1 clove garlic, minced

¾ cup (3 oz/90 g) soda cracker crumbs or fine dried bread crumbs

½ cup (2 oz/60 g) grated cheddar or Parmesan cheese

1 tablespoon chopped fresh oregano or 1 teaspoon dried oregano

½ teaspoon salt, plus salt to taste

¼ teaspoon freshly ground pepper

3 tablespoons heavy (double) cream

Cut or gently pull the stem from each mushroom, forming a hollow in the base of the cap to hold the stuffing; reserve the stems. Halve the squashes lengthwise and, using a teaspoon, scoop out the centers, leaving a shell about ⅓ inch (9 mm) thick; reserve the centers. Set the prepared vegetables aside.

Prepare a fire for indirect-heat cooking in a covered grill (see page 11).

Chop together the squash centers and mushroom stems. In a frying pan over medium-high heat, warm 2 tablespoons of the olive oil. When hot, add the chopped mixture, onion, and garlic and cook, stirring occasionally, until tender and any liquid released during cooking has evaporated, about 7 minutes. Scrape into a large bowl and add the crumbs, cheese, oregano, ½ teaspoon salt, pepper, and cream. Stir and toss with a fork to combine.

Brush the outsides of the squash shells and mushroom caps with the remaining 2 tablespoons oil; sprinkle with salt. Spoon about 2 teaspoons stuffing into each mushroom cap and 2 tablespoons into each squash shell, mounding slightly.

Place the stuffed vegetables on a grill screen in the center of the grill rack, cover, and open the vents halfway. Cook until the stuffing is browned on top and the vegetables are tender when pierced with a knife, about 20 minutes.

Transfer to a platter. Serve hot or at room temperature.

Mixed Vegetable Grill

SERVES 6

Here is a suggested medley of vegetables, but improvise and use whatever is in season and reasonably young and tender. Very firm vegetables will grill more quickly and evenly if you first cook them in boiling water until just tender, a step that can be done hours ahead.

¾ cup (6 fl oz/180 ml) olive oil

3 tablespoons fresh lemon juice

3 tablespoons chopped fresh cilantro
  (fresh coriander)

1 teaspoon salt

¼ teaspoon freshly ground pepper

2 fennel bulbs, trimmed and cut in
  half lengthwise

4 baby artichokes, trimmed

2 whole heads garlic, unpeeled

2 Belgian endives (chicory/witloof)

2 Anaheim chiles, halved lengthwise
  and seeded

8 oz (250 g) whole fresh shiitake
  mushrooms, brushed clean and
  stemmed

12–16 thin asparagus, about
  ¾ lb (375 g), tough ends removed

1 large red (Spanish) onion, cut crosswise into slices ½ inch (12 mm) thick

In a small bowl, whisk together the olive oil, lemon juice, cilantro, salt, and pepper; set aside.

Fill a large pot three-fourths full of salted water and bring to a rapid boil. Add the fennel bulbs and cook until just tender when pierced, 7–10 minutes. Using a slotted spoon, lift out and drain well; set aside. Drop in the artichokes and cook until just tender, 5–10 minutes. Scoop them out, drain well, and then cut them in half lengthwise; set aside. Blanch the garlic heads for about 5 minutes; scoop them out, drain well, and set aside. Finally, blanch the Belgian endives for about 1 minute; scoop out, drain well, and then halve lengthwise. Set aside. Have the chiles, mushrooms, asparagus, and onion at hand also.

Prepare a fire in a grill.

Arrange the vegetables directly on the grill rack or on an oiled grill screen placed on the rack. Grill the fennel halves, artichoke halves, whole garlic heads, and onion slices for about 12 minutes; the chile halves and mushrooms for about 10 minutes; the endive halves for about 8 minutes; and the asparagus for 4–8 minutes, depending upon size. As the vegetables cook, turn them two or three times and brush with the oil mixture.

Transfer to a platter and serve warm or at room temperature.

Eggplant and Fontina Sandwiches

SERVES 6

These have a good savory flavor and are delicious warm or at room temperature. They can even be reheated on the grill or in the oven the next day. If you can't find fontina cheese, use Monterey jack, moz-zarella, or any other mild cheese that will complement fresh sage.

1 large eggplant, about 3 inches
   (7.5 cm) in diameter and
   6–7 inches (15–18 cm) long
salt for sprinkling, plus ½ teaspoon salt
⅓ cup (3 fl oz/80 ml) olive oil

2 tablespoons fresh lemon juice
1 clove garlic, minced
1 tablespoon chopped fresh sage
   or 1 teaspoon dried sage
¼ teaspoon freshly ground pepper
5 oz (155 g) fontina cheese, thinly sliced
handful of fresh sage leaves (optional)

Prepare a fire in a grill.

Trim the eggplant and cut crosswise into slices about ½ inch (12 mm) thick. You should have 12 slices in all. Place the slices in a colander and salt them liberally to draw out the moisture. Let stand for 30 minutes.

Meanwhile, in a jar with a tight-fitting lid, combine the oil, lemon juice, garlic, chopped or dried sage, the ½ tea-spoon salt, and the pepper. Shake vigorously.

Rinse the eggplant slices and pat dry with paper towels. Arrange on the grill rack and grill, turning them once or twice and brushing with the oil mixture, until lightly browned, about 8 minutes. Top six of the slices with a piece of cheese and 2 or 3 sage leaves, if using, then cover with the remaining eggplant slices. Grill, turning once, until the cheese begins to melt, about 2 minutes longer.

Transfer to individual plates and serve.

Vegetable Skewers with Romesco Sauce

SERVES 6

In Spain, the zesty almond-pepper sauce known as romesco is a classic accompaniment to grilled fish, although it is equally delicious spooned over vegetables. Romesco is also good served with Polenta Wedges (page 210).

FOR THE ROMESCO SAUCE:

4 tablespoons (2 fl oz/60 ml)
   extra-virgin olive oil

2 slices coarse-textured white bread

¼ cup (1½ oz/45 g) blanched almonds

1 cup (6 oz/185 g) peeled, seeded, and
   chopped tomatoes (fresh or canned)

1 clove garlic, minced

2 teaspoons sweet paprika

¼ teaspoon red pepper flakes

3 tablespoons red wine vinegar

salt and freshly ground black pepper
   to taste

6 Asian (slender) eggplants (aubergines),
   1 lb (500 g) total weight, trimmed
   and cut crosswise into slices ¾ inch
   (2 cm) thick

24 fresh mushrooms, 1 lb (500 g) total
   weight, brushed clean and stem ends
   trimmed

6 long, thin zucchini (courgettes),
   1¼ lb (625 g) total weight, cut crosswise into slices 1 inch (2.5 cm) thick

12 cherry tomatoes, stems removed

3 tablespoons olive oil

flat-leaf (Italian) parsley sprigs (optional)

To prepare the sauce, in a frying pan over medium heat, warm 2 tablespoons of the olive oil. Add the bread and fry, turning once or twice with tongs, until golden on both sides, about 2 minutes. Transfer the bread to a food processor.

Add the almonds to the oil remaining in the frying pan and sauté, stirring often, until golden, about 2 minutes.

Transfer the almonds to the processor, along with the tomatoes, garlic, paprika, and red pepper flakes. In a small cup, combine the red wine vinegar and the remaining 2 tablespoons olive oil. With the processor motor running, pour in the olive oil mixture in a slow, steady stream. Season with salt and black pepper. Pour the sauce into a serving bowl and let stand for 1 hour before serving.

Prepare a fire in a grill.

Thread the eggplant slices, mushrooms, zucchini slices, and tomatoes onto 12 skewers, alternating the vegetables and dividing them evenly among the skewers. Brush the vegetables with the olive oil. Place on the grill rack and grill, turning occasionally, until tender when pierced, 10–15 minutes.

Place 2 skewers on each serving plate and garnish with parsley sprigs, if using. Pass the sauce at the table.

Ravioli with Spinach and Three Cheeses

SERVES 6

Briefly grilling cooked ravioli gives it a deliciously crisp, brown exterior that transforms the familiar pasta into a surprisingly different hors d'oeuvre.

FOR THE PASTA DOUGH:

2¼ cups (11½ oz/360 g) all-purpose (plain) flour
¼ teaspoon salt
3 eggs

FOR THE CHEESE FILLING:

3 cups (3 oz/90 g) spinach leaves, stems removed
1 cup (8 oz/250 g) ricotta cheese
½ cup (2 oz/60 g) shredded mozzarella cheese
1 tablespoon chopped fresh basil
salt and freshly ground pepper to taste

olive oil
½ cup (2 oz/60 g) grated pecorino romano cheese
2 tablespoons chopped fresh basil (optional)

To prepare the dough, in a food processor, combine the flour and salt. Pulse briefly to combine. With the motor running, add the eggs, one at a time, and process until mixed. The dough will be very soft. Transfer the dough to a lightly floured work surface and knead for a few minutes until smooth. Divide the dough into 4 equal portions and flatten each into a disk.

If using a pasta machine, set the rollers at the widest setting, dust a dough disk with flour, and feed it through the rollers. Fold in quarters, turn 90 degrees, and feed through again. Repeat, dusting the dough with flour as needed and decreasing the roller opening one notch

each time as the dough becomes smoother and silkier, until the dough is very thin. Set aside on a floured work surface. Repeat with the remaining dough portions. (Alternatively, dust a work surface lightly with flour. Working with 1 piece of dough at a time, flatten each disk with your hand and, using a rolling pin, roll the dough as thinly as possible.) Lightly sprinkle a kitchen towel with flour and place the pasta on it. Lightly sprinkle the pasta with flour and cover with another kitchen towel while you make the filling.

To prepare the filling, place the spinach in a saucepan with the rinsing water clinging to the leaves and place over medium heat. Cook until wilted, 2–3 minutes, then drain well and squeeze out the excess moisture with your hands. Chop the spinach and place in a bowl. Add the ricotta cheese, mozzarella cheese, basil, salt, and pepper and mix well.

Using a pastry brush, lightly coat 1 pasta sheet with water. Using a teaspoon, place mounds of the filling on the pasta sheet, spacing them about 3 inches (7.5 cm) apart. Place a second sheet of dough on top. Press down along the edges and around the mounds. Using a pastry wheel, cut between the mounds into 2½-inch (6-cm) squares. Repeat with the remaining pasta sheets and filling.

Prepare a fire in a grill.

Bring a large pot three-fourths full of salted water to a boil. Add the ravioli and cook until they rise to the surface and are tender, about 2 minutes. Drain well.

Brush the ravioli with olive oil, place them on an oiled grill screen, and grill, turning once, until golden brown and crisp, about 4 minutes total.

Transfer the ravioli to a serving platter and sprinkle with the pecorino romano cheese. Garnish with the basil, if desired, and serve hot.

Double Tomato Pizza

SERVES 4–6

For a crisper crust, grill the dough without any toppings for a minute or two, turn it over, add the toppings, and continue to cook.

1 recipe (10 oz/315 g) Pizza Dough (page 192)
olive oil for brushing and drizzling
3 large red or yellow tomatoes, sliced
3 plum (Roma) tomatoes, chopped
½ lb (250 g) fresh goat cheese, crumbled
2 tablespoons chopped garlic
2 tablespoons chopped fresh rosemary
salt and freshly ground pepper to taste

Prepare the pizza dough as directed.

Prepare a fire in a covered grill. Place a pizza stone on the grill rack.

On a lightly floured work surface, roll out the dough into a round about 12 inches (30 cm) in diameter.

Brush the surface of the dough with olive oil and then arrange the sliced tomatoes on top. Scatter the chopped tomatoes, goat cheese, and garlic over the sliced tomatoes. Sprinkle with the rosemary, salt, and pepper and drizzle lightly with olive oil.

Place the pizza directly on the hot pizza stone. Cover, open the vents, and grill, rotating the crust 180 degrees after about 4 minutes, until it is lightly browned, 8–10 minutes.

Transfer the pizza to a cutting board and cut into wedges. Serve immediately on warmed individual plates.

Grilled Onion Slices

SERVES 6

Grilled onions are quite sweet and not at all harsh. Green (spring) onions, which cook in just a few minutes, are delicious when grilled with the same butter-mustard basting sauce.

½ cup (4 oz/125 g) unsalted butter, melted
3 tablespoons Dijon mustard
2 teaspoons wine vinegar
1 tablespoon chopped fresh parsley or tarragon (optional)
3 large red onions, cut crosswise into slices ½ inch (12 mm) thick
salt and freshly ground pepper to taste

Prepare a fire in a grill.

In a small bowl, stir together the butter, mustard, vinegar, and the parsley or tarragon, if using.

Arrange the onion slices on the grill rack and sprinkle with salt and pepper. Grill, turning two or three times and brushing with the butter-mustard mixture, until tender and golden, about 10 minutes.

Leeks and Mushrooms

SERVES 6

For a subtle aromatic effect, soak ½ cup (1 oz/30 g) dried oregano in water for 5 minutes, drain well, and then sprinkle the herb over the hot coals.

6 leeks, including 2 inches (5 cm) of the tender greens, halved lengthwise
1 lb (500 g) fresh brown, white, or oyster mushrooms, brushed clean and trimmed
olive oil
balsamic vinegar
¼ cup (⅓ oz/10 g) chopped fresh oregano
½ teaspoon salt
¼ teaspoon freshly ground pepper
1 tablespoon grated orange zest

Prepare a fire in a grill.

Brush the leeks and the mushrooms with the olive oil and vinegar. Sprinkle with the oregano, salt, and pepper.

Arrange the vegetables on an oiled grill screen and grill, turning as necessary, until tender, about 6 minutes for the mushrooms and 10 minutes for the leeks.

Transfer the leeks and mushrooms to a platter. Drizzle with a little more oil and vinegar and sprinkle with the orange zest. Serve warm.

Asparagus with Orange Muscat Beurre Blanc

SERVES 4

This dish is special enough to serve as a first course and works best with spears about ½ inch (12 mm) thick.

1 lb (500 g) asparagus
¾ cup (6 fl oz/180 ml) orange muscat or other dessert wine such as Sauterne
¼ cup (2 fl oz/60 ml) dry vermouth

1 tablespoon peach or champagne vinegar
1 large shallot, minced
5 tablespoons (2½ oz/75 g) unsalted butter, at room temperature, cut into ½-inch (12-mm) cubes
¼ teaspoon freshly ground pepper
2 tablespoons minced fresh chives

Prepare a fire in a grill.

Snap off the tough ends of the asparagus spears. Using a vegetable peeler, peel the spears to within about 2 inches (5 cm) of the tips.

Bring a large frying pan three-fourths full of lightly salted water to a boil. Add the asparagus, reduce the heat to medium-low, and simmer until just tender, about 4 minutes. Drain and transfer to paper towels to dry.

In a small saucepan over medium-high heat, combine the dessert wine, vermouth, vinegar, and shallot and bring to a boil. Reduce the heat to low and simmer gently, uncovered, until reduced to about 1 tablespoon, about 20 minutes. Remove from the heat and set the pan aside.

Place the asparagus spears on a grill screen and grill, turning as necessary, to char evenly, about 4 minutes. Meanwhile, place the saucepan on the side of the grill rack to heat the wine mixture. As soon as it is steaming, add the butter all at once and swirl the pan or whisk the sauce continuously until the butter melts and emulsifies. Add the pepper and chives and swirl again.

Transfer the asparagus to a warmed serving platter and spoon the sauce over the top. Serve at once.

Eggplant Salad

SERVES 6

Sprinkle this smoky eggplant salad with chopped fresh parsley and serve as a first course or side dish. Add ½ cup (2 oz/60 g) toasted pine nuts with the olives, if desired. Grilled slices of coarse country bread go well with this dish.

2 medium-large eggplants (aubergines), trimmed, peeled, and cut into slices ¼ inch (6 mm) thick

3 yellow onions, cut into slices ½ inch (12 mm) thick

olive oil for brushing, plus ¼ cup (2 fl oz/60 ml) olive oil

4 cloves garlic, minced

1 cup (4 oz/125 g) diced celery

2 cups (12 oz/375 g) seeded and chopped tomatoes

1 cup (5 oz/155 g) oil-cured black olives, pitted

2 tablespoons red wine vinegar

salt and freshly ground pepper to taste

6 large red-leaf lettuce leaves

Prepare a fire in a covered grill.

🔥 Brush the eggplant and onion slices on both sides with olive oil. Place on an oiled grill screen, cover, open the vents, and grill, turning as necessary, until the eggplants are soft, 12–15 minutes, and the onions are slightly charred, about 5 minutes. Transfer to a platter and let cool.

🔥 In a food processor, combine the eggplants, onions, and garlic and pulse to chop coarsely. Transfer to a bowl and stir in the celery, tomatoes, olives, ¼ cup (2 fl oz/60 ml) olive oil, vinegar, salt, and pepper.

🔥 Line individual serving plates with the lettuce leaves, mound the salad on top, dividing evenly, and serve.

Bruschetta with White Beans and Fried Sage

SERVES 4

Many cultures serve some version of toasted bread with a savory topping, but the Italians seem to excel at it. Use a good country-style bread for this recipe, and bring out your best extra-virgin olive oil. The latter will marry beautifully with the crisp-fried sage and the earthy beans. To make this dish vegetarian, omit the prosciutto and increase the sage to 8 leaves.

FOR THE VINAIGRETTE:

½ teaspoon salt

¼ teaspoon freshly ground pepper

1 small clove garlic, minced

½ teaspoon Dijon mustard

2 tablespoons white wine vinegar

6 tablespoons (3 fl oz/90 ml) extra-virgin olive oil

2 tablespoons finely chopped fresh flat-leaf (Italian) parsley

2 oz (60 g) thinly sliced prosciutto, coarsely chopped

6 fresh sage leaves, julienned

1 can (15 oz/470 g) cannellini beans, rinsed and well drained

1 clove garlic, minced

¼ teaspoon salt

⅛ teaspoon freshly ground pepper

4 slices coarse country bread, each ½ inch (12 mm) thick

extra-virgin olive oil

Prepare a fire in a grill.

🔥 To prepare the vinaigrette, in a bowl, whisk together the salt, pepper, garlic, mustard, and vinegar. Slowly whisk in the oil until an emulsion forms, then whisk in the parsley.

🔥 In a small nonstick pan over medium-low heat, cook the prosciutto and sage, stirring occasionally, until crisp and golden, about 4 minutes. Remove from the heat.

🔥 In a bowl, combine the prosciutto, sage, beans, garlic, salt, and pepper. Add about 3 tablespoons of the vinaigrette and mix well. Taste and adjust the seasoning. (The remaining vinaigrette will keep, covered and refrigerated, for up to 1 week.)

🔥 Brush one side of the bread slices generously with olive oil. Place the slices, oiled side down, on the grill rack and grill until golden brown, about 3 minutes. Using tongs, transfer the bread slices, grilled side up, to a serving platter. Top with the bean mixture, dividing it evenly, and serve immediately.

Corn with Seasoned Butters

SERVES 6

Fresh corn still in the husk takes wonderfully to grilling. Serve it with one or all of the seasoned butters here and a platter full of ribs hot off the grill.

6 ears of corn
seasoned butter *(see below)*

Prepare a fire in a covered grill.

Working with 1 ear of corn at a time, carefully pull back the husks but leave them attached. Remove and discard the silk, then replace the husks around the ear. Soak the ears in cold water to cover for at least 20 minutes and then drain.

Carefully pull back the husks from each ear and spread the seasoned butter evenly over the kernels. Replace the husks.

Place the corn on the grill rack, cover, open the vents, and grill until the husks are browned and the kernels are tender, about 15 minutes. Transfer the corn to individual plates or a platter and serve hot.

FOR THE PECAN BUTTER:

⅓ cup (3 oz/90 g) unsalted butter, at room temperature
⅓ cup (1½ oz/45 g) ground pecans

To prepare the pecan butter, in a small bowl, using a fork or a wooden spoon, beat the butter until soft. Mix in the pecans to distribute evenly. Refrigerate if not using immediately.

FOR THE LIME BUTTER:

⅓ cup (3 oz/90 g) butter, at room temperature
1 tablespoon grated lime zest
1 tablespoon lime juice

To prepare the lime butter, in a small bowl, using a fork or a wooden spoon, beat the butter until soft. Mix in the lime zest and juice to distribute evenly. Refrigerate if not using immediately.

FOR THE CHILI BUTTER:

⅓ cup (3 oz/90 g) butter, at room temperature
2 tablespoons chili powder
1 teaspoon cumin seeds

To prepare the chili butter, in a small bowl, using a fork or a wooden spoon, beat the butter until soft. Mix in the chili powder and cumin seeds to distribute evenly. Refrigerate if not using immediately.

FOR THE ITALIAN HERB BUTTER:

⅓ cup (3 oz/90 g) unsalted butter, at room temperature
2 teaspoons minced fresh basil
2 teaspoons minced fresh oregano

To prepare the Italian herb butter, in a small bowl, using a fork or a wooden spoon, beat the butter until soft. Mix in the basil and oregano to distribute evenly. Refrigerate if not using immediately.

Slow-Cooked Onions with Tarragon Mustard Sauce

SERVES 4

Whole onions become especially sweet when prepared on a grill. Serve alongside grilled meat or poultry.

FOR THE TARRAGON MUSTARD SAUCE:
2 tablespoons white wine vinegar or
   tarragon vinegar
2 tablespoons Dijon mustard
⅓ cup (3 fl oz/80 ml) olive oil
2 tablespoons chopped fresh tarragon
   or 1 teaspoon dried tarragon
¼ teaspoon salt
pinch of freshly ground pepper

FOR THE ONIONS:
4 yellow onions
3 tablespoons olive oil
½ teaspoon salt
¼ teaspoon freshly ground pepper

Prepare a fire for indirect-heat cooking in a covered grill (see page 11).

To prepare the sauce, in a small bowl, whisk together the vinegar and mustard. Slowly add the olive oil, whisking constantly to form a smooth, creamy sauce. Whisk in the tarragon, salt, and pepper. Cover and set aside.

To prepare the onions, peel them, taking care to keep their layers intact at the root ends. Using a sharp knife and starting at the stem end, slice an X in each onion to within about 1 inch (2.5 cm) of the root end. In a large bowl, toss the onions with the olive oil, salt, and pepper.

Place the onions on the center of the grill rack, cover, and open the vents halfway. Cook, turning the onions every 15–20 minutes, until they are tender when pierced, 45–50 minutes total.

Transfer the onions to a platter and drizzle some of the sauce over them. Serve hot, warm, or at room temperature. Pass the remaining sauce at the table.

Tomatoes and Green Onions

SERVES 4–6

Firm tomatoes, even those that are slightly green, should be used for this recipe. They are less juicy and hold their shape better when grilled than fully ripe ones. Fresh basil is wonderful with tomatoes, but you could also use chopped tarragon or even parsley in the basting sauce. Serve warm or at room temperature.

⅓ cup (3 fl oz/80 ml) olive oil
1 tablespoon fresh lemon juice or wine vinegar
2 tablespoons chopped fresh basil
1 tablespoon chopped shallot
½ teaspoon salt
¼ teaspoon freshly ground pepper
3 large tomatoes, cut into slices ½–¾ inch (12 mm–2 cm) thick
10–12 green (spring) onions, trimmed, including 4 inches (10 cm) of tender green tops
fresh basil or parsley sprigs

Prepare a fire in a grill.

In a small bowl, stir together the oil, lemon juice or vinegar, chopped basil, shallot, salt, and pepper.

Arrange the tomatoes and green onions on a grill screen. Grill, turning them two or three times and brushing with the oil mixture, until lightly browned, about 5 minutes. If the onions are large, they might take 1 or 2 minutes longer.

Transfer the tomatoes and green onions to a platter and garnish with the basil or parsley sprigs.

207

Asparagus with Parmesan

SERVES 6

If the asparagus spears are thick, peel the stalks with a vegetable peeler, starting about 2 inches (5 cm) below the tips.

1½ lb (750 g) asparagus spears
⅓ cup (3 fl oz/80 ml) olive oil
3 tablespoons freshly grated Parmesan cheese
1 tablespoon grated lemon zest
salt and freshly ground pepper to taste

Prepare a fire in a grill.

Snap off the tough ends from the asparagus spears. Brush the spears with about half of the olive oil and place them directly on the grill rack or on an oiled grill screen. Grill, turning once, until the asparagus are slightly charred, about 10 minutes total.

Transfer to a serving platter and sprinkle with the remaining olive oil, the cheese, lemon zest, salt, and pepper. Serve hot.

Roasted Autumn Vegetables

SERVES 4

Offer this mélange of golden brown, crisp-crusted vegetables as an accompaniment to meat or poultry.

2 baking potatoes, about ½ lb (250 g) each
2 sweet potatoes, about ¾ lb (375 g) each
1 acorn squash, about 1½ lb (750 g)
2–3 tablespoons vegetable oil
1 teaspoon salt
½ teaspoon freshly ground pepper
¼ cup (2 oz/60 g) unsalted butter, melted
1 tablespoon chopped fresh sage or thyme, or 1 teaspoon dried sage or thyme, plus fresh sage or thyme sprigs for garnish (optional)

Prepare a fire for indirect-heat cooking in a covered grill (see page 11).

Using a vegetable peeler or a small, sharp knife, peel the baking potatoes, sweet potatoes, and acorn squash. Cut them all crosswise into slices about 1 inch (2.5 cm) thick. For the acorn squash, scrape out any seeds and fibers from the center of the slices and discard. In a large bowl, toss the prepared vegetables together with the vegetable oil, salt, and pepper. Set aside.

In a small bowl, stir together the melted butter and chopped or dried sage or thyme. Set aside.

Place the vegetables on the center of the grill rack, cover, and open the vents halfway. Cook for 15 minutes, then turn the slices. Cook for 15 minutes longer, then turn again and brush them with the butter mixture. Continue cooking until the vegetables are well browned and tender when pierced with a knife, 10–15 minutes longer.

Transfer to a platter and garnish with the sage or thyme sprigs, if using. Serve hot, warm, or at room temperature.

Polenta Wedges

SERVES 6

The polenta can be made on the stove top a day ahead and then grilled just before serving. If desired, sprinkle a handful of toasted pine nuts or chopped walnuts over the surface of the polenta as soon as it is poured into the baking pan.

olive oil for brushing
4 cups (32 fl oz/1 l) water
1⅓ cups (7 oz/220 g) white or yellow
   cornmeal
2 tablespoons chopped fresh basil
2 tablespoons chopped fresh tarragon
2 teaspoons unsalted butter, at room
   temperature
½ teaspoon salt
¼ cup (2 oz/60 g) drained and chopped
   oil-packed sun-dried tomatoes
   (optional)

Oil a 9-inch (23-cm) round baking pan with olive oil.

 Pour the water into a large saucepan. Whisk in the cornmeal, basil, tarragon, butter, salt, and the sun-dried tomatoes, if using. Bring to a boil over medium-high heat, whisking often. Reduce the heat to a simmer and continue whisking until the mixture is thick and smooth and pulls away from the sides of the pan, about 20 minutes. Pour the polenta into the prepared baking pan, cover loosely with plastic wrap, and refrigerate until firm, about 30 minutes.

 Prepare a fire in a grill.

 Cut the polenta into 6 wedges. Lightly brush the polenta wedges on both sides with olive oil and place on an oiled grill screen. Grill, turning once, until heated through and beginning to color, about 3 minutes on each side.

 Transfer the polenta wedges to a warmed platter and serve.

Corn and Pepper Salsa

SERVES 6

This salsa is easy to prepare and travels well. Serve with corn bread sticks or tortilla chips.

6 slices bacon
6 ears of corn, husks and silk removed
1 large red bell pepper (capsicum), seeded and diced
4 green (spring) onions, including tender green tops, minced

Prepare a fire in a grill.

In a frying pan over medium heat, cook the bacon until crisp, about 5 minutes. Using tongs, transfer the bacon to paper towels to drain; reserve about 3 tablespoons of the drippings.

Brush the ears of corn lightly with the reserved bacon drippings, then place on the grill rack and grill, rotating the ears every 2 minutes, until slightly charred and tender, about 6 minutes.

Transfer the corn to a cutting board and let cool. Then, working with 1 ear at a time, rest the ear on its stem end, and, using a sharp knife, cut down and away from you along the ear to strip off the kernels, turning the ear with each cut. Place the corn kernels in a bowl.

When all the ears are stripped, crumble the bacon and add to the bowl along with the bell pepper and green onions. Toss to mix well. Serve at room temperature.

Radicchio and Belgian Endive with Shaved Parmesan

SERVES 4

A number of varieties of radicchio are grown, but they all fall into two general types: round, or heading, radicchio, which has colorful ivory-and-burgundy leaves, and an elongated type, known as Treviso radicchio. Both are members of the chicory family, as is Belgian endive. Grilling these mildly bitter greens yields a surprisingly sweet result. If you cannot find them all in the market, use those you can find.

FOR BASTING:

¼ cup (2 fl oz/60 ml) extra-virgin olive oil

2 tablespoons balsamic vinegar

1 clove garlic, minced

1 teaspoon chopped fresh rosemary

½ teaspoon fresh thyme leaves

¼ teaspoon salt

¼ teaspoon freshly ground pepper

1 round head radicchio

1 large head or 2 small heads Treviso radicchio

1 head Belgian endive (chicory/witloof)

balsamic vinegar for drizzling

wedge of Parmesan cheese

Prepare a fire in a grill.

To prepare the basting mixture, in a small bowl, whisk together the oil, vinegar, garlic, rosemary, thyme, salt, and pepper. Halve or quarter the heads of radicchio and Belgian endive, depending on their size. The wedges should be about 2 inches (5 cm) in diameter at the widest point; small Treviso can be grilled whole. Dip each piece into a bowl of cold water and drain briefly in a colander.

Brush all sides of the wedges lightly with the basting mixture and place on the grill rack. Grill until they char slightly on the underside, 3½–5 minutes. Baste the tops, then turn the wedges over and baste the cooked side. Grill until lightly charred on the second side, 2–4 minutes longer, depending on size and variety. They should be deep brown and crisp on the surface and completely tender inside. Transfer to a serving platter and baste again.

To serve, drizzle each wedge with about ½ teaspoon balsamic vinegar. Using a vegetable peeler, shave generous curls of Parmesan over all. Serve warm or at room temperature.

Potatoes with Sun-Dried Tomato Pesto

SERVES 4–6

Cooked in aluminum foil, the potatoes steam while the pesto and cheese form a fragrant crust. When you open the foil packages, a delectable aroma fills the air. Serve as a side dish with grilled chicken or fish.

18 small new red potatoes, about
   1¾ lb (875 g), unpeeled
2 tablespoons Sun-Dried Tomato Pesto
   (page 295)
1 tablespoon freshly grated Parmesan
   cheese

Fill a large pot three-fourths full with salted water and bring to a boil over high heat. Add the potatoes and cook for 10 minutes. Drain well in a colander and set aside to cool.

🍃 Meanwhile, prepare a fire in a grill.

🍃 Oil six 6-inch (15-cm) squares of aluminum foil. Arrange 3 potatoes on the center of each foil square. Spoon 1 teaspoon of the pesto atop each portion of potatoes and then sprinkle each portion with ½ teaspoon of the Parmesan cheese. Enclose the potatoes in the foil and seal tightly closed.

🍃 Place the foil packages on the grill rack about 3 inches (7.5 cm) from the fire and grill, turning once, until the potatoes are cooked through, 12–16 minutes total.

🍃 Transfer the potato packages to a serving platter. Serve immediately, opening each package carefully with potholder-protected hands just before serving.

Vegetables with Two Dipping Sauces

SERVES 6–8

Here, grilled vegetables are served with a pair of full-flavored dipping sauces. You can substitute your favorite vegetables for the ones listed below. For easy entertaining, the sauces can be prepared the day before serving.

FOR THE TAPENADE:
¾ cup (4 oz/125 g) pitted Kalamata
   olives
4 or 5 anchovy fillets in olive oil
1 clove garlic, chopped
2 tablespoons capers
1 teaspoon chopped fresh basil
2 tablespoons chopped fresh flat-leaf
   (Italian) parsley
1 tablespoon fresh lemon juice
1 slice day-old white bread, torn into
   small pieces
1 cup (8 fl oz/250 ml) olive oil

FOR THE TOMATO SALSA:
1 yellow onion, minced
½ cup (¾ oz/20 g) chopped fresh
   cilantro (fresh coriander)
2 tomatoes, finely chopped
1 small red bell pepper (capsicum),
   seeded and chopped
salt and freshly ground pepper to taste

1 lb (500 g) cherry tomatoes, stems
   removed
⅓ lb (155 g) snow peas (mangetouts),
   trimmed
1 zucchini (courgette), cut into slices
   ¼ inch (6 mm) thick
1 red (Spanish) onion, cut into
   quarters through the stem end
   and layers separated
olive oil

To prepare the tapenade, in a food processor or blender, combine the olives, anchovies, garlic, capers, basil, parsley, lemon juice, and bread. Process until smooth. With the motor running, add the olive oil in a slow, steady stream and process until a thick paste forms. Spoon into a bowl, cover, and refrigerate until serving. You should have about 1¼ cups (10 oz/315 g).

🍃 To prepare the salsa, in a small bowl, toss together the onion, cilantro, tomatoes, and bell pepper. Season with salt and pepper. Cover and refrigerate. Toss again just before serving. You should have about 2 cups (12 oz/375 g).

🍃 Prepare a fire in a grill.

🍃 Thread the vegetables onto skewers, alternating them and dividing them evenly among 16 skewers. Lightly brush the vegetables with olive oil and place on a grill screen. Grill, turning once, until heated through and beginning to brown, 2–4 minutes total.

🍃 Transfer the vegetables to a serving platter. Serve warm with the tapenade and the salsa.

Grill-Roasted Garlic

SERVES 4

Slow cooking turns a head of garlic mellow, with each clove becoming soft and creamy. This makes a delicious accompaniment to Wine-Scented Leg of Lamb (page 169). To eat, squeeze the whole cloves free of their skins and onto crackers or thinly sliced French bread.

4 heads garlic
2 tablespoons olive oil
1 tablespoon chopped fresh thyme
   or ½ teaspoon dried thyme
½ teaspoon salt
¼ teaspoon freshly ground pepper

Prepare a fire for indirect-heat cooking in a covered grill (see page 11).

Using a sharp knife, slice off the top ¼–½ inch (6–12 mm) from each garlic head. Rub off some of the loose papery skin covering each head, taking care to keep the heads intact. In a small bowl, combine the garlic heads, olive oil, thyme, salt, and pepper. Toss to combine and coat the garlic evenly.

Place the garlic heads on the center of the grill rack, cover, and open the vents halfway. Cook, turning the garlic heads three or four times, until the cloves feel very soft when squeezed gently with tongs or your fingers, 35–40 minutes. Don't worry if the skin chars in spots.

Remove from the grill and serve warm.

Spicy Eggplant

SERVES 6

Serve this dish as a first course with wedges of feta cheese and Kalamata olives or as a tasty side dish.

9 Asian (slender) eggplants (aubergines) or 2 small globe eggplants, about 2 lb (1 kg) total weight
salt for sprinkling, if needed, plus salt to taste
6 tablespoons (3 fl oz/90 ml) olive oil
freshly ground black pepper to taste
3 cloves garlic, minced

1 tablespoon red wine vinegar
¼ teaspoon red pepper flakes
2 tablespoons chopped fresh parsley

Prepare a fire in a grill.

Trim the eggplants and cut crosswise into slices ¼ inch (6 mm) thick. If you are using globe eggplants, place the slices in a colander and salt them liberally to draw out the moisture. Let stand for 30 minutes. Rinse and pat dry with paper towels. If you are using Asian eggplants, there is no need to salt them.

Brush the eggplant slices with 4 tablespoons (2 fl oz/60 ml) of the olive oil. Season with salt and black pepper.

When the fire is ready, place the eggplant slices on the grill rack and grill, turning occasionally, until they are tender and golden, 10–12 minutes.

Meanwhile, in a small bowl, stir together the garlic, the remaining 2 tablespoons olive oil, and the vinegar.

Place the eggplant on a serving platter and drizzle the garlic-oil mixture over the top. Sprinkle with the red pepper flakes and parsley and serve.

Parmesan Pita Toasts

SERVES 4–6

Quick to grill over the still-glowing coals of an existing fire, these easy-to-assemble toasts can be placed on the rack after you've removed the main course. Two flour tortillas, stacked one on top of the other with the cheese in between, can be substituted for each pita bread.

4 pita breads, each about 6 inches
   (15 cm) in diameter
½ cup (2 oz/60 g) freshly grated
   Parmesan cheese
olive oil
salt to taste

Prepare a fire in a grill.

Cut the pita breads in half and gently open the pita "pockets." Sprinkle 1 tablespoon of the cheese inside each pocket, then press down firmly on the bread with your hand. Brush both sides of each pita half with the olive oil and sprinkle lightly with salt.

Arrange the pita halves on the grill rack. Grill, turning two or three times, until the bread is lightly browned and the cheese has melted slightly, 4–5 minutes total.

To serve, cut each half into wedges and arrange on a serving dish. Serve hot.

Bruschetta Primavera

SERVES 4–6

Use a long, slender baguette-type loaf for the bread and cut the slices on the diagonal. The brief grilling this recipe requires can easily be done at the last minute over an existing fire.

2 large tomatoes, peeled, seeded,
   and diced
¼ cup (⅓ oz/10 g) chopped fresh parsley
2 tablespoons chopped fresh basil
   or 1 teaspoon dried basil
1 large clove garlic, minced, plus
   4–6 cloves garlic, halved
½ teaspoon salt
¼ teaspoon freshly ground pepper
12 slices crusty bread, each about
   ½ inch (12 mm) thick *(see note)*
⅓–½ cup (3–4 fl oz/80–125 ml)
   olive oil

Prepare a fire in a grill.

In a small bowl, stir together the tomatoes, parsley, basil, minced garlic, salt, and pepper. Set aside.

Arrange the bread slices on the grill rack. Grill, turning two or three times, until the bread is golden brown on both sides, about 3 minutes total.

Remove from the grill and immediately rub one side of each slice with a cut garlic clove, pressing the garlic into the surface of the bread. Brush or drizzle the olive oil over the same side of the bread. Top each slice with about 2 tablespoons of the tomato mixture and place on a platter. Serve as soon as possible. If left to stand, the bread will gradually soften, although it will still taste good.

Herbed Two-Potato Skewers

SERVES 6

Crisp outside, soft and steamy inside, this dish goes well with grilled fish or chicken.

3 or 4 boiling potatoes, about 1 lb (500 g) total weight

2 small sweet potatoes or yams, about 1½ lb (750 g) total weight

½ cup (4 fl oz/125 ml) olive oil

2 tablespoons chopped fresh parsley

1 tablespoon chopped fresh tarragon or thyme, or 1 teaspoon dried tarragon or thyme

¼ teaspoon red pepper flakes

½ teaspoon freshly ground black pepper

½ teaspoon salt

Prepare a fire in a grill.

Place all the potatoes on a steamer rack over boiling water, cover, and steam until barely tender when pierced, 15–20 minutes. Transfer to a large bowl and cover with cold water. Let stand for about 2 minutes, then drain and pat dry with paper towels. Cut the potatoes into 1½-inch (4-cm) chunks and thread them onto skewers.

In a small bowl, whisk together the oil, parsley, tarragon or thyme, red pepper flakes, black pepper, and salt. Set aside.

Arrange the skewers on the rack. Grill, turning frequently and brushing occasionally with the oil-herb mixture, until the potato skins are well browned, about 10 minutes. Serve hot.

Fennel and Endive with Olive Vinaigrette

SERVES 6

The olive vinaigrette is a good match for the strongly flavored vegetables used here. You can also serve them plain, drizzled with just a little lemon juice. Garnish with the feathery tops of the fennel bulbs, if you like.

FOR THE OLIVE VINAIGRETTE:

½ cup (2½ oz/75 g) oil-cured black olives, pitted

½ cup (4 fl oz/125 ml) olive oil

1 clove garlic, minced

¼ teaspoon salt

¼ teaspoon freshly ground pepper

2 tablespoons white or red wine vinegar

FOR THE VEGETABLES:

3 large fennel bulbs

6 heads Belgian endive (chicory/witloof)

¼ cup (2 fl oz/60 ml) olive oil

½ teaspoon salt

¼ teaspoon freshly ground pepper

Prepare a fire for indirect-heat cooking in a covered grill (see page 11).

To prepare the vinaigrette, place the olives in a sieve and rinse briefly with cold water. Drain and pat dry with paper towels. Chop the olives finely and combine them in a small bowl with the olive oil, garlic, salt, and pepper. Whisk briskly until smooth and blended, then whisk in the vinegar. Cover and set aside.

To prepare the vegetables, trim off the stems and feathery tops and any bruised outer stalks from the fennel bulbs. Cut each fennel bulb and each endive in half lengthwise. In a large bowl, gently toss the fennel and the endive with the olive oil, salt, and pepper.

Place the fennel on the center of the grill rack, cover, and open the vents halfway. Cook for 15 minutes, then turn the fennel and place the endive on the rack. Re-cover and continue to cook, turning the vegetables again after 10 minutes, until they are lightly browned and tender when pierced, 10–15 minutes longer.

Transfer the vegetables to a platter and spoon some of the vinaigrette over them. Serve hot, warm, or at room temperature. Pass the remaining vinaigrette at the table.

Saganaki

SERVES 4

You will need to cook these traditional Greek packets over a relatively low fire, so that the cheese is molten before the vine leaves are completely charred. The packets make a nice cheese course after the main course, and the grill will have cooled down to the perfect temperature by then. The leaves can be discarded, but most people like to eat them. The briny, smoky flavor combines nicely with the soft, spreadable melted cheese. Italian fontina may be substituted for the Greek cheese, in which case a tiny pinch of salt should be added to each packet before wrapping.

8 brine-packed grape leaves
1 lb (500 g) kasseri or kefalotyri cheese
1 large clove garlic, minced
grated zest of 1 lemon
¼ teaspoon medium-ground pepper
olive oil
toasted wedges of coarse country bread
lemon wedges

Prepare a fire in a grill.

Trim off the tough base from the stem of each leaf and gently rinse and dry the leaves. Cut the cheese into 4 equal portions, each 2 by 4 inches (5 by 10 cm) and 1 inch (2.5 cm) thick.

Place 2 leaves on a work surface, slightly overlapping, and place 1 piece of the cheese in the center. Scatter one-fourth each of the garlic, lemon zest, and pepper on the cheese, and wrap up to form a secure packet. Place seam side down on a platter. Repeat with the remaining leaves, cheese, and toppings. (You can refrigerate the packets for up to 2 hours before grilling, removing them from the refrigerator 15 minutes before the fire is ready.)

Brush the packets lightly with olive oil, place on the edges of the grill rack, and grill, turning once, until the edges of the leaves start to char and the package feels soft when gently pressed, about 10 minutes total. The cheese should be just beginning to ooze from the edges.

Transfer to a platter or individual plates and serve immediately with toasted country bread and lemon wedges.

From the Kitchen

Salads are natural companions to grilled foods. The crisp, fresh flavors of raw vegetables and greens complement the smoky character of grilled fish, meat, poultry, or vegetables. A mound of Summer Succotash or Couscous Salad pairs well with a juicy steak or chicken breast. Earthy baked beans and pasta salads are classic favorites and round out any grilled menu.

Mixed Bean Salad with Balsamic Dressing

SERVES 6

Bursting with colors and flavors, this nutritious salad is made from a medley of beans. Hard-boiled eggs would make a nice garnish. Slices of toasted or grilled bread rubbed with garlic and doused with olive oil can be served on the side.

½ cup (3½ oz/105 g) dried black beans
½ cup (3½ oz/105 g) dried black-eyed peas
½ cup (3½ oz/105 g) dried adzuki beans
¼ cup (2 fl oz/60 ml) balsamic vinegar
2 teaspoons Dijon mustard
½ cup (4 fl oz/125 ml) extra-virgin olive oil
salt and freshly ground pepper to taste
½ lb (250 g) green beans, trimmed and cut into 1-inch (2.5-cm) lengths
1 small red (Spanish) onion, chopped
3 tablespoons chopped fresh parsley

Pick over and discard any damaged beans or stones. Rinse the dried beans separately. Place the beans in separate bowls, add plenty of water to cover, and let soak for about 3 hours.

Drain the beans and place in separate saucepans with water to cover by 2 inches (5 cm). Bring to a boil, reduce the heat to low and simmer, uncovered, until the skins begin to crack and beans are tender, about 1 hour for the black beans, 45 minutes for the black-eyed peas, and 30 minutes for the adzuki beans. Drain and combine the beans in a large bowl.

Meanwhile, in a small bowl, whisk together the vinegar, mustard, olive oil, salt, and pepper. Add to the warm beans, toss well, and let cool.

Bring a saucepan three-fourths full of salted water to a boil. Add the green beans and boil until tender, 4–5 minutes. Drain and let cool.

Add the green beans, onion, and parsley to the cooled mixed beans. Toss well and serve at room temperature or chilled.

Watercress and Orange Salad

SERVES 4

Laden with sunny Mediterranean flavors, this salad is a fine accompaniment to fish or lamb. Use only pale, very tender celery stalks and the small, tender leaves of the watercress sprigs. Avocado slices can be used in place of the orange slices.

1¼ lb (625 g) watercress, tough stems removed

2 oranges

4 celery stalks, thinly sliced crosswise

1 tablespoon fresh lemon juice

1 tablespoon white wine vinegar

1 tablespoon curry powder

salt and freshly ground pepper to taste

5 tablespoons (2½ fl oz/75 ml) extra-virgin olive oil

Place the watercress in a salad bowl.

Using a sharp knife, cut a thick slice off the top and bottom of 1 orange to expose the fruit. Stand the orange upright on a cutting board and thickly slice off the peel in strips, cutting around the contour of the orange to expose the flesh. Cut the orange crosswise into slices and remove any seeds. Repeat with the remaining orange. Add the orange slices to the bowl along with the celery.

In a small bowl, stir together the lemon juice, vinegar, curry powder, salt, and pepper until well mixed. Add the oil and stir vigorously until blended. Pour the dressing over the salad, toss well, and serve.

Italian Bread Salad with Tomatoes and Basil

SERVES 6

In Italy, yesterday's stale bread is sometimes made into today's fresh and flavorful panzanella *salad. Make sure to use a good-quality country-style bread for this salad—the coarser the better. Loaves made with unbleached flour are ideal, although those that also include whole-wheat or rye flour may also be used.*

1 small loaf coarse country bread, ½ lb (250 g), a few days old

1 cup (8 fl oz/250 ml) water

6 ripe tomatoes, seeded and cut into ½-inch (12-mm) dice

1 small red (Spanish) onion, thinly sliced

1 cucumber, peeled, halved lengthwise, seeded, and cut into ½-inch (12-mm) dice

2 cloves garlic, minced

3 tablespoons capers

½ cup (½ oz/15 g) lightly packed fresh basil leaves, torn into pieces

1 cup (8 fl oz/250 ml) Balsamic and Red Wine Vinegar Dressing *(page 295)*

salt and freshly ground pepper to taste

Cut the bread crosswise into slices 1 inch (2.5 cm) thick. Place in a large shallow container and pour the water evenly over the slices. Let stand for 1 minute. Carefully squeeze the bread between your hands until dry. Tear the bread into rough 1-inch (2.5-cm) pieces and spread out on paper towels to absorb any excess moisture for 10 minutes.

In a bowl, combine the tomatoes, onion, cucumber, garlic, capers, basil, and bread. Toss together to mix well. Add the dressing and toss again until evenly distributed. Cover and refrigerate for 1 hour.

Season with salt and pepper. Transfer to a platter or individual plates and serve at once.

⅓ cup (½ oz/15 g) chopped fresh
   cilantro (fresh coriander)
6 tablespoons (3 fl oz/90 ml)
   extra-virgin olive oil
5 tablespoons (2½ fl oz/75 ml) fresh
   lemon juice
1½ teaspoons ground cumin
½ teaspoon paprika
3 cloves garlic, minced
freshly ground pepper to taste

Preheat a broiler (griller).

Cut the bell peppers in half lengthwise and remove the stems, seeds, and
ribs. Place, cut side down, on a baking
sheet. Broil (grill) until the skins
blacken and blister. Remove from
the broiler, drape the peppers loosely
with aluminum foil, and let cool for
10 minutes. Using your fingers or a
small knife, peel off the skins. Cut the
peppers into ½-inch (12-mm) squares.

In a saucepan, bring the water to a
boil. Remove from the heat and add the
couscous and the ½ teaspoon salt. Stir
well, cover, and let stand for 10 minutes.
Uncover and transfer the couscous to
a large, shallow baking dish, fluffing
with a fork and spreading it evenly. Let
cool completely.

Transfer the couscous to a large bowl.
Scatter the bell peppers, tomatoes, cucumber, chile, and cilantro over the top.

In a small bowl, whisk together the
olive oil, lemon juice, cumin, paprika,
and garlic. Season with salt and pepper.
Add to the couscous and toss together
well. Taste and adjust the seasoning,
then serve.

Cabbage Salad with Cumin Seeds

SERVES 4

*Raw cabbage—either green or white—
makes an excellent salad. A chopped apple
and 2 tablespoons raisins are possible
additions. An alternative dressing can be
made using extra-virgin olive oil, pressed
garlic, anchovy paste, and vinegar.*

1 head savoy cabbage, about
   ¾ lb (375 g)
½ cup (4 fl oz/125 ml) heavy (double)
   cream
1 tablespoon red wine vinegar
1 tablespoon sugar
salt and white pepper to taste
1 tablespoon cumin seeds

Remove and discard the larger leaves
from the cabbage, then cut it lengthwise
into quarters. Cut each quarter into
long, very narrow strips. Set aside.

In a salad bowl, stir together the
cream, vinegar, sugar, salt, and white
pepper. Add the cabbage and mix gently. Sprinkle with the cumin seeds and
let stand for 30 minutes before serving
to allow the flavors to blend.

Couscous Salad with Cucumber, Peppers, and Tomatoes

SERVES 6

*This zesty salad can be made up to 2 hours
in advance; cover and refrigerate until you
are ready to serve.*

2 green bell peppers (capsicums)
1 cup (8 fl oz/250 ml) water
1 cup (6 oz/185 g) couscous
½ teaspoon salt, plus salt to taste
½ lb (250 g) cherry tomatoes, halved
1 cucumber, peeled, halved lengthwise,
   seeded, and cut into ½-inch
   (12-mm) dice
1 small red or green jalapeño or
   serrano chile, seeded and minced

Red Ginger Slaw

SERVES 4

The creaminess provided by the mayonnaise both carries and tames the pungent red ginger in this Asian-style slaw, while the hint of sesame provides a complementary flavor match for the cabbage and fennel. Red ginger is similar in flavor to the pickled pink ginger traditionally eaten with sushi, and the latter may be substituted if you cannot find the red variety. Look for the ginger, mirin, sesame oil, rice vinegar, and black sesame seeds at Asian markets. Serve the slaw with Star Anise and Pomegranate Flank Steak (page 144).

FOR THE DRESSING:

¼ cup (2 fl oz/60 ml) mayonnaise
¼ cup (1 oz/30 g) pickled
  red ginger
3 tablespoons soy sauce
2 tablespoons Asian sesame oil
2½ tablespoons rice vinegar
1½ tablespoons mirin
1 tablespoon sugar
1 small shallot, thinly sliced
2 large cloves garlic, thinly sliced
2 tablespoons coarsely chopped
  fresh basil

1 small head or ½ large head savoy
  cabbage, quartered lengthwise
1 fennel bulb, trimmed and quartered
  lengthwise
2 green (spring) onions, white and
  light green parts only, thinly sliced
1 tablespoon black sesame seeds
  (optional)

To make the dressing, in a food processor, combine the mayonnaise, red ginger, soy sauce, sesame oil, rice vinegar, mirin, sugar, shallot, garlic, and basil.

Process, stopping to scrape down the bowl sides as needed, until completely smooth.

🌿 Cut away the core portions from the cabbage and fennel quarters. One at a time, place cut side down and slice crosswise very thinly.

🌿 In a large bowl, combine the cabbage, fennel, and the dressing. Toss thoroughly, making sure the dressing works its way into all the nooks and crannies of the cabbage. Cover and refrigerate for up to 2 hours before serving.

🌿 To serve, mound the slaw on a serving platter. Scatter the green onions and sesame seeds, if using, over the top.

Fusilli Salad with Sweet Peppers and Mozzarella

SERVES 6

The array of sweet peppers now widely available to cooks gives this southern Italian pasta salad an especially colorful palette. The ingredients, except for the basil, can be assembled a few hours in advance and refrigerated. Creamy fontina may be substituted for the mozzarella.

3 red or yellow sweet peppers
  (capsicums), or a mixture
1 clove garlic
2 anchovy fillets in olive oil, drained
1 lb (500 g) fusilli
6 tablespoons (3 fl oz/90 ml)
  extra-virgin olive oil
2 tablespoons well-drained capers
  in brine
10 oz (315 g) mozzarella cheese, diced
12 fresh basil leaves, torn into small
  pieces
salt and freshly ground pepper to taste

Preheat the oven to 350°F (180°C).

🌿 Arrange the peppers on a rack in a baking pan and bake until tender when pierced with a fork, about 20 minutes. Remove the peppers from the oven and wrap them in aluminum foil. Leave them for about 5 minutes. Unwrap the peppers and, with your fingers, peel off the skins. Halve the peppers and remove the ribs and seeds. Cut lengthwise into strips about ⅜ inch (1 cm) wide; set aside.

🌿 Place the garlic and anchovies in a small bowl. With a fork, mash them together to form a smooth paste; set aside.

🌿 In a large pot, bring 5 qt (5 l) salted water to a boil. Add the fusilli and cook until al dente, about 10 minutes.

🌿 Drain the pasta and arrange it on a serving dish. Pour the olive oil over the pasta, add the anchovy-garlic paste and capers, and toss well. Let cool to room temperature.

🌿 Add the peppers, mozzarella, and basil. Season with salt and pepper; toss well. Serve at room temperature.

Tomatoes Stuffed with Eggs and Anchovies

SERVES 4

Ideal for hot-weather dining, these stuffed tomatoes can also be served chilled. For an even simpler dish, fill each tomato with a generous spoonful of homemade mayonnaise. Serve as a side dish or as a first course. Stuffed tomatoes make a wonderful addition to a buffet table, too; simply triple or quadruple the recipe as needed.

4 tomatoes
1 teaspoon Dijon mustard
salt to taste
¼ cup (2 fl oz/60 ml) extra-virgin
    olive oil
1 teaspoon minced fresh flat-leaf
    (Italian) parsley
1 teaspoon minced fresh mint
1 teaspoon minced fresh basil
4 anchovy fillets, cut into small pieces
3 hard-boiled eggs, peeled and cubed
4 thin slices lemon
12 capers
4 fresh curly-leaf parsley leaves

Slice the top off of each tomato. Using a spoon, gently remove the pulp and seeds. Lightly salt the insides and then invert onto a plate for 30 minutes to drain.

In a small bowl, stir together the mustard and salt until well mixed. Add the olive oil and stir vigorously until blended. Add the minced parsley, mint, basil, anchovies, and eggs; mix well.

Turn the tomatoes cut side up and place on a serving dish. Fill each tomato with one-fourth of the mixture. Place 1 lemon slice atop each tomato. Decorate each slice with 3 capers and a parsley leaf and serve.

Mixed Green Salad

SERVES 4

All kinds of greens work with this salad: butter (Boston) or Bibb lettuce, escarole (Batavian endive), oakleaf lettuce, young spinach leaves, dandelion, watercress, and radicchio.

FOR THE DRESSING:

2 cloves garlic, thinly sliced

1 tablespoon honey

salt to taste

1 tablespoon red wine vinegar or balsamic vinegar

¼ cup (2 fl oz/60 ml) extra-virgin olive oil

1 large handful green leaf lettuce leaves, about 3 oz (90 g), torn if large

1 large handful romaine (cos) lettuce leaves, about 3 oz (90 g), torn if large

1 small bunch arugula (rocket), tough stems removed

1 cucumber, peeled and thinly sliced

1 green bell pepper (capsicum), seeded and finely chopped

To prepare the dressing, in a small bowl, stir together the garlic, honey, and salt until well mixed. Add the vinegar and then the oil, stirring vigorously until blended. Let stand for about 10 minutes to allow the flavors to marry.

Arrange the lettuces and arugula in a salad bowl. Add the cucumber and bell pepper. Pour the dressing over the salad, toss, and serve.

Beet Salad with Orange-Tarragon Vinaigrette

SERVES 4

A simple dish that requires little time in the kitchen. It is marvelous served at room temperature with grilled fish. The smaller the beets, the better the dish will be. If fresh tarragon isn't available, substitute fresh parsley or chives.

12 small, young beets with greens
   attached
½ cup (4 fl oz/125 ml) water
½ cup (4 fl oz/125 ml) olive oil
¼ cup (2 fl oz/60 ml) red wine vinegar
¼ cup (2 fl oz/60 ml) fresh orange juice
3 tablespoons chopped fresh tarragon
salt and freshly ground pepper to taste

Preheat an oven to 350°F (180°C).

🔥 Cut off the greens from the beets, leaving about ½ inch (12 mm) of the stems. Discard the tough, damaged outer leaves. Thoroughly wash the beets and greens. Chop the greens coarsely. Place the whole beets and the greens in a baking dish with a lid. Add the water, cover the dish, and place in the oven. Bake until the beets are tender, 40–50 minutes (the amount of time will depend upon the size of the beets).

🔥 Remove from the oven and set aside to cool. Trim off the stem and root ends. Peel the beets; the skins will slip off easily. Slice the beets thinly and place on a serving plate. Using a slotted spoon, transfer the greens to the plate and arrange around the beets.

🔥 In a small bowl, stir together the oil, vinegar, orange juice, and 2 tablespoons of the tarragon. Season with salt and pepper.

🔥 Pour the vinaigrette evenly over the beets and greens. Garnish with the remaining 1 tablespoon tarragon. Serve at room temperature.

Creamy Red Potato Salad with Celery Seeds

SERVES 6–8

The red skins on the potatoes add extra color and texture to this salad. Fresh celery and celery seeds add a double dose of flavor. Serve on a bed of mixed greens, if you like. This salad is perfect with grilled chicken.

3 lb (1.5 kg) red potatoes, unpeeled

FOR THE DRESSING:

¾ cup (6 fl oz/180 ml) sour cream
¾ cup (6 fl oz/180 ml) mayonnaise
2 celery stalks, finely diced
1 tablespoon celery seeds
2 tablespoons chopped green (spring)
   onion, plus 1 tablespoon finely chopped
5 tablespoons (⅓ oz/10 g) chopped
   fresh parsley
1 teaspoon dry mustard
½ teaspoon salt
¼ teaspoon white pepper

Fill a large pot three-fourths full of salted water and bring to a boil over high heat. Add the potatoes and cook until tender but slightly resistant when pierced with a fork, 25–30 minutes. Drain and let cool, then cut the unpeeled potatoes into 1-inch (2.5-cm) cubes. Place in a bowl.

🔥 To prepare the dressing, in a small bowl, combine the sour cream, mayonnaise, celery, celery seeds, the 2 tablespoons green onion, 4 tablespoons of the parsley, mustard, salt, and white pepper. Using a large spoon, mix well.

🔥 Pour the dressing over the potatoes and mix gently to coat evenly. Taste and adjust the seasoning. Transfer to a serving bowl and garnish with the remaining 1 tablespoon parsley and the 1 tablespoon finely chopped green onion.

🔥 Before serving, cover and refrigerate for 1–2 hours to chill and blend the flavors.

Caesar Salad

SERVES 4

Capers give this famous salad an Italian accent. If possible, steep the garlic cloves in the olive oil for at least an hour before using them.

⅓ cup (3 fl oz/80 ml) extra-virgin olive oil

4 cloves garlic, sliced lengthwise

4 thick slices coarse country bread, crusts removed and bread cut into ¾-inch (2-cm) cubes

1 head romaine (cos) lettuce, separated into leaves

4 anchovy fillets

2 tablespoons capers

1 egg

1 tablespoon fresh lemon juice

1 tablespoon Worcestershire sauce

1 teaspoon coarse-grain mustard

1½ oz (45 g) Parmesan cheese, cut into shavings

In a frying pan over high heat, combine the oil and garlic and fry the garlic until brown, about 4 minutes. Remove the garlic and discard. Add the bread cubes to the pan and fry over high heat, stirring often, until browned. Transfer to paper towels to drain.

Tear the large and medium-sized lettuce leaves coarsely and leave the small leaves whole. Put the lettuce in a large salad bowl. In a smaller bowl, mash the anchovies with a fork. Rinse the capers under cold running water, drain, and pat dry with paper towels. Add to the anchovies along with the bread cubes and toss to mix.

Bring a small saucepan filled with water to a boil, gently slip in the egg, remove from the heat, and let stand for 1 minute. Remove the egg from the pan, immerse it in cold water, and break it into a small bowl. Add the lemon juice, Worcestershire sauce, and mustard and stir vigorously until well blended. Add the anchovy mixture to the lettuce. Pour the dressing over the salad, scatter the Parmesan over the top, toss delicately, and serve.

Boston Baked Beans

SERVES 6–8

*Centuries ago, Native Americans baked
beans with local maple syrup and bear fat
in handmade clay pots in underground
pits. The Pilgrims made their own version
of these beans, substituting molasses and
salt pork. This modern version is less sweet
and takes less baking time. Serve with
warm slices of steamed brown bread.*

3 cups (21 oz/655 g) dried small
   white (navy) beans
¼ lb (125 g) salt pork, in one piece
4 thin yellow onion slices
⅓ cup (4 oz/125 g) molasses
½ cup (3½ oz/105 g) firmly packed
   brown sugar
1½ teaspoons salt
½ teaspoon freshly ground pepper
2 teaspoons dry mustard

Pick over and discard any damaged
beans or stones. Rinse the beans. Place
in a bowl, add plenty of water to cover,
and let soak for about 3 hours.

Drain the beans and place in a saucepan with water to cover by 2 inches
(5 cm). Bring to a boil, reduce the heat
to low, and simmer, uncovered, until
almost tender, 25–35 minutes. Drain,
reserving the liquid.

Preheat an oven to 300°F (150°C).

Using a sharp knife, cut a crisscross
pattern ¼ inch (6 mm) deep in the
top of the salt pork. Add to a saucepan
of boiling water and boil for 1 minute,
then drain.

Spoon the beans into a 2-qt (2-l)
baking dish. Top with the salt pork and
onion slices. In a saucepan, combine
the molasses, brown sugar, salt, pepper,
mustard, and 1 cup (8 fl oz/250 ml)
of the bean cooking liquid. Heat, stirring, to dissolve the sugar. Pour evenly
over the beans and add just enough

additional bean cooking liquid to cover
the beans.

Cover the dish and bake for 4 hours.
Remove the cover, scoop up the pork
so it rests on top of the beans, and

continue to bake, uncovered, until the
beans are cooked through and caramel-
colored and the salt pork is golden,
1½–2 hours longer. If you like, slice the
salt pork and serve it alongside.

Chickpea Salad with Olives and Herbs

SERVES 6–8

Adapted from a dish native to the south of France, this recipe can also be made with small white (navy) beans, pinto beans, black beans, cranberry (borlotti) beans, or red or white kidney beans.

1 cup (7 oz/220 g) dried chickpeas (garbanzo beans)
¼ cup (2 fl oz/60 ml) red wine vinegar
6 tablespoons (3 fl oz/90 ml) extra-virgin olive oil
4 cloves garlic, minced
1 tablespoon minced fresh mint
1 tablespoon minced fresh basil
1 tablespoon minced fresh thyme
1 tablespoon minced fresh rosemary
1 tablespoon minced fresh oregano
salt and freshly ground pepper to taste
¼ cup (1½ oz/45 g) Niçoise or Kalamata olives, pitted and coarsely chopped

¼ cup (1½ oz/45 g) green olives, pitted and coarsely chopped
1 small bunch green (spring) onions, including 2 inches (5 cm) of the green tops, thinly sliced

Pick over and discard any damaged chickpeas or stones. Rinse the chickpeas. Place in a bowl, add plenty of water to cover, and let soak for about 3 hours.

🍃 Drain the chickpeas and place in a saucepan with water to cover by 2 inches (5 cm). Bring to a boil, reduce the heat to low, and simmer, uncovered, until tender, about 1 hour. Drain and let cool.

🍃 In a large bowl, whisk together the vinegar, olive oil, garlic, all the herbs, salt, and pepper. Add the cooled beans, black and green olives, and green onions and mix well.

🍃 Transfer to a serving bowl and serve at room temperature.

Brown Rice Tabbouleh

SERVES 6–8

Tabbouleh, a salad eaten throughout much of the Middle East, is traditionally made with bulgur, parsley and other herbs, vine-ripened tomatoes, and crunchy cucumbers. Here, brown rice is used to make this healthful, substantial summer salad.

⅔ cup (4½ oz/140 g) brown rice
2 cups (16 fl oz/500 ml) water
½ teaspoon salt, plus salt to taste
½ cup (4 fl oz/120 ml) extra-virgin olive oil
4 or 5 cloves garlic, minced
1 cup (8 fl oz/250 ml) fresh lemon juice
1 bunch green (spring) onions, including tender green tops, cut crosswise into slices ¼ inch (6 mm) thick
2 bunches fresh parsley, chopped

¼ cup (⅓ oz/10 g) chopped fresh mint
4 tomatoes, cut into ¼-inch (6-mm) dice
1 cucumber, peeled, seeded, and cut into ¼-inch (6-mm) dice
freshly ground pepper to taste
romaine (cos) leaves or warmed pita bread

Rinse the rice well and drain. Place in a heavy saucepan with the water and the ½ teaspoon salt. Bring to a boil, reduce the heat to low, cover, and cook, without stirring, for 45 minutes; do not remove the cover. After 45 minutes, uncover and check to see if the rice is tender and the water is absorbed. If not, re-cover and cook for a few minutes longer until the rice is done. Then uncover, drizzle with ¼ cup (2 fl oz/60 ml) of the olive oil and fluff gently with a fork to coat the grains. Let cool completely.

🍃 Place the cooled rice in the bottom of a large salad bowl. Mix together the remaining ¼ cup (2 fl oz/60 ml) olive oil, the garlic, and lemon juice and drizzle over the rice. Layer the next 5 ingredients in the order given: green onions, parsley, mint, tomatoes, and cucumber. Sprinkle lightly with salt and pepper and cover with plastic wrap. Refrigerate for at least 4 hours or for up to 24 hours.

🍃 Bring the salad to room temperature. Sprinkle with salt and toss well. Serve with romaine leaves or warmed pita bread for scooping up bitefuls of the salad.

Butter Lettuce and Tarragon Salad

SERVES 4

Fresh and light, this salad makes a nice side dish to fish or meat. If it is to accompany fish, substitute lemon juice for the vinegar. Slices of hard-boiled egg are an attractive garnish. Minced fresh basil and flat-leaf (Italian) parsley can be added to the dressing, if you wish.

2 small heads butter (Boston) lettuce, separated into leaves
2 tablespoons minced fresh tarragon
2 tablespoons minced fresh chives
1 tablespoon red wine vinegar
1 tablespoon Dijon mustard
salt to taste
¼ cup (2 fl oz/60 ml) extra-virgin olive oil

Discard the largest and darkest lettuce leaves; use only the most tender ones. If the leaves are large, tear them into pieces. Arrange in a salad bowl and sprinkle with the tarragon and chives.

In a small bowl, stir together the vinegar, mustard, and salt until well mixed. Add the oil and stir vigorously with a fork until blended. Pour the dressing over the lettuce, toss well, and serve.

Summer Succotash

SERVES 6

When lima beans and sweet corn are ripe from the garden, succotash appears on New England dinner tables. If fresh lima beans are not available, you can use dried lima beans: Soak for a few hours, drain, then simmer in water to cover by 2 inches (5 cm) until not quite tender, about 35 minutes. Add the bacon and cook until the beans are tender, then proceed with the recipe.

¼ lb (125 g) thickly sliced bacon, finely diced
1½ cups (8 oz/250 g) shelled fresh lima beans
boiling water to cover
kernels from 3 ears of corn (about 2 cups/12 oz/375 g)
½ lb (250 g) green beans, trimmed and cut into 1-inch (2.5-cm) lengths
salt to taste
2 tablespoons unsalted butter
½ cup (4 fl oz/125 ml) milk
½ cup (4 fl oz/125 ml) heavy (double) cream
pinch of sugar
freshly ground pepper to taste

In a saucepan, combine the bacon and lima beans with boiling water to cover generously. Cook until the lima beans are almost tender, 15–20 minutes.

Add the corn, green beans, and salt and cook until the green beans are tender, 7–10 minutes. Drain and let cool.

In a sauté pan over medium heat, melt the butter. Add the cooled vegetables and cook for 2 minutes.

In a measuring cup, combine the milk and cream. Add ¼ cup (2 fl oz/60 ml) of the milk mixture to the vegetables. Add the sugar and season with salt and pepper. Simmer over medium-high heat, stirring occasionally, until most of the liquid is gone. Continue adding the milk mixture ¼ cup (2 fl oz/60 ml) at a time and cooking until it is almost gone before adding more liquid. When all the liquid has been absorbed, transfer to a warmed serving dish and serve immediately.

Pasta Salad with Tomato and Celery

SERVES 4

This typical pasta salad lends itself to many other types of pasta, such as conchiglie (shells) or rigatoni (tubes). The only rule is that the pasta must be short and wide. Fresh oregano is a pleasant alternative to the basil. For a more filling salad, add cubed mozzarella cheese.

2 tablespoons capers
3 tomatoes, peeled and finely chopped
1 yellow bell pepper (capsicum), seeded and finely chopped
3 celery stalks, thinly sliced
8 fresh basil leaves, shredded
1 teaspoon fresh lemon juice
salt to taste

5 tablespoons (3 fl oz/80 ml) extra-virgin olive oil
½ lb (250 g) fusilli

Rinse the capers and pat dry with paper towels. Place in a large salad bowl with the tomatoes, bell pepper, celery, and basil.

In a small bowl, stir together the lemon juice and salt until well mixed. Add the oil and stir vigorously until blended.

Meanwhile, fill a large saucepan three-fourths full with salted water and bring to a boil. Add the pasta and boil until al dente, about 8 minutes or according to package directions. Drain, cool under cold running water, drain again, and then add to the salad bowl.

Pour the dressing over the salad, toss well, and serve.

Potato Salad with Sun-Dried Tomato Cream

SERVES 6

This is a wonderful side dish to accompany grilled meats and vegetables.

2½ lb (1.25 kg) white potatoes, unpeeled

FOR THE DRESSING:

½ cup (4 fl oz/125 ml) sour cream
½ cup (4 oz/125 g) nonfat plain yogurt
2 tablespoons Sun-Dried Tomato Pesto *(page 295)*
1 tablespoon white wine vinegar
1 teaspoon balsamic vinegar
1 teaspoon Dijon mustard
2 tablespoons capers, rinsed and patted dry
¼ teaspoon salt
pinch of freshly ground pepper

2 tablespoons chopped fresh parsley

Fill a large pot three-fourths full with salted water and bring to a boil over high heat. Add the potatoes and cook until tender but slightly resistant when pierced with a fork, 25–30 minutes. Drain and let cool slightly, then peel and cut into slices or cubes 1½ inches (4 cm) thick. Place in a bowl.

In a small bowl, combine all the ingredients for the dressing and mix well. Taste and adjust the seasoning.

Pour the dressing over the potatoes and mix gently until evenly coated. Taste again for seasoning.

Transfer to a serving bowl and garnish with chopped parsley. Refrigerate for 1–2 hours before serving to chill and blend the flavors.

Cucumber Salad with Dill

SERVES 4

A lovely summertime dish typical of the southern Mediterranean, this salad can be served as a side dish or an appetizer. A few slices of onion are an interesting addition, and a bed of greens makes an attractive presentation.

4 cucumbers
salt for sprinkling
3 cloves garlic
⅔ cup (5 oz/155 g) plain yogurt
1 tablespoon fresh lemon juice
2 tablespoons minced fresh dill
white pepper to taste
3 tablespoons extra-virgin olive oil

Peel and thinly slice the cucumbers, then place the slices on a flat plate. Salt lightly and prop up the plate so it is slightly tilted, allowing the accumulating moisture to drain off easily. Let stand for about 1 hour.

Pass the garlic cloves through a garlic press into a small bowl. Add the yogurt, lemon juice, and dill. Season with salt and white pepper and stir until well mixed. Add the olive oil and stir vigorously until blended.

Place the drained cucumber slices in a salad bowl, pour the dressing over the top, and toss gently. Refrigerate for about 1 hour to allow the flavors to marry, then serve.

Black Bean Salad with Peppers and Corn

SERVES 6–8

This striking dish is perfect for summer entertaining. It can be made several hours ahead of time and is an excellent accompaniment to grilled fish, chicken, or steaks.

1 cup (7 oz/220 g) dried black beans
kernels from 1 ear of corn
½ red bell pepper (capsicum), seeded
1 green bell pepper, seeded
1 yellow bell pepper, seeded
1 small red (Spanish) onion
1 clove garlic, minced
3 tablespoons chopped fresh parsley
½ cup (4 fl oz/125 ml) olive oil
4–5 tablespoons (2–2½ fl oz/60–75 ml)
   red wine vinegar
salt and freshly ground pepper to taste

Pick over and discard any damaged beans or stones. Rinse the beans. Place in a bowl, add plenty of water to cover, and let soak for about 3 hours.

Drain the beans and place in a saucepan with water to cover by 2 inches (5 cm). Bring to a boil over high heat, reduce the heat to low, and simmer until the skins begin to crack and the beans are tender, 1–1¼ hours. Drain and let cool.

Bring a saucepan three-fourths full of salted water to a boil. Add the corn kernels and cook for 1 minute. Drain and let cool.

Cut all of the bell peppers and the red onion into ¼-inch (6-mm) dice. In a salad bowl, combine the bell peppers, onion, corn kernels, garlic, and parsley and toss to mix. Add the olive oil, vinegar, salt, and pepper and toss again. Add the beans, toss well, and serve.

Desserts

On the Grill

Fruits are the basis of the most common grilled desserts. The heat of the coals naturally dies down a bit after the main course has been cooked, and most fruit desserts are best grilled over gentle heat. (It's a good idea to brush the grill clean before starting the dessert.) Tropical and subtropical fruits lend themselves splendidly to grilling. Mango with Vanilla Bean Sabayon is an excellent example of how delectable these fruits can be. A grilled Brie has even been included here, for those who insist upon a cheese course.

Nectarines, Mascarpone, and Pistachios

SERVES 6

A wide variety of fruits take well to grilling: bananas, melon slices, figs, peaches, nectarines, plums, pears, pineapple slices, and more.

6 large, ripe nectarines, halved and pitted
melted unsalted butter
¾ cup (6 oz/185 g) mascarpone cheese
3 tablespoons sugar
⅓ cup (1½ oz/45 g) chopped pistachio nuts, plus extra for garnish

Prepare a fire in a grill.

Brush the nectarine halves with butter and place, cut sides down, on a grill screen. Grill, turning once, until heated through and just tender but not mushy, about 10 minutes total.

Meanwhile, in a bowl, stir together the cheese, sugar, and the ⅓ cup (1½ oz/45 g) pistachios.

Transfer the nectarine halves, cut sides up, to individual bowls, placing 2 halves in each bowl. Spoon the cheese mixture into the hollows, dividing evenly.

Serve hot or warm, sprinkled with pistachios.

Mango with Vanilla Bean Sabayon

SERVES 4

This luscious sabayon is very quick to make if you assemble all the ingredients ahead of time. Since making it is a very visual experience, it's nice if your grill has an outside burner you can use for preparing it. The sabayon may also be served alone, in wineglasses or over a few berries, if desired. It is a vanilla lover's dream. The ideal time to put the mangoes on the grill is when the fire has begun to die down after grilling the main course.

2 large, ripe mangoes
canola, grapeseed, or other
   flavorless oil
freshly ground pepper to taste

FOR THE SABAYON:
3 egg yolks
3 tablespoons sugar
⅓ cup (3 fl oz/80 ml) Vermouth,
   Riesling, or other medium-sweet
   white wine
1 teaspoon balsamic vinegar
1 vanilla bean, split lengthwise

4 small mint sprigs
½ cup (2 oz/60 g) fresh raspberries

Prepare a fire in a grill.

Using a vegetable peeler, peel the mangoes. With a sharp knife, make a few cuts into a mango to locate the pit. Then place the mango on a cutting board and cut downward vertically along each side, following the contour of the pit, to remove the flesh. Repeat with the second mango. You should have 4 large pieces of mango. Place the mango pieces flat side down and make lengthwise cuts ½ inch (12 mm) apart in each one, starting 1 inch (2.5 cm) from the top end and extending all

the way through the bottom end, to create a fan shape. Brush both sides of each mango piece with a little oil, and sprinkle one side sparingly with pepper. Set aside.

To make the sabayon, in a large, heat-proof bowl (preferably copper), whisk together the yolks and sugar until completely blended and slightly pale. Whisk in the wine and vinegar until thoroughly combined. Using the tip of a sharp knife, scrape the seeds from the vanilla bean into the bowl. (Reserve the pods for another flavoring use.)

Place the bowl over (not touching) gently simmering water in a saucepan and whisk constantly until the eggs begin to thicken. Continue whisking until the sabayon is very thick, and when tested with an instant-read thermometer registers 180°F (82°C). As the sauce cooks, it will become light and fluffy and will triple in bulk. Remove from the heat and whisk for 3 minutes longer, to stabilize the foam. Serve immediately or within 20 minutes (the sauce will thicken as it cools, so it will "dollop," rather than pour).

Splay the bottoms of the mango fans slightly to bring more of the fruit's surface into contact with the grill rack, and place the fans on the edges of the rack, flat side down and perpendicular to the bars. Grill until nicely charred with the marks of the grill, 5–10 minutes (the timing depends on the heat of the fire). Using a metal spatula, gently flip the mango halves over and grill until golden on the second side, 5–10 minutes longer.

Transfer the mango fans to warmed individual plates and smother them with generous spoonfuls of the sabayon. Garnish each plate with a sprig of mint and a few berries. Serve at once.

Pound Cake with Raspberry Sauce

SERVES 6

Serve this wonderful dessert to top off a barbecue. A wire grilling basket makes turning the cake easy. Sweetened sliced strawberries, peaches, or nectarines can be used in place of the raspberry sauce. Seek out a high-quality pound cake at your favorite bakery.

FOR THE RASPBERRY SAUCE:
⅓ cup (3½ oz/105 g) red currant jelly
2 cups (8 oz/250 g) fresh or frozen
   raspberries

1 pound cake, at least 9 inches (23 cm)
   long
2–3 tablespoons unsalted butter, at
   room temperature (optional)

Prepare a fire in a grill.

To prepare the raspberry sauce, in a small saucepan over medium heat, warm the jelly until it is fully melted, 2–3 minutes. Place the raspberries in a bowl and stir in the melted jelly. Let cool to room temperature, then transfer to the refrigerator to chill.

Cut the pound cake into 12 slices, each ¾ inch (2 cm) thick, and place obliquely in a grilling basket or on the grill rack. Toast, turning once, until the pieces are darkened on the edges and the marks of the basket or grill rack begin to show, about 2 minutes on each side. Remove the slices from the grill and spread with butter, if desired.

Place the toasted slices on a platter or individual plates. Spoon the chilled sauce in a line across the slices and serve the cake warm.

Foil-Wrapped Oranges in Dark Rum

SERVES 4

This is a grown-up dessert because the alcohol in the rum does not cook off completely, resulting in a very pleasant wallop. You can, however, bring the rum to a boil in a small saucepan for 1 minute before you pour it over the oranges, leaving just the warm, complex character of the rum itself. Select a Jamaican or other full-bodied dark rum for the best flavor. Think of this as hot buttered rum with oranges—a nice toddy before bed.

4 large oranges

4 tablespoons (2 fl oz/60 ml)
   dark rum

2 tablespoons plus 2 teaspoons dark
   brown sugar

½ teaspoon ground cinnamon

2 tablespoons unsalted butter

4 scoops vanilla or chocolate
   ice cream

Prepare a fire in a grill.

Cut out four 12-inch (30-cm) squares of aluminum foil. Working with 1 orange at a time, and using a small, sharp knife, cut a slice off the top and bottom to expose the fruit. Stand the orange upright and thickly slice off the peel in strips, following the contour of the fruit to expose the flesh.

Cut 1 orange crosswise into about 8 rounds, each ⅓ inch (9 mm) thick. With the tip of the knife, pick out and discard any seeds. Reassemble the orange in its original shape in the center of a foil square. Pull up the sides slightly and spoon in 1 tablespoon of the rum, 2 teaspoons of the brown sugar, ⅛ teaspoon of the cinnamon, and ½ tablespoon of the butter. Bunch up the foil into a purse shape, and pinch the neck closed. Repeat with the remaining oranges and foil. (At this point, the oranges can be left at room temperature for up to 2 hours or refrigerated overnight.)

Place the orange packets at the farthest edges of the grill rack; they should not be placed directly over hot coals. Grill gently for about 15 minutes, then open the top of a packet. The sugar should have melted and caramelized. If not, leave on the grill for a few minutes longer.

Transfer the packets to a platter and let cool for 5–15 minutes. Serve over bowls of the ice cream, being sure to catch the delicious juices that escape when the oranges are unwrapped.

Pear Bruschetta

SERVES 6

Sprinkle the pears with chopped pistachios or almonds just before serving, if desired.

6 slices brioche or similar dense, rich
    bread, each about ½ inch (12 mm)
    thick
3 large, ripe Bosc pears, peeled, cored,
    and sliced
melted unsalted butter
½ cup (5 oz/155 g) raspberry jam

Prepare a fire in a covered grill.

🍃 Brush the bread slices and the pear slices on both sides with melted butter, arrange on an oiled grill screen, and place the screen on the grill rack. Cover, open the vents, and grill, turning once, until the bread slices are just toasted, about 4 minutes total, and the pear slices are warm and soft, 4–6 minutes total. Watch the bread closely, as it can char easily.

🍃 Transfer the bread slices to a platter and spread the raspberry jam over the tops, dividing evenly. Arrange the pear slices decoratively on the jam. Serve warm.

Mixed Fruit Grill with Spiced Lemon Cream

SERVES 6–8

Apples and pears are delicious grilled, but you can substitute any of your fresh, seasonal favorites. Note that apples and pears take about twice as long to cook as summer fruits such as apricots and peaches. To prepare most fruits, halve them, then pit or core. If the skin is tough, peel before cooking.

FOR THE SPICED LEMON CREAM:
¾ cup (6 fl oz/180 ml) heavy (double)
    cream, chilled
1 tablespoon nonfat dry milk
¼ cup (3 oz/90 g) honey
2 teaspoons finely grated lemon zest
1 tablespoon fresh lemon juice
¼ teaspoon ground cinnamon

FOR THE FRUIT:
4 apples, preferably Golden Delicious
4 firm but ripe pears, preferably Bosc
3 tablespoons unsalted butter, melted
2 tablespoons sugar

Prepare a fire in a grill.

🍃 To prepare the spiced lemon cream, in a small bowl, combine the cream and the dry milk. Using a wire whisk or an electric mixer, beat until stiff peaks form, then fold in the honey, lemon zest, lemon juice, and cinnamon. Cover and refrigerate until serving.

🍃 To prepare the fruit, halve, peel, and core the apples and pears. Place the fruit in a large bowl and toss with the melted butter and sugar.

🍃 Arrange the fruit, cut side down, on a grill screen. Grill, turning every 10 minutes, until lightly browned and tender but not mushy when pierced, 25–30 minutes total.

🍃 To serve, transfer to a platter or individual plates. Serve warm or at room temperature. Pass the lemon cream at the table.

Pound Cake Kabobs with Chocolate-Coffee Sauce

SERVES 6

FOR THE CHOCOLATE-COFFEE SAUCE:
4 oz (125 g) unsweetened chocolate, chopped
¼ cup (2 oz/60 g) unsalted butter
1 cup (8 oz/250 g) sugar
½ cup (4 fl oz/125 ml) evaporated milk
2 tablespoons coffee liqueur
1 teaspoon vanilla extract (essence)

6 slices pound cake, each 1 inch (2.5 cm) thick, cut into 1-inch (2.5-cm) cubes
3 bananas, peeled and cut into 1-inch (2.5-cm) lengths
melted unsalted butter for brushing
whipped cream (optional)

Prepare a fire in a grill.

To prepare the sauce, combine the chocolate and butter in the top pan of a double boiler or in a heatproof bowl. Place over (not touching) simmering water in a pan. Stir until smooth.

Using a rubber spatula, scrape the chocolate mixture into a clean saucepan. Stir in the sugar and evaporated milk and bring to a simmer over medium-high heat, stirring until the sugar dissolves and the sauce is heated through. Stir in the liqueur and vanilla and remove from the heat.

Thread the cake and banana pieces alternately onto 6 skewers, dividing them evenly. Brush with the butter, place on the grill rack, and grill, turning once, until the cake is lightly toasted, about 2 minutes total.

Gently rewarm the chocolate sauce over low heat. Pour a pool of the sauce onto 6 individual plates, dividing evenly. Add a dollop of whipped cream, if desired. Place 1 skewer on each plate, drizzle with some of the warmed sauce, and serve hot.

Rum-Raisin Bananas with Ice Cream

SERVES 6

½ cup (3 oz/90 g) raisins
¼ cup (2 fl oz/60 ml) dark rum, or as needed to cover
½ cup (3½ oz/105 g) firmly packed light brown sugar
6 large, firm but ripe bananas, peeled and halved lengthwise
melted unsalted butter
1 qt (1 l) good-quality vanilla ice cream

In a small bowl, combine the raisins with rum to cover. Let stand for about 30 minutes.

Prepare a fire in a grill.

Spread the brown sugar on a plate. Brush the bananas with butter and then roll in the sugar. Set the bananas on an oiled grill screen, place on the grill rack, and grill, turning as necessary, until warm and soft and beginning to color, about 4 minutes total.

Divide the ice cream evenly among individual bowls or plates, placing 2 scoops in each. Top with the banana halves and sprinkle with the rum-soaked raisins. Serve immediately.

Mixed Berry Tart

SERVES 6

You can shape the dough into a rectangle, if you like, or make individual tartlets. Grilling time will vary, so bake until the pastry is firm to the touch and golden brown on the bottom. Serve the tart with sweetened whipped cream.

1 teaspoon plus 3 tablespoons granulated sugar

scant 1 cup (8 fl oz/250 ml) lukewarm water (110°F/43°C)

2½ teaspoons (1 package) active dry yeast

2¾ cups (14 oz/440 g) all-purpose (plain) flour

½ teaspoon salt

2 tablespoons unsalted butter, at room temperature

1 cup (8 oz/250 g) mascarpone cheese

⅓ cup (2½ oz/75 g) firmly packed light brown sugar

6 cups (1½ lb/750 g) strawberries, stems removed and halved if large

2 cups (8 oz/250 g) blueberries

1 cup (10 oz/315 g) strawberry jam

¼ cup (2 fl oz/60 ml) water

In a small bowl, stir the 1 teaspoon granulated sugar into the warm water. Sprinkle the yeast over the top and let stand until foamy, about 5 minutes.

🔥 In a food processor, combine the flour, the 3 tablespoons granulated sugar, and the salt and pulse briefly to combine. Add the butter and the yeast mixture and process until a soft, slightly sticky dough forms, about 10 seconds.

🔥 Turn out the dough onto a lightly floured work surface and knead until smooth, about 5 minutes. If the dough is too sticky, work in additional flour, 1 tablespoon at a time, until smooth. Gather the dough into a ball, place in a bowl, cover the bowl tightly with buttered plastic wrap, and let the dough rise in a warm place until doubled in bulk, 45–60 minutes.

🔥 Punch down the dough and let stand for 5 minutes. Turn out onto the floured work surface and knead for a few minutes until smooth. Stretch and pat the dough into a round about 12 inches (30 cm) in diameter.

🔥 Prepare a fire in a grill. Place a pizza stone on the grill rack.

🔥 In a small bowl, stir together the mascarpone cheese and the brown sugar. Spread the cheese mixture over the dough, then the strawberries, and finally the blueberries. In a small saucepan over medium heat, combine the jam and water and stir until melted. Brush the jam mixture over the berries.

🔥 Place the tart directly on the hot pizza stone. Cover, open the vents, and grill, rotating the tart 180 degrees after about 5 minutes, until the crust is golden, 8–10 minutes.

🔥 Transfer to a serving plate, cut into wedges, and serve warm.

Tropical Fruits with Toasted Coconut

SERVES 6

1 cup (4 oz/125 g) shredded or flaked dried coconut

3 large, ripe mangoes

melted unsalted butter

6 pineapple slices, each ½ inch (12 mm) thick

2 star fruits, cut into slices ¼ inch (6 mm) thick

½ cup (3 oz/90 g) chopped crystallized ginger

Preheat the oven to 325°F (165°C).

🔥 Spread the coconut on a nonstick baking sheet and toast in the oven, shaking the baking sheet a few times to prevent burning, until lightly browned, about 8 minutes. Set aside.

🔥 Prepare a fire in a grill.

🔥 Working with 1 mango at a time and holding it upright on a cutting board, cut the flesh off the flat sides of the pit in 2 large slabs, cutting as close to the pit as possible. Do not peel. Brush the cut side of each mango slice with melted butter, then brush the pineapple slices and star fruit slices on both sides with melted butter.

🔥 Arrange the mango slices, cut sides down, on an oiled grill screen along with the pineapple and star fruit slices. Place on the grill rack and grill, turning the pineapple and star fruit slices once (do not turn the mango slices), until the fruits are warm and soft, 3–4 minutes total. The fruits may brown slightly.

🔥 Transfer to a serving dish and sprinkle with the crystallized ginger and toasted coconut. Serve warm.

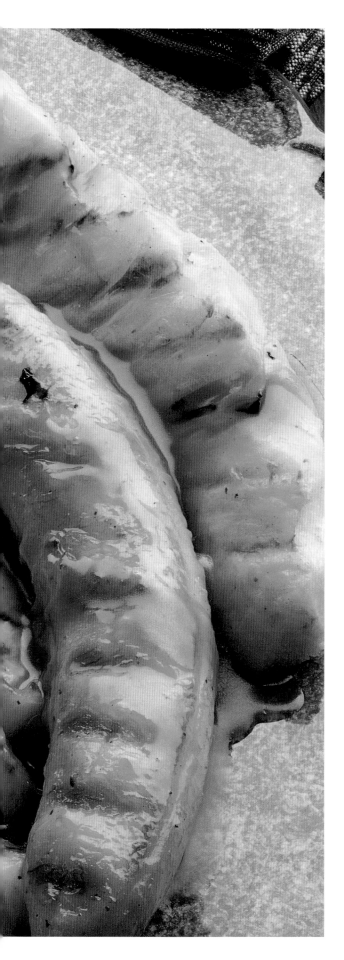

Bananas and Pineapple with Butterscotch Sauce

SERVES 6–8

This unusual dessert is attractive garnished with strips of orange zest. For a splurge, serve the warm grilled fruit over vanilla ice cream.

FOR THE BUTTERSCOTCH SAUCE:
½ cup (4 oz/125 g) unsalted butter
1 cup (7 oz/220 g) firmly packed
  brown sugar
½ cup (4 fl oz/125 ml) heavy (double)
  cream
pinch of salt
½ teaspoon vanilla extract (essence)

FOR THE FRUIT:
4 firm but ripe bananas
6–8 fresh pineapple spears, ½–1 inch
  (12 mm–2.5 cm) thick, or canned
  pineapple spears, drained
6 tablespoons (3 oz/90 g) unsalted
  butter
2 tablespoons granulated sugar
¼ teaspoon ground nutmeg

Prepare a fire in a grill.

To prepare the butterscotch sauce, in a small saucepan over medium heat, melt the butter. Add the brown sugar and cream and bring to a boil, whisking almost constantly. Remove from the heat and stir in the salt and vanilla. Cover to keep warm. (If made ahead, let cool, then cover and refrigerate for up to 1 week. Reheat over low heat before serving.)

To prepare the fruit, peel the bananas. Place the bananas and the pineapple spears on a platter and set aside. In a small saucepan over medium heat, combine the butter, granulated sugar, and nutmeg, and stir frequently until melted and smooth. Remove from the heat and pour over the fruit. Turn the fruit to coat evenly with the butter mixture.

Arrange the pineapple spears and the bananas on the grill rack and grill, turning every 2–3 minutes, until the fruit is lightly browned and the bananas are just tender when pierced with the tip of a sharp knife, 10–12 minutes total.

Remove from the grill and arrange on a warmed platter. Reheat the sauce to serving temperature, if necessary. Spoon some of the warm butterscotch sauce over the fruit. Pass the remaining sauce at the table.

Brie with Papaya

SERVES 6

Brie's protective coating makes the cheese a natural for the grill. Select a wedge that gives slightly when pressed. If desired, omit the papaya, sprinkle the grilled Brie with slivered blanched almonds, and serve with a large bunch of green grapes and slices of French bread.

1 ripe papaya, about 1 lb (500 g),
  peeled, halved, seeded, and cut
  lengthwise into slices ½ inch
  (12 mm) thick
melted unsalted butter for brushing
1 wedge Brie cheese, ½ lb (250 g)
¼ cup (2 oz/60 g) sugar

Prepare a fire in a grill.

Brush the papaya slices with melted butter. Place the papaya slices and the cheese on an oiled grill screen and place on the grill rack. Grill, turning the papaya and cheese once, for 2–4 minutes total for the cheese and 4 minutes total for the papaya. The cheese should be warm and just beginning to run, and the papaya slices should be warm and soft.

Transfer the cheese and papaya slices to a serving platter and sprinkle the papaya with the sugar. Serve warm.

From the Kitchen

Many cooks like to rely on desserts that can be prepared ahead of time, to avoid last-minute cooking as the meal winds down. Present fruit in its natural state, accompanied by a sauce of white chocolate and lime, or baked into a cobbler, crisp, or gratin. Cookies and bars, which are easy to make and travel well, are perfect for a barbecue at the beach or park. Ice cream is a satisfying finale to any grilling session, whether on its own or served along-side a grilled fruit dessert.

Summer Fruits in White Chocolate–Lime Sauce

SERVES 6–8

Use only the best-quality white chocolate and sweet ripe fruits. The sauce can be made up to 3 days ahead, covered, and refrigerated. Soften it in a microwave oven or in the top pan of a double boiler or a heatproof bowl placed over (not touching) barely simmering water.

12 oz (375 g) white chocolate, chopped into ½-inch (12-mm) pieces
2 cups (16 fl oz/500 ml) heavy (double) cream
2 teaspoons grated lime zest
4 cups (1 lb/500 g) sliced mixed ripe summer fruits such as apricots, nectarines, and peaches (½-inch/ 12-mm slices)

2 cups (8 oz/250 g) mixed berries such as raspberries, blackberries, stemmed strawberries, and gooseberries
curls of lime zest or fresh mint sprigs

Place the white chocolate in a food processor or blender. Pour the cream into a small saucepan and place over medium heat. When tiny bubbles begin to appear around the edge of the pan, remove from the heat and pour the cream over the chocolate. Process until smooth. Add the lime zest and process for a few seconds longer. Let cool to room temperature. The sauce should have the consistency of a very thick cream.

Arrange the fruit on a rimmed serving plate or in a bowl. Serve the cooled sauce alongside the fruit, and garnish it with lime-zest curls or mint sprigs.

Nectarines Poached in Champagne

SERVES 8

Midsummer, when nectarines are at their peak, is the best time to make this simple and elegant dessert. Select large, firm (but not green) nectarines with rosy gold skins. Substitute peaches if you wish, or use a mixture of both. Amaretti are Italian almond-flavored macaroons; look for them in Italian or other specialty-food stores.

8 large nectarines, about 4 lb (2 kg)
16 amaretti
3 cups (24 fl oz/750 ml) champagne
  or sparkling wine
⅔ cup (5 oz/155 g) sugar
Raspberry Sauce *(page 250)*

Fill a large saucepan three-fourths full of water and bring to a rapid boil. Add the nectarines and reduce the heat to a bare simmer. Simmer, uncovered, for 2 minutes. Then, using a slotted spoon, transfer the fruit to a bowl of cold water. Slip off the skins, using a paring knife to remove any skin that does not come off easily.

Cut the nectarines in half and remove the pits. Place 1 cookie in each cavity left by the pit. Arrange the halves, cut sides down, in a single layer in a non-aluminum baking pan (you may have to use several pans). Pour the champagne or sparkling wine evenly over the nectarines and sprinkle with the sugar. Place a piece of waxed paper or parchment (baking) paper over the fruit, being careful that it doesn't hang over the pan and touch the heat element. Place the pan over low heat and bring to a gentle simmer. Cook just until the nectarines are very tender but not falling apart, 15–20 minutes. Turn off the heat and let cool completely in the pan.

To serve, ladle some of the sauce on individual rimmed plates. Using a slotted spoon, carefully place 2 nectarine halves on top of the sauce. Dribble more sauce over the top and serve.

Tropical Papaya Boats

SERVES 4

For the best results, use peak-of-ripeness fruits for the sweetest flavor. The boats can be assembled up to 4 hours in advance of serving, covered with plastic wrap, and refrigerated. If you do prepare the dessert ahead of time, sprinkle the bananas with lemon or lime juice to keep them from turning brown. Star fruits, if available, make a wonderful garnish. Also called carambola, the star fruit is a tropical yellow-green fruit that is generally available from late summer through winter.

2 papayas, each about 6 inches
   (15 cm) long
juice of 1 small lime
2 kiwifruits, peeled and sliced crosswise
1 cup (6 oz/185 g) fresh pineapple
   chunks
1 mango
1 banana, peeled and sliced crosswise

Cut the papayas in half lengthwise and scoop out the seeds. Set 1 half on each individual plate, hollow side up. Sprinkle evenly with the lime juice.

 Arrange the kiwifruit slices and pineapple chunks attractively in the papaya halves.

 Peel the mango. Cut the flesh lengthwise off the pit in thick slices, cutting as close to the pit as possible. Add the mango slices and banana slices to the papaya halves and serve.

African Fruit Salad

SERVES 8

Here is a naturally sweet, refreshing dessert that is a common finale to dinner parties in former French West Africa. Use only the ripest, fullest-flavored fruits: bananas that have just turned yellow and only the sweetest pineapple. If you cannot find the large-sized fruits called for in the recipe, equivalent weights of smaller fruits can be used. You can make the salad up to 4 hours ahead of time, then cover with plastic wrap and refrigerate. Add the bananas just before serving, however, or they will turn brown. The fruits must all be cut into very small pieces for the dish to be at its best.

1 large papaya, 1 lb (500 g) or larger
2 mangoes, about 1 lb (500 g) each
1 large pineapple, 3–4 lb (1.5–2 kg)
2 large bananas

Halve the papaya and scoop out its seeds; peel the halves. Cut the flesh into small pieces and place in a large serving bowl.
Peel the mangoes. Slice as much of the flesh off each pit as possible, being careful to capture any juices. Cut the flesh into small pieces. Add the pieces and their juices to the bowl holding the papaya.
Using a sturdy, sharp knife, cut the top and bottom off the pineapple. Set the pineapple upright on a cutting board. Working from the top to the bottom, slice off the dark, prickly outside skin. Cut out any remaining eyes or dark spots. (A strawberry huller works well for this.) Cut the pineapple lengthwise into quarters, being careful to capture any juices. Cut lengthwise again to remove the tough inner core on each quarter. Cut the pineapple into small pieces, again being careful to capture any juices. Add the pineapple and juices to the other fruits. Toss well, cover, and refrigerate until well chilled.

Just before serving, peel the bananas and cut into small pieces. Add to the bowl, toss well, and serve.

Berry and Banana Salad

SERVES 4

Wild berries picked in the woods are the most fragrant, and it is best to wash them with a little white wine instead of water, to preserve their perfume. This salad can also be dressed with white wine and sugar, or cream and sugar.

½ lb (250 g) strawberries, stemmed and thinly sliced lengthwise
½ lb (250 g) blueberries
2 bananas, peeled and thinly sliced
¾ cup (4 oz/125 g) confectioners' (icing) sugar
juice of 1 orange
juice of ½ lemon

Combine the berries and bananas in a salad bowl. In a small bowl, stir together the sugar and the orange and lemon juices until the sugar dissolves. Pour the dressing over the fruit and serve.

Chocolate-Dipped Frozen Bananas

MAKES ABOUT 40 SLICES

A confection for children—and anyone who is still a child at heart.

1½ cups (7½ oz/235 g) hazelnuts (filberts)
12 oz (375 g) bitter or semisweet chocolate, chopped
¼ cup (2 oz/60 g) unsalted butter
4 large, firm bananas

Preheat an oven to 300°F (150°C). Spread the hazelnuts in a shallow pan and place in the oven until lightly toasted and the skins begin to loosen from the nuts, 10–12 minutes. Remove from the oven and pour the hot nuts into a kitchen towel. Rub the towel against the nuts to flake off as much of the skins as possible. Chop the nuts. Alternatively, place the toasted hazelnuts in a food processor fitted with the metal blade. Process with on-off pulses until the nuts are coarsely chopped, then pour into a large wire-mesh sieve and shake vigorously; the skins will flake off.

🍴 Place the chocolate and butter in a bowl set over (but not touching) gently simmering water, or in the top pan of a double boiler set over gently simmering water. Stir occasionally until the mixture is smooth. Remove from the heat, but leave over the hot water.
🍴 On a sturdy tray, set out about 40 fluted paper cups 2 inches (5 cm) in diameter. Sprinkle about 1 teaspoon of the chopped nuts into the bottom of each cup.
🍴 Peel the bananas and cut each one crosswise into 10 slices, each about 1 inch (2.5 cm) thick. Spear a slice onto a metal or wooden skewer and dip into the chocolate, coating it. Place in a paper cup and sprinkle with another 1 teaspoon or so of nuts. Repeat with the remaining banana slices, chocolate, and nuts.
🍴 Place the tray in the freezer for at least 2 hours or as long as 24 hours. Thaw for 2 minutes before serving.

Three-Berry Cobbler

SERVES 6–8

Cobblers conjure up memories of irresistible aromas in warm, friendly kitchens. This one combines blackberries, raspberries, and strawberries under a sweet biscuit crust.

FOR THE FILLING:
1½ cups (6 oz/185 g) strawberries
1½ cups (6 oz/185 g) raspberries
1½ cups (6 oz/185 g) blackberries
½ cup (4 oz/125 g) sugar

FOR THE BISCUIT TOPPING:
⅓ cup (3 oz/90 g) unsalted butter or margarine, at room temperature
⅓ cup (3 oz/90 g) sugar, plus 1–2 teaspoons sugar (optional)
2 cups (10 oz/315 g) all-purpose (plain) flour
½ teaspoon salt

1 teaspoon baking powder
½ cup (4 fl oz/125 ml) milk

Preheat the oven to 375°F (190°C). Grease a deep 1½- or 2-qt (1.5- or 2-l) baking dish with butter or margarine, or spray with vegetable cooking spray.
🍴 To prepare the filling, remove the stems from the strawberries and then slice the berries. Place in the prepared baking dish. Add the raspberries and blackberries. Sprinkle the sugar over the berries and toss to mix. Set aside.
🍴 To prepare the biscuit topping, combine the butter or margarine and the ⅓ cup (3 oz/90 g) sugar in a bowl. Using a wooden spoon, a whisk, or an electric mixer set on medium-high speed, beat until fluffy, 3–4 minutes. In another bowl, sift together the flour, salt, and baking powder. Add the flour mixture alternately with the milk to the butter mixture, stirring with a fork just until the flour disappears. Do not overmix or the biscuit topping will become heavy.
🍴 Turn the dough out onto a floured work surface and roll out or pat into the shape and size of the baking dish. Lift the dough onto the baking dish to cover the fruit; it should reach just slightly short of the dish sides. Crimp or flute the edges of the dough to form an attractive rim. Cut several slits in the top for steam to escape. Sprinkle with 1–2 teaspoons sugar, if desired.
🍴 Bake until the top is golden and the berries are bubbling, about 50 minutes. Transfer to a rack to cool. Serve hot, warm, or at room temperature.

Mixed Summer Fruit Compote

SERVES 6

Use the best of summer's fruit. For a more complex-tasting sauce, substitute a fruit wine such as blueberry or cherry for ¼ cup (6 fl oz/180 ml) of the water. You can serve the compote plain or garnished with a dollop of whipped cream or vanilla yogurt.

2 lb (1 kg) mixed summer fruits such as pitted cherries, raspberries, blueberries, strawberries, red currants, or pitted apricots, peaches, or nectarines
¾ cup (5½ oz/170 g) superfine (caster) sugar
1½ cups (12 fl oz/375 ml) water, plus 2 tablespoons water
1 tablespoon cornstarch (cornflour)

Cut the larger fruits into smaller pieces; leave the berries whole. Set aside.

In a 2-qt (2-l) saucepan set over medium heat, combine the sugar and the 1½ cups (12 fl oz/375 ml) water. Stir until the sugar dissolves, then bring the liquid to a boil.

Add the fruits to the sugar syrup and lower the heat so that the mixture simmers. Cook until the fruits are soft but have not begun to disintegrate, 3–4 minutes. Using a slotted spoon, transfer the fruits to a serving bowl. Allow the liquid to continue to simmer.

In a small cup, stir together the cornstarch and the 2 tablespoons water. Whisk it into the simmering liquid. Stir constantly until the liquid is clear and has thickened slightly, 2–3 minutes. Remove from the heat and let cool for 15 minutes, then pour over the fruit.

Cover and refrigerate to chill well before serving. Spoon into shallow bowls to serve.

Melba Summer Pudding

SERVES 6–8

Traditionally this English pudding calls for soaking the bread in milk or cream. In this lighter version, the bread is merely brushed with cream—an optional step. If you like, glaze the pudding with melted red currant jelly.

2 teaspoons unsalted butter or margarine, at room temperature

1½ lb (750 g) peaches

juice of 1 lemon

3 cups (12 oz/375 g) fresh or slightly thawed frozen raspberries, plus fresh raspberries for garnish (optional)

½ cup (4 oz/125 g) sugar

8 slices slightly stale challah or other rich, slightly sweet egg bread, crusts removed

⅓ cup (3 fl oz/80 ml) heavy (double) cream mixed with ¼ teaspoon vanilla extract (essence) (optional)

whipped cream (optional)

fresh mint leaves (optional)

Heavily grease a 2-qt (2-l) mixing bowl or pudding mold with the butter or margarine.

🥄 Bring a saucepan three-fourths full of water to a boil. Immerse the peaches for 30 seconds. Using a slotted spoon, transfer to a work surface. When cool enough to handle, slip off the skins. Halve, pit, and slice the peaches. Place in a bowl and toss with the lemon juice. In another bowl, toss together the raspberries and sugar.

🥄 Brush both sides of each bread slice with the cream-vanilla mixture, if using. Line the prepared bowl or mold with 6 of the bread slices, overlapping them slightly and leaving a small opening in the bottom.

🥄 Spoon about 3 tablespoons of the raspberries into the bread-lined mold.

Add a layer of peaches, then top with more of the raspberries. Repeat the layers until the fruits are used up. Place the remaining 2 bread slices on top, piecing as needed to cover completely. Cover with plastic wrap and weight with a small plate that fits inside the mold, pressing firmly to compress the pudding. Place a 1-lb (500-g) weight on the plate and refrigerate for 24 hours.

🥄 Remove the weight, plate, and plastic wrap. Dip the mold in very warm water, almost to the rim, for about 45 seconds, then loosen the edges with a knife. Invert onto a serving plate.

🥄 If desired, garnish with the whipped cream, raspberries, and mint leaves. Slice and serve.

Raspberry-Blackberry Gratin

SERVES 8

This beautiful dish consists of summer berries and a simple French custard called sabayon. You can use any berries you wish, but the combination of raspberries and plump, sweet blackberries is a showstopper. Make this in a single ovenproof dish or in individual baking dishes. Prepare the custard at least 4 hours before serving.

3 egg yolks from extra-large eggs
1 tablespoon water
½ cup (4 oz/125 g) sugar
½ cup (4 fl oz/125 ml) framboise (raspberry brandy)
2 cups (16 fl oz/500 ml) heavy (double) cream, chilled
3 cups (12 oz/375 g) raspberries
3 cups (12 oz/375 g) blackberries

Combine the egg yolks, water, and sugar in a metal bowl set over (not touching) gently simmering water, or in the top pan of a double boiler set over simmering water. Whisk constantly until the mixture is foamy and begins to thicken slightly, 2–3 minutes. Immediately remove from the heat and strain through a fine-mesh sieve into a 2-qt (2-l) metal bowl. (The metal bowl will help cool the mixture more quickly.) Stir in the framboise, cover, and refrigerate for at least 4 hours or overnight.

Just before serving, position the rack 3–4 inches (7.5–10 cm) from the heat source in a broiler (griller) and preheat the broiler.

Using chilled beaters and a large chilled bowl, whip the cream until stiff peaks form. Gently fold the cream into the chilled custard. Scatter all of the berries over the bottom of a 2-qt (2-l) ovenproof baking dish with at least 1-inch (2.5-cm) sides. Place the dish on a heavy-duty baking sheet or in a shallow baking pan to make for easier removal from the broiler. Gently pour and spoon the custard over the berries.

Broil (grill) until the top is browned and bubbling, 1½–2 minutes. Serve immediately.

Blueberry Crisp

SERVES 6

Tart blueberries and a slightly crunchy, sweet topping come together in this easy-to-make dessert. Serve with vanilla ice cream.

4 cups (1 lb/500 g) fresh or frozen blueberries
1 tablespoon fresh lemon juice
¾ cup (6 oz/185 g) firmly packed light brown sugar
½ cup (2½ oz/75 g) all-purpose (plain) flour
½ teaspoon ground cinnamon
¼ cup (2 oz/60 g) unsalted butter, at room temperature, cut into pieces
¾ cup (2½ oz/75 g) old-fashioned rolled oats

Preheat the oven to 375°F (190°C). Grease a shallow 1½-qt (1.5-l) baking dish with butter or margarine, or spray with vegetable cooking spray.

Spread the fresh or frozen blueberries evenly over the bottom of the prepared baking dish and sprinkle with the lemon juice.

In a bowl, using a fork, mix together the brown sugar, flour, cinnamon, butter, and rolled oats until well combined. Sprinkle evenly over the blueberries.

Bake until the top is golden and the blueberries are bubbling, about 30 minutes. Transfer to a rack and serve hot or warm.

Chocolate-Chunk and Cherry Cookies

MAKES ABOUT 2 DOZEN

Use big hunks of premium chocolate to make these chocolate-rich cookies extra special. Dried cherries or cranberries provide sophisticated flavor; if they're unavailable, raisins or currants can be substituted with excellent results.

1 cup (5 oz/155 g) all-purpose (plain) flour

¾ teaspoon baking powder

⅛ teaspoon baking soda (bicarbonate of soda)

⅛ teaspoon salt

½ cup (4 oz/125 g) plus 2 tablespoons unsalted butter, at room temperature

¾ cup (6 oz/185 g) firmly packed dark brown sugar

1 teaspoon vanilla extract (essence)

1 egg

8 oz (250 g) semisweet (plain) chocolate, cut into ½-inch (12-mm) pieces (about 1½ cups)

6 oz (185 g) dried sour cherries, dried Bing cherries, or dried cranberries, chopped (about 1½ cups)

Preheat the oven to 350°F (180°C).

Sift together the flour, baking powder, baking soda, and salt into a bowl; set aside. Combine the butter, brown sugar, and vanilla in a large bowl. Using an electric mixer set on high speed, beat until fluffy. Beat in the egg. Reduce the speed to low, add the flour mixture, and mix in just until incorporated. Mix in the chocolate and cherries or cranberries on low speed.

Drop the batter by slightly rounded tablespoonfuls onto ungreased baking sheets, spacing 2 inches (5 cm) apart. Bake until golden brown, about 16 minutes. Transfer the cookies to wire racks to cool. Store in an airtight container at room temperature for up to 4 days.

Lemon-Coconut Squares

MAKES 16

Coconut adds a special twist in this recipe for a picnic favorite, but feel free to vary the flavor by substituting chopped almonds or hazelnuts (filberts). To make a stripe pattern on the cookies, place strips of parchment paper atop the cooled cookies, then dust with confectioners' sugar.

FOR THE CRUST:

1 cup (5 oz/155 g) all-purpose (plain) flour

¼ cup (2 oz/60 g) granulated sugar

¼ teaspoon salt

6 tablespoons (3 oz/90 g) chilled unsalted butter, cut into ½-inch (12-mm) pieces

¾ cup (2½ oz/75 g) toasted flaked coconut

FOR THE FILLING:

¾ cup (6 oz/185 g) granulated sugar

2 eggs

3 tablespoons fresh lemon juice

1 tablespoon grated lemon zest

½ teaspoon baking powder

pinch of salt

confectioners' (icing) sugar

Preheat the oven to 350°F (180°C). Line an 8-inch (20-cm) square baking pan with aluminum foil. Butter the foil.

To prepare the crust, in a food processor, combine the flour, granulated sugar, and salt. Process briefly until well mixed. Add the butter and coconut and process until the mixture resembles fine meal. Transfer to the prepared pan and press into the bottom to form a crust. Bake until light brown around the edges, about 35 minutes.

Meanwhile, to prepare the filling, combine the granulated sugar, eggs, lemon juice and zest, baking powder, and salt in a food processor or blender. Process until smooth.

When the crust is ready, pour the filling onto the hot crust. Continue to bake until the filling begins to brown around the edges and is just springy to the touch, about 35 minutes longer. Let cool in the pan on a wire rack.

Using the foil, lift the sheet from the pan and place on a work surface. Gently peel back the foil sides. Cut into 16 squares. Using a sieve, dust the tops with confectioners' sugar. Remove the squares from the foil. Store in an airtight container in the refrigerator for up to 5 days.

Preheat the oven to 350°F (180°C). Butter an 8-inch (20-cm) square baking pan.

🍃 Combine the butter, brown sugar, espresso powder, and vanilla in a large bowl. Using an electric mixer set on high speed, beat until light and fluffy. Beat in the eggs, one at a time, then beat at high speed until very fluffy, about 2 minutes. Reduce the speed to low, add the flour, and mix in. Continuing to mix on low speed, fold in the nuts and white chocolate just until blended. Spread the batter in the prepared pan.

🍃 Bake until a toothpick inserted in the center comes out clean, about 40 minutes. Let cool in the pan on a wire rack. Cut into 24 bars. Wrap individually in plastic wrap and store at room temperature for up to 3 days.

Cappuccino-Walnut Brownies

MAKES 25

Instant coffee is the secret to the intense flavor. The chocolate glaze is optional.

FOR THE BROWNIES:

4 oz (125 g) unsweetened chocolate, chopped

6 tablespoons (3 oz/90 g) unsalted butter

2 teaspoons instant coffee powder

½ cup (2½ oz/75 g) all-purpose (plain) flour

¾ teaspoon ground cinnamon

¼ teaspoon salt

2 eggs

1½ cups (10½ oz/330 g) firmly packed brown sugar

1 cup (4 oz/125 g) walnut pieces

White Chocolate and Macadamia Nut Blondies

MAKES 2 DOZEN

Rich, gooey, and delicious, these treats make a tasty conclusion to a grilled picnic lunch. Drizzle the blondies with caramel glaze if you're feeling indulgent.

½ cup (4 oz/125 g) unsalted butter, at room temperature

1¼ cups (9 oz/280 g) firmly packed golden brown sugar

2 teaspoons instant espresso powder

1 teaspoon vanilla extract (essence)

2 eggs

1 cup (5 oz/155 g) all-purpose (plain) flour

¾ cup (4 oz/125 g) macadamia nuts, coarsely chopped

3–4 oz (90–125 g) white chocolate, coarsely chopped

FOR THE GLAZE:

3 oz (90 g) semisweet (plain) chocolate, chopped

6 tablespoons (3 oz/90 g) unsalted butter

1 teaspoon instant coffee powder

½ heaping teaspoon ground cinnamon

Preheat the oven to 350°F (180°C). Line a 9-inch (23-cm) square pan or 7-by-11-inch (18-by-28-cm) baking dish with aluminum foil. Butter the foil, then dust with flour.

🍃 To prepare the brownies, combine the chocolate, butter, and coffee powder in a small, heavy saucepan. Stir over low heat until melted and smooth. Let cool slightly.

🍃 Sift together the flour, cinnamon, and salt into a bowl; set aside. In a large bowl, whisk the eggs until foamy. Whisk in the brown sugar and then the chocolate mixture. Mix in the flour mixture just until blended. Fold in the walnuts. Spread the batter in the prepared pan.

🍃 Bake until just springy to the touch and a toothpick inserted in the center comes out with a few crumbs attached, about 40 minutes. Let cool in the pan on a wire rack.

🍃 To prepare the glaze, combine the chocolate, butter, coffee powder, and cinnamon in the top pan of a double boiler or in a heatproof bowl set over (not touching) simmering water in a pan. Stir until melted and smooth. Remove from over the water and refrigerate, stirring occasionally, until just spreadable but not set, about 15 minutes.

🍃 Spread the glaze on the cooled brownies. Let stand until set, about 15 minutes. Using the foil, lift the sheet of brownies from the pan. Peel back the foil sides. Cut into 25 squares or diamonds. Wrap individually in plastic wrap and store in the refrigerator for up to 3 days.

S'More Bars

MAKES ABOUT 2 DOZEN

The ritual campfire combination of graham cracker, chocolate, and marshmallow is re-created in an unforgettable cookie. A nice make-ahead option for a casual, family-style barbecue.

FOR THE CRUST:

5 whole graham crackers

¾ cup (4 oz/125 g) all-purpose (plain) flour

½ cup (3½ oz/105 g) firmly packed golden brown sugar

½ cup (4 oz/125 g) chilled unsalted butter, cut into ½-inch (12-mm) pieces

1 egg, lightly beaten

FOR THE TOPPING:

6 tablespoons (3 fl oz/90 ml) heavy (double) cream

9 oz (280 g) milk chocolate, chopped

1 cup (2 oz/60 g) miniature marshmallows

Preheat the oven to 350°F (180°C). Line an 8-inch (20-cm) square baking pan with aluminum foil.

To prepare the crust, crumble the graham crackers into a food processor. Process finely. Add the flour and brown sugar and process to mix. Add the butter and process until the mixture resembles fine meal. Add the egg and process only until the mixture is evenly moist. Transfer the mixture to the prepared pan and press into the bottom to form a crust.

Bake until the top is just firm to the touch, about 20 minutes. Let cool completely in the pan on a wire rack.

To prepare the topping, place the cream in a heavy saucepan and bring to a simmer. Remove from the heat. Add the chocolate and stir until melted and smooth. Mix in the marshmallows. Spread the chocolate mixture evenly over the cooled crust. Cover and refrigerate until firm, at least 2 hours.

Using the foil, lift the sheet from the pan. Peel back the foil sides. Cut into bars 2 inches (5 cm) long by 1¼ inches (3 cm) wide. Remove the bars from the foil. Store in an airtight container in the refrigerator for up to 5 days.

Oatmeal, Date, and Walnut Cookies

MAKES ABOUT 4 DOZEN

A great recipe for a big batch of long-keeping, old-fashioned cookies. You can alter the baking time according to your preference for chewy or crisp cookies.

2 cups (10 oz/315 g) all-purpose (plain) flour

1 tablespoon ground cinnamon

1 teaspoon baking soda (bicarbonate of soda)

1 teaspoon salt

¾ cup (6 oz/185 g) unsalted butter, at room temperature

1 cup (8 oz/250 g) granulated sugar

1 cup (7 oz/220 g) firmly packed dark brown sugar

2 whole eggs, plus 1 egg yolk

3 tablespoons milk

2 teaspoons vanilla extract (essence)

2½ cups (7½ oz/235 g) old-fashioned rolled oats or quick-cooking oats

½ lb (250 g) pitted dates, chopped (about 1½ cups)

2 cups (8 oz/250 g) walnuts, coarsely chopped

Preheat the oven to 375° (190°C). Butter baking sheets.

Sift together the flour, cinnamon, baking soda, and salt into a bowl; set aside. Place the butter in a large bowl. Using an electric mixer set on high speed, beat until light and fluffy. Beat in the granulated sugar and brown sugar. Add the whole eggs, egg yolk, milk, and vanilla and beat until light and fluffy, about 2 minutes. Reduce the speed to low, add the flour mixture, and mix just until incorporated. Mix in the oats, dates, and walnuts on low speed.

Drop the batter by rounded tablespoons onto the prepared baking sheets, spacing 2 inches (5 cm) apart. Bake until light brown, about 12 minutes for chewy cookies and about 15 minutes for crisp cookies. Let cool on the baking sheets for 1 minute. Transfer the cookies to wire racks to cool completely. Store in an airtight container in the refrigerator for up to 1 week.

Pistachio-Orange Biscotti

MAKES ABOUT 3 DOZEN

Serve these cookies with mixed grilled fruits.

1¾ cups (9 oz/280 g) all-purpose (plain) flour

½ teaspoon baking soda (bicarbonate of soda)

½ teaspoon baking powder

⅛ teaspoon salt

½ cup (4 oz/125 g) unsalted butter, at room temperature

1 cup (8 oz/250 g) granulated sugar

2 tablespoons grated orange zest

1½ teaspoons vanilla extract (essence)

2 eggs

1½ cups (6 oz/185 g) unsalted shelled pistachio nuts

Sift together the flour, baking soda, baking powder, and salt into a bowl; set aside. Combine the butter, sugar, orange zest, and vanilla in a large bowl. Using an electric mixer set on high speed, beat until light and fluffy. Mix in the eggs, one at a time, beating well after each addition. Reduce the speed to low, add the pistachios, and mix in. Add the flour mixture and mix just until incorporated. Cover and refrigerate until well chilled, about 1 hour.

Preheat the oven to 350°F (180°C). Butter and flour a large baking sheet.

Divide the dough in half. Using lightly floured hands, roll each half on a lightly floured surface into a log 1½ inches (4 cm) in diameter. Arrange the logs on the prepared baking sheet, spacing them 5 inches (12 cm) apart.

Bake until light brown and firm to the touch, about 30 minutes (the logs will spread during baking). Remove from the oven and let cool slightly on the baking sheet. Leave the oven set at 350°F (180°C).

Using a spatula, carefully transfer the logs to a work surface. Using a serrated knife, cut on the diagonal into slices ¾ inch (2 cm) thick. Arrange the slices cut side down on the baking sheet and bake until golden brown, about 15 minutes. Transfer the cookies to wire racks to cool. Store in an airtight container at room temperature for up to 2 weeks.

Hazelnut-Orange Brownies

MAKES 9

These sophisticated treats will keep for up to 3 days when well wrapped individually.

¾ cup (4 oz/125 g) hazelnuts (filberts)

3 oz (90 g) unsweetened chocolate, chopped

6 tablespoons (3 oz/90 g) unsalted butter

2 eggs

1 cup (8 oz/250 g) sugar

1 tablespoon grated orange zest

¾ teaspoon vanilla extract (essence)

pinch of salt

¼ cup (1½ oz/45 g) all-purpose (plain) flour

Preheat the oven to 350°F (180°C). Butter and flour an 8-inch (20-cm) square baking dish.

🍂 Spread the hazelnuts on a baking sheet and bake until beginning to color, 5–10 minutes. Wrap the warm nuts in a kitchen towel and rub to remove the skins. Chop coarsely and set aside.

🍂 Combine the chocolate and butter in a heavy saucepan over low heat and stir until melted and smooth. Set aside.

🍂 Place the eggs in a large bowl and whisk until foamy. Whisk in the sugar, orange zest, vanilla, and salt until thoroughly incorporated. Stir in the chocolate mixture. Add the flour and mix just until blended. Fold in the hazelnuts. Spread the batter in the prepared dish.

🍂 Bake until the top is just springy to the touch and a toothpick inserted in the center comes out with a few moist crumbs attached, about 30 minutes. Let cool in the dish on a wire rack. Cut into 9 squares and serve.

Citrus Gelato

**MAKES ABOUT 3³/4 CUPS
(30 FL OZ/ 940 ML); SERVES 4–6**

*Small scoops of this gelato can be served
in frozen hollowed-out orange halves.*

2 oranges
2 lemons
3 cups (24 fl oz/750 ml) whole milk
8 egg yolks
1 cup (8 oz/250 g) sugar
3 tablespoons light corn syrup

Using a vegetable peeler, remove the
zest from the oranges and lemons in
strips. Place the strips in a medium-
sized, heavy saucepan and add the milk.
Bring to a simmer over medium-high
heat. Remove from the heat.

In a metal bowl, whisk together the
egg yolks, sugar, and corn syrup until
blended. Form a kitchen towel into a
ring and place the bowl on top to prevent it from moving. Gradually pour the
hot milk mixture into the yolk mixture,
whisking constantly. Return the mixture to the same saucepan and place
over medium-low heat. Cook, stirring
slowly and continuously with a wooden
spatula, until the custard thickens and
leaves a path on the back of the spatula
when a finger is drawn across it, about
6 minutes; do not allow to boil.

Pour the custard through a medium-
mesh sieve set over a clean bowl.
Refrigerate until cold, about 1 hour.

Transfer the custard to an ice-cream
maker and process according to the
manufacturer's instructions. For the best
texture, serve the gelato immediately.
Or transfer to a container, cover, and
freeze until firm, at least 4 hours or for
up to 3 days.

Orange Ice Cream with Truffles

**MAKES ABOUT 5 CUPS
(40 FL OZ/1.25 L); SERVES 8**

FOR THE TRUFFLES:
3 tablespoons sugar
2 egg yolks
⅓ cup (3 fl oz/80 ml) plus 2 tablespoons
  heavy (double) cream
4 oz (125 g) bittersweet chocolate,
  chopped

FOR THE ICE CREAM:
2 small oranges
2 cups (16 fl oz/500 ml) heavy (double)
  cream
1 cup (8 fl oz/250 ml) half-and-half
  (half cream)
6 egg yolks
⅔ cup (5 oz/155 g) sugar
1 cup (8 fl oz/250 ml) fresh orange juice
2 teaspoons grated orange zest

To prepare the truffles, in a small metal
bowl, whisk together the sugar and egg
yolks until blended. In a small, heavy
saucepan over medium-high heat, bring
the ⅓ cup (3 fl oz/80 ml) cream to a simmer. Gradually whisk the hot cream into
the yolk mixture. Return the mixture
to the same saucepan over medium-low
heat and cook, stirring continuously, until
the custard thickens, about 2 minutes.
Remove from the heat and stir in the
chocolate until melted. Then mix in the
2 tablespoons cream. Freeze, uncovered,
until firm enough to hold a shape, about
3 hours. Drop the truffle mixture by tea-
spoonfuls onto an aluminum foil–lined
baking sheet. Freeze until ready to use.

To prepare the ice cream, using a
vegetable peeler, remove the zest from
the oranges in long, wide strips and
place in a large, heavy saucepan. Add
1 cup (8 fl oz/250 ml) of the cream and
the half-and-half and bring to a simmer
over medium-high heat. Remove from
the heat.

In a metal bowl, whisk together the
egg yolks and sugar until blended. Gradually whisk in the hot cream mixture.
Return the mixture to the same saucepan
and place over medium-low heat. Add
the orange juice and cook, stirring continuously, until the custard thickens
slightly, about 5 minutes; do not boil.

Pour the custard through a medium-
mesh sieve set over a clean bowl. Stir in
the remaining 1 cup (8 fl oz/250 ml)
cream and the grated orange zest.
Refrigerate until cold, about 1 hour.

Transfer the custard to an ice-cream
maker and process according to the
manufacturer's instructions. Transfer half
of the ice cream to a 1½–2-qt (1.5–2-l)
rectangular container; top with a layer
of truffles, spacing them slightly apart.
Cover with the remaining ice cream.
Top with more truffles in the same
manner, pressing them gently into the
ice cream. Cover and freeze until firm,
at least 4 hours or for up to 3 days.

Dark Chocolate Gelato

MAKES ABOUT 1 QT (1 L); SERVES 6

Serve this gelato right out of the machine to highlight its ultra-creamy texture.

2 cups (16 fl oz/500 ml) milk
5 egg yolks
¾ cup (6 oz/185 g) sugar
2 tablespoons light corn syrup
4 oz (125 g) bittersweet chocolate, chopped
¼ cup (¾ oz/20 g) unsweetened cocoa powder

Pour the milk into a heavy saucepan. Bring to a simmer over medium-high heat. Remove from the heat.

In a metal bowl, whisk together the egg yolks, sugar, and corn syrup until blended. Gradually pour the hot milk into the yolk mixture, whisking constantly. Return the mixture to the same saucepan and place over medium-low heat. Cook, stirring slowly and continuously with a wooden spatula, until the custard thickens and leaves a path on the back of the spatula when a finger is drawn across it, about 6 minutes; do not allow to boil.

Pour the custard through a medium-mesh sieve set over a clean metal bowl. Add the chocolate and cocoa and stir until the chocolate melts. Refrigerate until cold, about 1 hour.

Transfer the custard to an ice-cream maker and process according to the manufacturer's instructions. For the best texture, serve the gelato immediately. Or transfer to a container, cover, and freeze until firm, at least 4 hours or for up to 3 days.

Fresh Peach Ice Cream

**MAKES ABOUT 5 CUPS
(40 FL OZ/1.25 L); SERVES 8**

For the best possible flavor, use only the ripest, juiciest peaches for this summertime treat.

2 cups (12 oz/375 g) peeled and finely chopped ripe peaches
½ cup (4 oz/120 g) sugar
¼ cup (2½ oz/75 g) light corn syrup
1½ cups (12 fl oz/375 ml) half-and-half (half cream)
1 cup (8 fl oz/250 ml) heavy (double) cream
4 egg yolks
½ teaspoon vanilla extract (essence)

Place the peaches in a large, heavy saucepan. Add ¼ cup (2 oz/60 g) of the sugar and the corn syrup and place over medium heat. Stir until the sugar melts and the peaches are heated through, about 4 minutes. Pour into a large bowl and set aside. Add the half-and-half and ½ cup (4 fl oz/125 ml) of the cream to the same saucepan. Bring to a simmer over medium-high heat. Remove from the heat.

In a metal bowl, whisk together the egg yolks and the remaining ¼ cup (2 oz/60 g) sugar until blended. Gradually pour the hot half-and-half mixture into the yolk mixture, whisking constantly. Return the mixture to the saucepan and place over medium-low heat. Cook, stirring slowly and continuously with a wooden spatula, until the custard thickens and leaves a path on the back of the spatula when a finger is drawn across it, about 5 minutes; do not allow to boil.

Pour the custard through a medium-mesh sieve into the peach mixture. Transfer three-fourths of the peach mixture to a food processor or blender and purée until smooth. Pour the purée back into the remaining peach mixture. Add the vanilla and the remaining ½ cup (4 fl oz/125 ml) cream and whisk to blend. Refrigerate until cold, about 1 hour.

Transfer the peach mixture to an ice-cream maker and process according to the manufacturer's instructions. Transfer the ice cream to a container; cover and freeze until firm, at least 4 hours or for up to 3 days.

Toasted Almond Ice Cream

MAKES ABOUT 5 CUPS (40 FL OZ/1.25 L); SERVES 8

Sautéing the almonds in butter intensifies the flavor of this simple ice cream.

2 tablespoons unsalted butter
½ cup (2½ oz/75 g) coarsely chopped almonds
3 cups (24 fl oz/750 ml) half-and-half (half cream)
6 egg yolks
¾ cup (6 oz/185 g) sugar
2 tablespoons light corn syrup
1 teaspoon vanilla extract (essence)
½ teaspoon almond extract (essence)

In a large, heavy saucepan over medium-high heat, melt the butter. Add the almonds and sauté, stirring often, until the almonds are golden and the butter browns, about 5 minutes; do not burn. Add the half-and-half and bring just to a simmer. Remove from the heat.

In a metal bowl, whisk together the egg yolks, sugar, and corn syrup until blended. Gradually pour the hot half-and-half mixture into the yolk mixture, whisking constantly. Return the mixture to the same saucepan and place over medium-low heat. Cook, stirring slowly and continuously with a wooden spatula, until the custard thickens and leaves a path on the back of the spatula when a finger is drawn across it, about 5 minutes; do not allow to boil.

Pour the custard through a medium-mesh sieve into a clean bowl for a smooth texture, or do not strain for a crunchy texture. Stir in the vanilla and almond extracts. Refrigerate the custard until cold, about 1 hour.

Transfer the custard to an ice-cream maker and process according to the manufacturer's instructions. Transfer the ice cream to a container; cover and freeze until firm, at least 4 hours or for up to 3 days.

Crimson Plum-Raspberry Sorbet

MAKES ABOUT 5 CUPS (40 FL OZ/1.25 L); SERVES 8

The bright color of this sorbet is a good indication of its equally intense fresh fruit flavor. Garnish with fresh raspberries and fresh mint leaves, if you like.

1 cup (8 oz/250 g) sugar
⅔ cup (5 fl oz/160 ml) water
2 tablespoons light corn syrup
1 package (1 lb/500 g) frozen unsweetened raspberries, thawed
1 lb (500 g) ripe plums, preferably red-fleshed, halved, pitted, and sliced

In a small, heavy saucepan over low heat, combine the sugar, water, and corn syrup. Stir until the sugar dissolves, about 3 minutes. Increase the heat to high and bring to a boil. Remove from the heat and set the syrup aside.

In a food processor or blender, process the raspberries and their juices until smooth. Strain the purée through a coarse sieve set over a bowl to remove the seeds. Press firmly on the solids with a rubber spatula to extract as much liquid as possible; discard the solids.

Return the berry purée to the processor or blender. Add the plums and purée until smooth. Add the reserved syrup and process to mix well. Transfer to a bowl and refrigerate until cold, about 1 hour.

Transfer the sorbet mixture to an ice cream maker and process according to the manufacturer's instructions. Transfer the sorbet to a container; cover and freeze until firm, at least 4 hours or for up to 3 days.

Mango Sorbet

MAKES ABOUT 2¹/₂ CUPS (20 FL OZ/ 625 ML); SERVES 3 OR 4

This is the ideal finish to a grilled spicy Asian meal.

2 large ripe mangoes
6 tablespoons (3 oz/90 g) sugar
¼ cup (2½ oz/75 g) light corn syrup

Using a small, sharp knife, make 4 lengthwise slits through the skin of each mango, cutting the skin into quarters. Peel off the skin and discard. Then slice the flesh from both sides of the large flat pit, as well as from around its edges.

Place the mango flesh in a food processor or blender; purée until smooth. Measure the purée; you should have 1⅔ cups (13 fl oz/410 ml). Return the purée to the processor or blender. Add the sugar and corn syrup and process to mix well. Pour the purée into a bowl and refrigerate until cold, about 1 hour.

Transfer the sorbet mixture to an ice-cream maker and process according to the manufacturer's instructions. Transfer the sorbet to a container; cover and freeze until firm, at least 4 hours or for up to 3 days.

Strawberry-Rhubarb Sherbet

MAKES ABOUT 5 CUPS (40 FL OZ/1.25 L); SERVES 8

Inspired by a favorite pie, this fruit combination also makes great sherbet.

2 tablespoons water
1 teaspoon unflavored gelatin
1 package (1 lb/500 g) frozen unsweetened sliced rhubarb, thawed
1 package (1 lb/500 g) frozen unsweetened whole strawberries, thawed
1½ cups (12 oz/375 g) sugar

1½ cups (12 fl oz/375 ml) milk
½ cup (5 oz/155 g) light corn syrup

Pour the water into a small cup. Sprinkle the gelatin over the water. Let stand for 5 minutes to soften.

Meanwhile, in a large, heavy saucepan, combine the rhubarb and strawberries with their juices and the sugar. Place over medium heat and stir until the sugar dissolves, about 3 minutes. Continue cooking, stirring occasionally, until the rhubarb is tender, about 5 minutes.

Reduce the heat to low, add the gelatin mixture, and stir until the gelatin dissolves, about 1 minute.

In a food processor or blender, process the rhubarb mixture until smooth. Pour the purée into a large bowl. Add the milk and corn syrup and stir to blend. Refrigerate until cold, about 1 hour.

Transfer the sherbet mixture to an ice-cream maker and process according to the manufacturer's instructions. Transfer the sherbet to a container; cover and freeze until firm, at least 4 hours or for up to 3 days.

Lemon Ice Cream with Lemon-Ginger Sauce

MAKES ABOUT 6 CUPS (48 FL OZ/1.5 L); SERVES 8

Lemon lovers will delight in this tangy citrus ice cream.

FOR THE ICE CREAM:

2 cups (16 fl oz/500 ml) half-and-half (half cream)

2 cups (16 fl oz/500 ml) heavy (double) cream

6 egg yolks

1¼ cups (10 oz/315 g) granulated sugar

1 tablespoon grated lemon zest

¾ cup (6 fl oz/180 ml) fresh lemon juice

FOR THE SAUCE:

½ cup (4 oz/125 g) granulated sugar

½ cup (3½ oz/105 g) firmly packed golden brown sugar

⅓ cup (3 fl oz/80 ml) water

¼ cup (2 fl oz/60 ml) fresh lemon juice

3 tablespoons unsalted butter

1 teaspoon grated lemon zest

2 tablespoons minced crystallized ginger

To prepare the ice cream, pour the half-and-half and 1 cup (8 fl oz/250 ml) of the cream into a large, heavy saucepan. Bring to a simmer over medium-high heat. Remove from the heat.

In a large metal bowl, whisk together the egg yolks, granulated sugar, and lemon zest until blended. Gradually pour the hot half-and-half mixture into the yolk mixture, whisking constantly. Return the mixture to the same saucepan and place over medium-low heat. Cook, stirring slowly and continuously with a wooden spatula, until the custard thickens and leaves a path on the back of the spatula when a finger is drawn across it, about 5 minutes; do not allow to boil.

Pour the custard into a clean bowl; do not strain. Whisk in the lemon juice and the remaining 1 cup (8 fl oz/250 ml) cream. Refrigerate the custard until cold, about 1 hour.

Transfer the custard to an ice-cream maker and process according to the manufacturer's instructions. Transfer the ice cream to a container; cover and freeze until firm, at least 4 hours or for up to 3 days.

To prepare the sauce, in a heavy saucepan over medium heat, combine the sugars, water, lemon juice, butter, and lemon zest. Stir until the sugars dissolve, about 3 minutes. Simmer, stirring occasionally, until reduced to 1 cup (8 fl oz/ 250 ml), about 15 minutes. Remove from the heat and let cool completely. Stir in the ginger.

To serve, scoop the ice cream into 8 balloon-shaped wineglasses. Drizzle 1–2 tablespoons sauce over each serving.

Basic Recipes

Perhaps the easiest way to express your creativity in grilling is to marinate food before you cook it. Steeping meat, poultry, seafood, or vegetables from a few minutes to several hours in a mixture usually consisting of some kind of acidic liquid (citrus fruit juice, wine, or vinegar), oil, herbs, and spices imparts flavors that complement the natural taste of food. A marinade or barbecue sauce also adds moisture to food, particularly if it is also used for basting.

Dry marinades are blends of herbs or spices without added liquid. They are rubbed over food several hours before grilling, after coating the food with oil.

Meat, poultry, seafood, or vegetables may be flavored after grilling with barbecue, peanut, and other sauces, as well as flavored butters, called compound butters.

Also included here are a pesto and a vinegar dressing, two recipes that are also used in this book.

Red or White Wine Marinade

MAKES ABOUT 5 CUPS (40 FL OZ/1.25 L), ENOUGH FOR LARGE ROAST, LEG OF LAMB, OR WHOLE CHICKEN

This recipe can be made with red wine for beef and lamb or white wine for poultry. Large roasts and whole chickens can marinate anywhere from 1–3 days; the longer they marinate, the more flavor they will gain.

1 bottle, about 3½ cups (28 fl oz/ 875 ml), dry red or white wine
½ cup (4 fl oz/125 ml) olive oil
1 onion, finely chopped
¼ cup (⅓ oz/10 g) chopped fresh parsley
2 large cloves garlic, minced
1 tablespoon chopped fresh thyme, rosemary, or tarragon, or 2 teaspoons dried herb of choice
1 teaspoon salt
½ teaspoon freshly ground pepper

In a large bowl, whisk together all the ingredients. Use immediately or refrigerate in a tightly covered jar for up to 2 days.

Citrus Marinade

MAKES ABOUT 1 CUP (8 FL OZ/250 ML), ENOUGH FOR 2–3 LB (1–1.5 KG) VEAL OR PORK CHOPS, STEAKS, OR FISH FILLETS

Citrus juice gives a clean, satisfying flavor to chicken, veal, or fish. Use an herb that is compatible with the food you are marinating, such as thyme or tarragon for veal, sage for pork, dill or tarragon for fish. Let steaks, chops, and fish fillets marinate for at least an hour, or all day if you wish. Large cuts can marinate for a day or two.

½ cup (4 fl oz/125 ml) olive oil
¼ cup (2 fl oz/60 ml) fresh lemon juice

1 clove garlic, minced
2 tablespoons finely chopped shallots or green (spring) onions
2 teaspoons grated lemon zest
2 teaspoons chopped fresh thyme, tarragon, dill, or sage, or 1 teaspoon dried herb of choice
½ teaspoon salt
½ teaspoon freshly ground pepper

In a small bowl, whisk together all the ingredients. Use immediately or refrigerate in a tightly covered jar for up to 2 days.

Soy-Ginger Marinade

MAKES ABOUT 1⅓ CUPS (11 FL OZ/330 ML), ENOUGH FOR ABOUT 3 LB (1.5 KG) MEAT, FISH, OR POULTRY

Here, soy sauce, sherry, and ginger are combined to make an American version of Japanese teriyaki marinade, which is good on flank steak, skirt steak, chicken, pork, and firm-fleshed fish. Marinate steaks, chops, or chicken in the refrigerator for at least 3 hours, or up to all day if you wish; marinate fish fillets for 1–2 hours. Large pieces of meat or poultry can marinate for a day or two.

½ cup (4 fl oz/125 ml) soy sauce
½ cup (4 fl oz/125 ml) dry sherry
⅓ cup (3 fl oz/80 ml) vegetable oil
2 tablespoons sugar
2 cloves garlic, minced
1 tablespoon peeled and grated fresh ginger

In a small bowl, combine the soy sauce, sherry, vegetable oil, sugar, garlic, and ginger. Whisk until blended. If possible, let stand at room temperature for about 1 hour before using, to allow the flavors to blend.

Dry Marinades

EACH RECIPE MAKES ABOUT ¼ CUP (1 OZ/30 G) IF MADE WITH FRESH HERBS, ENOUGH FOR 4–5 LB (2–2.5 KG) BEEF, PORK, OR LAMB, OR 2 LB (1 KG) FISH

Dry mixtures of salt, pepper, herbs, and spices rubbed over food several hours before grilling are good flavor enhancers. Rub the meat, poultry, or fish lightly with oil before coating it with the marinade. These marinades will keep, if refrigerated and tightly covered, up to 3 days.

FOR LAMB, BEEF, AND CHICKEN:

2 tablespoons chopped fresh rosemary
   or 2 teaspoons dried rosemary
2 large cloves garlic, minced
1½ teaspoons salt
1 teaspoon freshly ground pepper
finely grated zest of 1 lemon or lime

FOR FISH:

2 tablespoons chopped fresh dill
   or 2 teaspoons dried dill
2 teaspoons mild paprika
1 tablespoon grated lemon zest
1 teaspoon salt
1 teaspoon freshly ground pepper
¼ teaspoon cayenne pepper

FOR PORK:

2 tablespoons chopped fresh thyme
   or 2 teaspoons dried thyme
1 tablespoon chopped fresh sage
   or 1 teaspoon dried sage
2 teaspoons salt
1 teaspoon freshly ground pepper
¼ teaspoon ground allspice or cloves
2 cloves garlic, minced

Select the list of ingredients that complements the food you are marinating. In a small bowl, stir together the ingredients.

Red or White Wine Barbecue Sauce

MAKES ABOUT 2 CUPS (16 FL OZ/500 ML), ENOUGH FOR ABOUT 4 LB (2 KG) MEAT OR POULTRY

You can use this herbal, wine-based mixture as a marinade or a baste for chicken, pork, lamb, or beef.

1½ cups (12 fl oz/375 ml) dry red
   or white wine
½ cup (4 fl oz/125 ml) red or white
   wine vinegar
⅓ cup (3 fl oz/80 ml) olive oil
1 yellow onion, finely chopped
2 tablespoons Worcestershire sauce
2 tablespoons chopped fresh rosemary
   or thyme, or 2 teaspoons dried
   rosemary or thyme
2 teaspoons finely grated lemon zest
½ teaspoon salt
pinch of red pepper flakes

In a saucepan over high heat, combine the wine, wine vinegar, olive oil, onion, Worcestershire sauce, rosemary or thyme, lemon zest, salt, and pepper flakes. Bring to a boil, stirring once or twice to combine the ingredients. Reduce the heat to low, cover partially, and simmer until the onion has wilted and the sauce has reduced slightly, about 15 minutes.

• Remove from the heat and let cool. Use immediately, or transfer to a container, cover tightly, and refrigerate for up to 4 days.

Spicy Mop Sauce

MAKES ABOUT 2 CUPS (16 FL OZ/500 ML), ENOUGH FOR ABOUT 4 LB (2 KG) MEAT OR POULTRY

This flavorful concoction belongs to the family of vinegar-based Carolina mop sauces, so-called because they are popular in North and South Carolina and are traditionally swabbed over a slab of meat with an old-fashioned string mop. The sauces vary from sweet and tangy to fiery hot. This one is at once a dash sweet and moderately hot, but you can adjust the amount of sugar and pepper to suit your taste. It's a great marinade for beef, pork, or chicken.

1 teaspoon peppercorns
1¼ cups (10 fl oz/310 ml)
   cider vinegar
⅔ cup (5 fl oz/160 ml) water
3 tablespoons sugar
½ teaspoon salt
1 teaspoon red pepper flakes

Place the peppercorns on a work surface and crush them coarsely by firmly pressing and rolling the bottom of a heavy frying pan or saucepan over them.

• In a nonaluminum saucepan over high heat, combine the crushed peppercorns, vinegar, water, sugar, salt, and pepper flakes. Bring to a boil, stirring once or twice. Remove from the heat and let stand, uncovered, for at least 1 hour before using, to allow the flavors to blend. For longer storage, let cool completely, then transfer to a nonaluminum container, cover tightly and refrigerate for up to 1 week.

Midwestern Barbecue Sauce

MAKES ABOUT 2¼ CUPS (18 FL OZ/560 ML),
ENOUGH FOR 5–6 LB (2.5–3 KG) MEAT OR POULTRY

The Midwest abounds with thick tomato-based barbecue sauces that are a touch hot and sweet, and wonderful on pork ribs, beef brisket, or chicken. Because the sauces contain sugar and thus can burn easily, they are usually brushed on during the last 15–20 minutes of cooking. This is also a good dipping sauce to pass at the table.

2 tablespoons vegetable oil
1 yellow onion, chopped
½ cup (2½ oz/75 g) finely chopped
   celery
1¼ cups (10 fl oz/310 ml) tomato
   ketchup
½ cup (4 fl oz/125 ml) cider vinegar
½ cup (4 fl oz/125 ml) water
⅓ cup (3 oz/90 g) sugar
½ teaspoon cayenne pepper
½ teaspoon salt

In a saucepan over medium-high heat, warm the oil. When hot, add the onion and celery and cook, stirring, until the vegetables have softened, about 7 minutes.
• Add the ketchup, vinegar, water, sugar, cayenne, and salt and stir well. Bring to a boil, then reduce the heat to low, cover partially, and simmer until the sauce has thickened slightly, 15–20 minutes.
• Remove from the heat and let cool. Use immediately, or transfer to a container, cover tightly, and refrigerate for up to 5 days.

Basic Barbecue Sauce

MAKES ABOUT 2½ CUPS (20 FL OZ/625 ML)

A traditional American barbecue sauce, good on chicken, spareribs, and hamburgers. Because the sauce contains sugar it burns easily and should be brushed on for the last 10–15 minutes of cooking. Pass any remaining sauce at the table.

2 tablespoons vegetable oil
1 onion, finely chopped
3 cloves garlic, minced
1½ cups (12 fl oz/375 ml) tomato
   ketchup
½ cup (4 fl oz/125 ml) cider vinegar
¼ cup (2 fl oz/60 ml)
   Worcestershire sauce
⅓ cup (3 oz/90 g) sugar
1 tablespoon chili powder
½ teaspoon cayenne pepper

Heat the oil in a saucepan over medium heat and add the onion and garlic. Cook gently, stirring, for about 5 minutes. Add the ketchup, vinegar, Worcestershire sauce, sugar, chili powder, and cayenne to taste (the more cayenne you use, the hotter it will be). Reduce the heat and simmer, partially covered, until the sauce has thickened slightly, about 20 minutes.

Peanut Dipping Sauce

MAKES ABOUT 1¾ CUPS (14 FL OZ/440 ML)

Slightly sweet and slightly hot, this Asian-influenced dipping sauce complements grilled pork or poultry right from the fire. It is also good with firm-fleshed fish, such as swordfish, and on cold chicken or turkey. Pass it in a bowl at the table.

½ cup (4 fl oz/125 ml) water
1 teaspoon cornstarch (cornflour)
½ cup (5 oz/155 g) smooth or
   chunky peanut butter
¼ cup (2 fl oz/60 ml) fresh lime juice
⅓ cup (3 fl oz/80 ml) soy sauce
¼ cup (2 fl oz/60 ml) Asian sesame oil
2–3 tablespoons sugar
½–1 teaspoon red pepper flakes
¼ teaspoon hot chile oil
¼ cup (⅓ oz/10 g) chopped fresh
   cilantro (fresh coriander)
¼ cup (¾ oz/20 g) chopped green
   (spring) onion

In a saucepan, combine the water and cornstarch and stir until the cornstarch has dissolved. Add the peanut butter, lime juice, soy sauce, sesame oil, sugar, pepper flakes, and chile oil and whisk until smooth. Bring to a boil over medium-high heat, whisking frequently. Reduce the heat to low and simmer, uncovered, until the sauce has thickened slightly, about 3 minutes.
• Remove from the heat and let cool. Stir in the cilantro and green onion. Use immediately, or transfer to a container, cover tightly, and refrigerate for up to 3 days.

Compound Butters

A slice of flavored butter placed on a hot-from-the-grill steak, hamburger, chop, fish fillet, or piece of chicken melts to form an almost-instant bit of sauce. Compound butters keep for several days in the refrigerator or may be frozen for several months. The herb butter is especially good on steaks, chops, and hamburgers, while the lemon butter enhances fish and chicken. Pork and beef are good with the mustard butter.

FOR HERB BUTTER:

½ cup (4 oz/125 g) unsalted butter,
  at room temperature
2 tablespoons chopped fresh tarragon,
  sage, or cilantro (fresh coriander)
  or 2 teaspoons dried tarragon or sage
2 tablespoons chopped fresh parsley
½ teaspoon salt
½ teaspoon freshly ground pepper

FOR LEMON BUTTER:

½ cup (4 oz/125 g) unsalted butter,
  at room temperature
4 tablespoons chopped fresh parsley
2 tablespoons fresh lemon juice
2 teaspoons finely grated lemon zest
½ teaspoon salt
¼ teaspoon freshly ground pepper

FOR MUSTARD BUTTER:

½ cup (4 oz/125 g) unsalted butter,
  at room temperature
3 tablespoons Dijon mustard
2 tablespoons chopped shallots
  or green (spring) onions
1 tablespoon chopped fresh parsley
1–2 teaspoons fresh lemon juice
½ teaspoon salt
¼ teaspoon freshly ground pepper

Select the compound butter that complements the food you are serving. In a bowl, beat the butter with a wooden spoon or handheld mixer until smooth, then gradually beat in all the remaining ingredients. Form the butter mixture into a rough log about 4 inches (10 cm) long and 1 inch (2.5 cm) in diameter. Wrap in plastic wrap and chill until firm. To serve, cut into slices ½ inch (12 mm) thick.

Sun-Dried Tomato Pesto

MAKES ABOUT ½ CUP (4 FL OZ/125 ML)

A blender can be used to make this pesto, although it may not combine the ingredients as efficiently as a food processor.

1 clove garlic
½ cup (4 oz/125 g) coarsely chopped
  sun-dried tomatoes packed in olive
  oil, well drained
2 tablespoons chopped fresh basil
¼ teaspoon salt
⅛ teaspoon freshly ground pepper
2 tablespoons olive oil
2 tablespoons hot water, if needed

Start the motor of a food processor fitted with the metal blade. Add the garlic and process until minced. Add the tomatoes, basil, salt, pepper, and olive oil and process until a thick paste forms. If the paste is too thick, thin it with the hot water or a little more oil.
• Store refrigerated in a tightly covered container for up to 1 week.

Balsamic and Red Wine Vinegar Dressing

MAKES ABOUT ½ CUP (4 FL OZ/125 ML)

This versatile dressing is delicious with any salad of mixed greens, beans, or legumes. To vary the flavor, use all red wine vinegar or all balsamic vinegar, as you wish. Then taste and adjust with more oil or vinegar, if needed. Be sure to whisk the dressing well before using.

5 tablespoons (3 fl oz/80 ml)
  extra-virgin olive oil
1 tablespoon red wine vinegar
1 tablespoon balsamic vinegar
salt and freshly ground pepper to taste

In a small bowl, whisk together the olive oil, red wine vinegar, and balsamic vinegar. Season with salt and pepper.

Glossary

The following entries provide a reference source for this book, offering definitions of essential or unusual ingredients and explanations of related techniques.

Artichokes

The flower buds of a type of thistle native to the Mediterranean have, at their center, a tender, gray-green base topped by a prickly, inedible choke. The center is enclosed by a cluster of tough, pointed leaves. Before artichokes are used in a recipe, their stems and outer leaves are trimmed and their chokes are removed. Baby artichokes need only light trimming of their outer leaves before they are cooked.

Asparagus

Belonging to the lily family, these long, slender stalks have compact buds at one end. The most common variety is green; white spears are occasionally available. Asparagus are at their peak in April and May. Look for firm, brightly colored spears with tightly furled tips.

To trim asparagus, cut or snap off any tough, woody ends from the spears and discard. If the spears are thick, using a vegetable peeler and starting about 2 inches (5 cm) below the tip, peel off the skin.

Belgian Endive

Leaf vegetable with refreshing, slightly bitter, spear-shaped leaves. The leaves, white to pale yellow green in color, are tightly packed in cylindrical heads 4–6 inches (10–15 cm) long.

Bell Pepper

This sweet-fleshed, bell-shaped member of the pepper family, also known as capsicum, is most common in the unripe green form. Ripened red, yellow, and orange varieties are available, and creamy pale yellow and purple-black specimens may also be found.

To prepare a raw bell pepper, cut it in half lengthwise with a sharp knife. Pull out the stem section from each half, along with the cluster of seeds attached to it. Remove any remaining seeds and any thin white membranes, or ribs, to which they are attached. Cut the pepper halves as called for in the specific recipe.

Bread Crumbs

Fresh or dried bread crumbs are often used to add body and texture to fillings or to coat foods before cooking.

To prepare bread crumbs, begin with a good-quality rustic loaf that is made of unbleached wheat flour and has a firm, coarse-textured crumb. For fresh crumbs, cut away the crusts and let the loaf dry out overnight. The next day, crumble the bread by hand into a blender or food processor fitted with the metal blade and process until fine crumbs form. For dried crumbs, spread the fresh crumbs on a baking pan. Dry slowly in an oven set at its lowest temperature for about 1 hour. Fine dried bread crumbs are also sold prepackaged.

Chiles

A number of chiles are used to flavor marinades, bastes, and sauces. *Anaheim chiles*, slender and 6–8 inches (15–20 cm) long, are sharp and astringent, and vary in heat from mild to medium hot. Sold fresh in their green state, Anaheims are also available ripened until red and dried. *Jalapeño chiles* are medium to fiery hot fresh chiles with a distinctively sharp flavor. Usually dark green, jalapeños measure about 1½ inches (4 cm) long. Ripe red jalapeño chiles are also available. *Ancho chiles* are the dried form of the poblano. About 4½ inches (11.5 cm) long, they have wide shoulders, wrinkled, deep reddish brown skin, and a relatively mild, bittersweet flavor.

Coconut Milk

Often mistakenly thought to be the liquid found inside whole coconuts, coconut milk is a rich, sweet extract made from shredded fresh coconut. It is available canned in Asian markets and well-stocked food stores.

Eggplant

This vegetable-fruit, also known as aubergine, has tender, mildly earthy, sweet flesh. The shiny skins of eggplants vary in color from purple to red and from yellow to white, and their shapes range from small and oval to long and slender to large and pear shaped. The large, purple *globe eggplant* is the most common variety. It tends to have a slightly bitter edge and is usually sliced and lightly salted to draw out the bitter juices and excess moisture before cooking. Slender, purple *Asian eggplants* are sweeter and more tender and have fewer, smaller seeds.

Fennel

Crisp, refreshing bulb vegetable with a mild licorice or anise flavor. Before fennel is used in recipes, the stems and feathery tops and any bruised outer stalks are cut off the bulb. The bulb is then cut as directed in recipes, and the fine, feathery leaves are often used fresh as a garnish.

Fish Sauce

This thin, amber-colored liquid is made from salted and fermented fish. It is used in Southeast Asian cuisine much as soy sauce is used to season Japanese and Chinese dishes. Fish sauce varies from country to country, but all sauces may be used interchangeably. One of the most commonly available varieties is Thai fish sauce, called *nam pla*.

Garlic

Pungent bulb used both raw and cooked as a flavoring ingredient in cuisines around the world. Garlic is well suited for use in marinades, bastes, and sauces, and the whole heads can be grilled. For the best flavor, purchase whole heads of dry garlic and separate individual cloves from the head as needed; it is best not to purchase more than you will use in 1 or 2 weeks, as garlic can lose its flavor with prolonged storage.

To peel a garlic clove, place on a work surface and cover with the flat side of a large chef's knife. Press down firmly but carefully on the side of the knife to crush the clove slightly; the dry skin will the slip off easily.

Ginger, Fresh

The rhizome of the tropical ginger plant yields a sweet, strong-flavored spice. Whole rhizomes, mistakenly called roots, have a brown, papery skin that is usually peeled before the flesh is used.

Hot-Pepper Sauce

Bottled commercial cooking and table sauces made from fresh or dried hot red chiles make excellent seasonings and accompaniments for grilled foods. Many varieties are available; Tabasco is the most commonly known brand.

Leeks

A member of the onion family, moderate-flavored leeks are long and cylindrical, with a white root end and dark green leaves. If possible, select leeks that are small to medium. Grown in sandy soil, these multilayered vegetables require a thorough cleaning.

To clean leeks, trim off the roots. Trim off the dark green leaves where they meet the pale green part of the stem. Starting about 1 inch (2.5 cm) from the root end, slit each leek lengthwise. Vigorously swish the leek in a bowl of cold water. Drain and rinse again; check to make sure that no dirt remains between the tightly packed pale portion of the leaves.

Lemongrass

A Southeast Asian plant is the source of these stiff, reedlike stalks that are now also grown outside of Asia. The stalks impart a marked citrusy perfume to foods when used as skewers for grilling or when peeled, chopped, and added to recipes as an ingredient.

Mirin

This popular Japanese seasoning is made from fermented sweet rice. The amber-colored liquid is used to flavor marinades, bastes, and sauces.

Herbs

Many fresh and dried herbs can be used to season grilled foods. If using dried herbs, it is best to crush them first in the palm of the hand to release their flavor. Or they can be warmed in a frying pan and crushed using a mortar and pestle. The following are among the herbs that appear in this book.

Basil

Sweet, spicy herb popular in Italian and Thai cooking. It is best used fresh.

Bay Leaves

Pungent, spicy, dried whole leaves of the bay laurel tree. Two varieties are available. The French has a milder, sweeter flavor than California bay leaves. Remove and discard the leaves from a dish before serving.

Chives

Long, thin green shoot with a mild flavor reminiscent of onions, to which it is related. Fresh chives are preferred over dried.

Cilantro

Green, leafy herb resembling flat-leaf (Italian) parsley, with a sharp, aromatic, somewhat astringent flavor. Popular in Latin American and Asian cuisines, it is also called fresh coriander and Chinese parsley.

Dill

Fine, feathery leaves with a sweet flavor. Available fresh or dried.

Mint

Refreshing herb available in many varieties, with spearmint being the most common. Used fresh or dried to flavor a wide range of dishes, both savory and sweet.

Oregano

Pungent and spicy herb, also known as wild marjoram. It is used fresh or dried to season many savory dishes, particularly tomatoes and other vegetables.

Rosemary

Mediterranean herb with an aromatic flavor particularly suited to grilled foods such as poultry, meat, and vegetables. Used fresh or dried.

Sage

Fresh or dried herb with a pungent flavor that goes especially well with lamb, pork, and chicken.

Tarragon

Fragrant, distinctively sweet herb used fresh or dried as a seasoning for seafood, chicken, light meats, and vegetables.

Thyme

Fragrant, clean-tasting herb with small leaves. Used fresh or dried as a seasoning for poultry, light meats, seafood, and vegetables.

Mushrooms

Grilling brings out the rich, earthy taste of mushrooms and enhances their meaty texture. Many mushrooms are suitable for outdoor cooking. *Cultivated white mushrooms* are a common variety with white caps and white stems. *Cremini mushrooms* are cultivated mushrooms that have brown caps and white stems. They resemble cultivated white mushrooms, but are often more flavorful. *Portobello mushrooms* are the mature form of the cremini mushroom. Their large, dark brown caps are 4–6 inches (10–15 cm) in diameter and have a robust texture. *Oyster mushrooms* are white, gray, or pinkish and have lily-shaped caps. They have a tender texture, and their mild flavor is faintly reminiscent of oysters.

Mustards

Dijon and coarse-grain mustards give spark to grilled foods, marinades, and sauces. True Dijon mustard, made in Dijon, France, and non-French blends labeled "Dijon-style" are generally made with brown mustard seeds. They are pale in color, fairly hot, and sharp tasting. Darker coarse-grained mustards have a granular texture due to the roughly ground mustard seeds.

Oils

For grilling foods, oils—used on their own or as part of marinades, bastes, or sauces—not only prevent foods from sticking to the grill, but can also subtly enhance their flavor. *Extra-virgin olive oil*, extracted from olives on the first pressing without use of heat or chemicals, is prized for its pure, fruity taste and golden to pale green hue. Products labeled *pure olive oil* are less aromatic and flavorful and are suitable for all-purpose cooking. *Vegetable oils*, such as canola, safflower, and corn, are employed for their high cooking temperatures and bland flavor. *Asian sesame oil* is pressed from sesame seeds that have been toasted, resulting in a dark, strong oil used primarily as a flavoring ingredient. *Chile oil* is a popular seasoning that consists of olive, sesame, or vegetable oil in which hot chiles have been steeped.

Onions

Used as an ingredient or as a seasoning, onions of many varieties bring pungent-sweet distinction to outdoor cooking. *Green onions*, also called spring onions or scallions, are harvested immature, leaves and all, before their bulbs have formed. The green and white parts are both enjoyed for their mild but still pronounced onion flavor. *Red (Spanish) onions* are a mild, sweet variety with purplish red skin and red-tinged white flesh. *Yellow onions* are the common, white-fleshed, strong-flavored variety distinguished by their dry, yellowish brown skin.

Polenta

This Italian term refers to a cooked porridge made of specially ground cornmeal and to the cornmeal itself. Cooked polenta may be enriched with butter, cream, cheese, or eggs. When cooled, its consistency is firm enough for it to be shaped and grilled.

Salt

Kosher salt and coarse salt are well suited for use in dry and wet marinades and seasonings. Sea salt is an acceptable substitute.

Shallot

Small member of the onion family with brown skin, white-to-purple flesh, and a flavor resembling a cross between sweet onion and garlic.

Shrimp

Raw shrimp (prawns) are generally sold with the heads removed but with the shells still intact. Before cooking, they are often peeled and their thin, veinlike intestinal tracts removed.

To peel and devein shrimp, use your thumbs to split open the thin shell along the concave side, between the two rows of legs. Grasp the shell and gently peel away. Using a small knife, make a shallow slit along the outer curved back of the peeled shrimp, just deep enough to expose the long, veinlike intestinal tract. With the tip of the knife or your fingers, lift up and pull out the vein, discarding it.

Soy Sauce

Asian seasoning and condiment made from soybeans, wheat, salt, and water. Japanese brands tend to be markedly less salty than Chinese.

Sweet Potatoes

These tuberous vegetables are not true potatoes, though they resemble them in form. They have light to deep red skin and pale yellow to orange flesh.

Tomatillo

Small, green vegetable-fruit that resembles the tomato but is not related to it. Fresh tomatillos come encased in brown papery husks. Before using tomatillos, peel and discard the husks, then briefly rinse the tomatillos to remove the slightly sticky residue on the surface.

Tomatoes

When tomatoes are at their seasonal peak—in summer—seek out the best sun-ripened tomatoes you can find. At other times of the year, plum tomatoes, sometimes called Roma tomatoes, are likely to have the best flavor and texture.

To peel fresh tomatoes, bring a saucepan of water to a boil. Using a small, sharp knife, cut out the core from the stem end. Then cut a shallow X in the skin at the base of the tomato. Place the tomato in the boiling water for about 20 seconds; remove and dip in a bowl of cold water. Starting at the X, peel the skin, using your fingertips and, if needed, the knife blade. Cut as directed in individual recipes.

To seed a tomato, cut it in half crosswise. Squeeze gently to force out the seed sacs.

Vinegars

Used to add piquant, tart flavor to marinades, bastes, and sauces, vinegar is made when certain strains of yeast cause wine or another alcoholic liquid—such as apple cider—to ferment for a second time and turn it acidic. The best-quality *wine vinegars* begin with good quality wine. Red wine vinegar, like the wine from which it is made, has a more robust flavor than vinegar produced from white wine. *Cider vinegar* has the sweet tang and golden color of apple cider. Flavored vinegars such as *tarragon vinegar* are made by adding herbs or, in some cases, fruits such as raspberries. *Balsamic vinegar*, a specialty of Modena, Italy, is made from grape must and can be aged for many years. *Rice vinegar*, a clear vinegar made from rice wine, has a fresh, clean, light taste; it is available unseasoned and seasoned with sugar and salt. Japanese rice vinegars tend to be milder than Chinese varieties.

Worcestershire Sauce

This traditional English seasoning or condiment consists of an intensely flavorful, savory, and aromatic blend of many ingredients, including molasses, soy sauce, garlic, onion, and anchovies. It is popular as a marinade ingredient or as a table sauce for grilled foods, especially meats.

Zest

The thin, brightly colored, outermost layer of a citrus fruit's peel contains most of its aromatic essential oils, which are a lively source of flavor for marinades, bastes, and sauces. Zest may be removed from lemons, limes, and oranges with a simple tool known as a zester. Draw the zester across the skin to remove the zest in thin strips. Zest can also be removed with a fine handheld grater or in wide strips with a vegetable peeler or a paring knife held almost parallel to the fruit's skin.

Spices

Derived from the aromatic seeds, bark, or roots of various plants, the following savory, hot, and sweet spices add distinctive flavor to grilled dishes. The following are among the spices that appear in this book.

Cayenne Pepper

Very hot ground spice derived from dried cayenne chiles.

Chili Powder

Commercial blend of spices featuring ground dried chiles along with such other seasonings as cumin, oregano, cloves, coriander, pepper, and salt. It is best purchased in small quantities as flavor diminishes rapidly after opening.

Cinnamon

Popular spice derived from the aromatic bark of a type of evergreen tree. It is sold as whole dried strips, as well as ground.

Cumin

This Middle Eastern spice has a strong, dusky flavor. Sold ground or as whole, small, crescent-shaped seeds.

Curry Powder

Generic term for blends of spices commonly used to flavor East Indian–style dishes. Most curry powders are made with coriander, cumin, chili powder, fenugreek, and turmeric; other additions may include cardamom, cinnamon, cloves, allspice, fennel, and ginger. Curry powder is best purchased in small quantities.

Juniper Berries

Aromatic, small dried berries of the juniper tree, used as a seasoning in marinades for meat or poultry.

Mustard Seeds

Small, spherical seeds of the mustard plant, used to season marinades and sauces, as well as to make homemade mustards.

Peppercorns

The most common savory spice is best purchased as whole peppercorns and ground in a peppermill as needed. They can also be coarsely crushed. Black peppercorns derive from the slightly underripe pepper berries, whose hulls oxidize as they dry.

Red Pepper Flakes

Coarse flakes of dried red chiles, including seeds, which add moderately hot flavor to the foods they season.

Saffron

Intensely aromatic, golden orange spice made from the dried stigmas of a species of crocus. It is used to perfume and color many classic Mediterranean and East Indian dishes. Sold as threads (the dried stigmas) or in powdered form.

Sweet Paprika

Powdered spice derived from the dried paprika pepper. Available in hot and mild forms, as well as sweet.

Turmeric

Pungent, earthy ground spice that imparts a vibrant yellow color to any dish.

Index

acorn squash, stuffed 186
African fruit salad 267
aioli, double-garlic, chicken breasts with 80
all-American barbecued chicken 94
all-American beef short ribs 133
almond ice cream, toasted 286
anchovies
 Niçoise sauce 72
 tomatoes stuffed with eggs and 232
anise-marinated fish 33
apples
 -mint relish, turkey burgers with 112
 mixed fruit grill with spiced lemon cream 254
aromatics 13
artichokes
 mixed vegetable grill 195
 preparing 296
arugula, pizza with pears, pancetta, and 189
asparagus
 lemon-dill salmon and 43
 mixed vegetable grill 195
 with orange muscat buerre blanc 200
 with Parmesan 208
 trimming 296
avocados
 pork tenderloins with guacamole 152

bacon
 -wrapped Cornish hens 106
 -wrapped scallop and salmon skewers 52
balsamic and red wine vinegar dressing 295
bananas
 African fruit salad 267
 and berry salad 267
 chocolate-dipped frozen 268
 and pineapple with butterscotch sauce 261
 rum-raisin, with ice cream 257
basil, walnut, and mint pesto 38
bass, Greek-style whole, with olives and feta 29
beans
 Boston baked 237
 chickpea salad with olives and herbs 238
 salad, black, with peppers and corn 244
 salad, mixed, with balsamic dressing 224
 summer succotash 241
 white, bruschetta with fried sage and 202
beef
 brisket, Kansas City 128
 chuck roast, bourbon-marinated 140
 cooking time for 16, 17
 dry marinade for 293
 flank steak, peppery 130
 flank steak, sesame 139
 flank steak, star anise and pomegranate 144
 hamburgers with grilled mushrooms and
  jalapeño ketchup 130
 hamburgers with grilled tomatoes 118
 kabobs with pineapple relish 124
 rib eye, rotisserie, with crispy crust 144
 rib-eye steak, charred, with salsa verde 135
 rib roast, old-fashioned 121
 short ribs, all-American 133
 short ribs, Korean 142
 skirt steak, gingered 123
 skirt steak, Mexican-style 136
 skirt steak with cumin and sweet onion salsa 121
 steak, cumin, with spicy salsa 127
 steak fajitas 118

steak salad, Far Eastern 122
 steak sandwiches with chive butter 129
 steak with balsamic vinegar and black
  pepper 132
 steak with sauce poivrade 139
 tenderloin, marinated, with tarragon butter 124
 tenderloin pepper steaks 143
 top round with jalapeño marinade 116
beets
 relish, tuna with 24
 salad with orange-tarragon vinaigrette 234
Belgian endive
 and fennel with olive vinaigrette 221
 mixed vegetable grill 195
 and radicchio with shaved Parmesan 212
berries. *See also individual berries*
 and banana salad 267
 tart, mixed 258
 three-berry cobbler 268
biscotti, pistachio-orange 280
black bean salad with peppers and corn 244
blackberries
 -raspberry gratin 273
 three-berry cobbler 268
blondies, white chocolate and macadamia nut 276
blueberries
 berry and banana salad 267
 crisp 273
 mixed berry tart 258
Boston baked beans 237
bourbon-marinated chuck roast 140
bread
 bruschetta with white beans and fried sage 202
 country, and pork tenderloin skewers 163
 crumbs 296
 garlic bruschetta, Provençal mussels with 54
 melba summer pudding 271
 Parmesan pita toasts 218
 pear bruschetta 254
 salad, Italian, with tomatoes and basil 227
Brie with papaya 261
brined turkey 109
brisket, Kansas City beef 128
brochettes
 chicken liver 78
 lamb and eggplant, with Provençal dressing 174
 of roasted pepper–wrapped scallops 58
brownies
 cappuccino-walnut 276
 hazelnut-orange 281
brown rice tabbouleh 238
bruschetta
 garlic, Provençal mussels with 54
 pear 254
 primavera 218
 with white beans and fried sage 202
Buffalo chicken wings 88
burgers
 beef, with grilled mushrooms and jalapeño
  ketchup 130
 beef, with grilled tomatoes 118
 cooking time for 16, 17
 lamb, grilled, with mint, tomatoes, and garlic 180
 lamb and eggplant 170
 turkey, with apple-mint relish 112
butter lettuce and tarragon salad 241
butters
 compound 295
 seasoned 204
butterscotch sauce 261

cabbage
 red ginger slaw 230
 salad with cumin seeds 228
Caesar salad 236
cakes. *See* pound cake
cappuccino-walnut brownies 276
celery, pasta salad with tomato and 242
champagne, nectarines poached in 264
charcoal grills 9, 10, 12
charmoula, shrimp with 55
cheese
 Brie with papaya 261
 feta, Greek-style whole bass with olives and 29
 feta and cucumber salad, lamb sandwich
  with 180
 fontina and eggplant sandwiches 196
 mascarpone, nectarines, and pistachios 248
 mozzarella, fusilli salad with sweet peppers
  and 230
 mozzarella, prosciutto-wrapped figs stuffed
  with 157
 Parmesan pita toasts 218
 ravioli with spinach and 198
 saganaki 222
cherry and chocolate-chunk cookies 274
chicken
 all-American barbecued 94
 breasts, lemon 77
 breasts, tropical 85
 breasts with black olive butter 94
 breasts with double-garlic aioli 80
 breasts with Niçoise sauce 72
 cooking time for 16, 17
 deviled 87
 dry marinade for 293
 flattened, with a Greek flavor 90
 grill-roasted, with potato fans 78
 hickory-smoked 93
 Jamaican jerk 75
 kabobs 93
 lemon-rosemary 75
 liver brochettes 78
 and mushroom kabobs 87
 mustard-grilled 97
 Pacific Rim, with peanut sauce 88
 paillards with grilled tangerines and green
  onion oil 97
 Provençal, on skewers 77
 rotisserie Cuban, with orange, mint, and
  garlic 80
 with sage 82
 Southwestern barbecued 70
 tandoori 82
 teriyaki 85
 thighs in yogurt-curry marinade 72
 wings, Buffalo 88
chickpea salad with olives and herbs 238
chili butter 204
chive butter, steak sandwiches with 129
chocolate
 cappuccino-walnut brownies 276
 -chunk and cherry cookies 274
 -coffee sauce 257
 -dipped frozen bananas 268
 gelato, dark 285
 hazelnut-orange brownies 281
 orange ice cream with truffles 282
 s'more bars 279
chutney, dried-fruit 151
citrus gelato 282

citrus marinade 292
clams 16, 17
cobbler, three-berry 268
coconut
    -lemon squares 274
    toasted, tropical fruits with 258
cookies
    cappuccino-walnut brownies 276
    chocolate-chunk and cherry 274
    hazelnut-orange brownies 281
    lemon-coconut squares 274
    oatmeal, date, and walnut 279
    pistachio-orange biscotti 280
    s'more bars 279
    white chocolate and macadamia nut
        blondies 276
corn
    black bean salad with peppers and 244
    and pepper salsa 211
    with seasoned butters 204
    summer succotash 241
Cornish hens
    bacon-wrapped 106
    with ginger butter 101
couscous salad with cucumber, peppers, and
    tomatoes 228
crimson plum-raspberry sorbet 286
crisp, blueberry 273
Cuban chicken, rotisserie, with orange, mint,
    and garlic 80
Cuban tuna tacos, spicy 47
cucumbers
    brown rice tabbouleh 238
    couscous salad with peppers, tomatoes, and 228
    and feta salad, lamb sandwich with 180
    salad, orange-and-miso-glazed sea bass with 44
    salad with dill 244
cumin steak with spicy salsa 127
curried pork satay 160

date, oatmeal, and walnut cookies 279
desserts
    African fruit salad 267
    bananas and pineapple with butterscotch
        sauce 261
    berry and banana salad 267
    blueberry crisp 273
    Brie with papaya 261
    cappuccino-walnut brownies 276
    chocolate-chunk and cherry cookies 274
    chocolate-dipped frozen bananas 268
    citrus gelato 282
    crimson plum-raspberry sorbet 286
    dark chocolate gelato 285
    foil-wrapped oranges in dark rum 252
    fresh peach ice cream 285
    hazelnut-orange brownies 281
    lemon-coconut squares 274
    lemon ice cream with lemon-ginger sauce 291
    mango sorbet 289
    mango with vanilla bean sabayon 250
    melba summer pudding 271
    mixed berry tart 258
    mixed fruit grill with spiced lemon cream 254
    mixed summer fruit compote 270
    nectarines, mascarpone, and pistachios 248
    nectarines poached in champagne 264
    oatmeal, date, and walnut cookies 279
    orange ice cream with truffles 282
    pear bruschetta 254

pistachio-orange biscotti 280
pound cake kabobs with chocolate-coffee
    sauce 257
pound cake with raspberry sauce 250
raspberry-blackberry gratin 273
rum-raisin bananas with ice cream 257
s'more bars 279
strawberry-rhubarb sherbet 289
summer fruits in white chocolate–lime
    sauce 262
three-berry cobbler 268
toasted almond ice cream 286
tropical fruits with toasted coconut 258
tropical papaya boats 265
white chocolate and macadamia nut
    blondies 276
deviled chicken 87
direct heat 11
double tomato pizza 198
dry marinades 293
duck
    cooking time for 17
    guava-glazed 109
    with orange and vermouth 98

eggplant
    and fontina sandwiches 196
    and lamb brochettes with Provençal dressing 174
    and lamb burgers 170
    mixed vegetable pasta 191
    Provençal chicken on skewers 77
    ratatouille from the grill 184
    ratatouille pizza 192
    salad 202
    spicy 217
    vegetable skewers with romesco sauce 197
eggs, tomatoes stuffed with anchovies and 232
electric grills 9
equipment 14–15. See also grills

fajitas, steak 118
Far Eastern steak salad 122
fennel
    and endive with olive vinaigrette 221
    -marinated salmon 40
    mixed vegetable grill 195
    red ginger slaw 230
feta
    and cucumber salad, lamb sandwich with 180
    Greek-style whole bass with olives and 29
figs, prosciutto-wrapped, stuffed with smoked
    mozzarella 157
fish. See also anchovies
    anise-marinated 33
    bass, Greek-style whole, with olives and feta 29
    cooking time for 16, 17
    dry marinade for 293
    flounder with orange salsa 48
    in grape leaves 33
    halibut, Veracruz style 38
    halibut with grilled pipérade 22
    halibut with red pepper butter 27
    in Indian ginger masala 30
    kabob, North African 30
    salmon, fennel-marinated 40
    salmon and asparagus, lemon-dill 43
    salmon and scallop skewers, bacon-wrapped 52
    salmon skewers 44
    salmon with mustard glaze and Asian
        vinaigrette 48

salmon with sour orange and red onion mojo 35
sea bass, orange-and-miso-glazed, with cucumber
    salad 44
snapper with cilantro butter 24
swordfish, Middle Eastern, with lemon and
    thyme 35
swordfish drizzled with balsamic-butter sauce 28
swordfish with lemon, garlic, and olive oil 40–41
swordfish with lime and cilantro sauce 37
swordfish with tomatillo salsa 27
trout with prosciutto and sage 51
tuna, fresh, pasta with 47
tuna salad, Mediterranean 36
tuna tacos, spicy Cuban 47
tuna with beet relish 24
with walnut, mint, and basil pesto 38
flare-ups, controlling 10–11
flattened chicken with a Greek flavor 90
flounder with orange salsa 48
fontina and eggplant sandwiches 196
fruits. See also individual fruits
    compote, mixed summer 270
    grill, mixed, with spiced lemon cream 254
    salad, African 267
    summer, in white chocolate–lime sauce 262
    tropical, with toasted coconut 258
fusilli salad with sweet peppers and mozzarella 230

garlic
    aioli, double- 80
    grilled lamb burgers with mint, tomatoes,
        and 180
    grill-roasted 216
    mayonnaise 175
    peeling 296
gas grills 9, 11, 12
gelato
    citrus 282
    dark chocolate 285
ginger
    gingered skirt steak 123
    slaw, red 230
grape leaves
    fish in 33
    saganaki 222
Greek-style whole bass with olives and feta 29
green onions
    oil 97
    and tomatoes 207
green salad, mixed 233
grills
    caring for 10
    choosing 9
    fuels for 12
    starting fire in 10
    types of 9
guacamole, pork tenderloins with 152
guava-glazed duck 109

halibut
    with grilled pipérade 22
    with red pepper butter 27
    Veracruz style 38
ham, hickory-smoked fresh 149
hamburgers. See burgers
hazelnut-orange brownies 281
herb butter
    basic 295
    Italian 204

hickory-smoked
  chicken 93
  ham, fresh 149
  ribs 158
  turkey thighs 105
hoisin pork loin 159

ice cream. *See also* gelato
  almond, toasted 286
  lemon, with lemon-ginger sauce 291
  orange, with truffles 282
  peach, fresh 285
  rum-raisin bananas with 257
Indian ginger masala, fish in 30
indirect heat 11
Italian bread salad with tomatoes and basil 227
Italian herb butter 204

jalapeño chiles
  ketchup 130
  marinade, beef top round with 116
jerk chicken, Jamaican 75

kabobs. *See also* brochettes; skewers
  beef, with pineapple relish 124
  chicken 93
  chicken and mushroom 87
  fish, North African 30
  lamb, saffron 169
  lamb tikka 176
  pound cake, with chocolate-coffee sauce 257
  turkey, with peanut dipping sauce 106
Kansas City beef brisket 128
ketchup, jalapeño 130
Korean short ribs 142

lamb
  burgers, grilled, with mint, tomatoes, and
    garlic 180
  chops, rosemary-smoked 170
  cooking time for 16, 17
  dry marinade for 293
  and eggplant brochettes with Provençal
    dressing 174
  and eggplant burgers 170
  fillet of, with roasted peppers and onions 173
  grilled, salad of potatoes, garlic mayonnaise,
    and 175
  kabobs, saffron 169
  leg of, butterflied, with Mediterranean rub 173
  leg of, grilled butterflied, with mint mustard 179
  leg of, wine-scented 169
  and potato skewers 179
  rack of, herbed 166
  sandwich with feta and cucumber salad 180
  shoulder chops with sweet ginger, soy, and
    shallot glaze 176
  tikka 176
leeks
  cleaning 297
  and mushrooms 200
lemon
  butter 295
  chicken breasts 77
  citrus gelato 282
  -coconut squares 274
  cream, spiced 254
  -dill salmon and asparagus 43
  ice cream with lemon-ginger sauce 291
  -rosemary chicken 75

lemongrass skewers, Thai shrimp on 60
lime
  butter 204
  and cilantro sauce, swordfish with 37
liver brochettes, chicken 78
lobster
  with citrus butter 65
  cooking time for 17
  tails, Catalan style 66

macadamia nut and white chocolate blondies 276
Madeira, pork loin with 152
mangoes
  African fruit salad 267
  sorbet 289
  tropical fruits with toasted coconut 258
  with vanilla bean sabayon 250
marinades
  citrus 292
  dry 293
  red or white wine 292
  soy-ginger 292
mascarpone, nectarines, and pistachios 248
Mediterranean rub, butterflied leg of lamb
  with 173
Mediterranean tuna salad 36
melba summer pudding 271
Mexican-style skirt steak 136
Middle Eastern swordfish with lemon and
  thyme 35
Midwestern barbecue sauce 294
mint mustard, grilled butterflied leg of lamb
  with 179
mop sauce, spicy 293
mozzarella
  fusilli salad with sweet peppers and 230
  prosciutto-wrapped figs stuffed with 157
mushrooms
  and chicken kabobs 87
  grilled, hamburgers with jalapeño ketchup
    and 130
  and leeks 200
  mixed vegetable grill 195
  portobello, on salad greens 190
  and shrimp skewers 66
  and summer squashes, stuffed 192–193
  vegetable skewers with romesco sauce 197
mussels
  cooking time for 16, 17
  Provençal, with garlic bruschetta 54
mustard butter 295
mustard-glazed sausages with sauerkraut relish 165
mustard-glazed ribs 150
mustard-grilled chicken 97

nectarines
  mascarpone, pistachios, and 248
  poached in champagne 264
  summer fruits in white chocolate–lime sauce 262
Niçoise sauce, chicken breasts with 72
North African fish kabob 30

oatmeal, date, and walnut cookies 279
olives
  chickpea salad with herbs and 238
  tapenade 215
  vinaigrette, fennel and endive with 221
onions
  slices, grilled 200
  slow-cooked, with tarragon mustard sauce 206

orange
  citrus gelato 282
  -Cognac butter, oysters with 65
  duck with vermouth and 98
  foil-wrapped, in dark rum 252
  -and-ginger-glazed pork roast 160
  ice cream with truffles 282
  -and-miso-glazed sea bass with cucumber
    salad 44
  muscat buerre blanc, asparagus with 200
  salsa, flounder with 48
  -tarragon vinaigrette, beet salad with 234
  and watercress salad 227
oysters
  cooking time for 16, 17
  with orange-Cognac butter 65
  with soy-citrus vinaigrette 60
oyster sauce, crisp tofu with 186

Pacific Rim chicken with peanut sauce 88
pancetta, pizza with pears, wilted arugula,
  and 189
papaya
  African fruit salad 267
  boats, tropical 265
  Brie with 261
Parmesan pita toasts 218
pasta
  with fresh tuna 47
  fusilli salad with sweet peppers and
    mozzarella 230
  mixed vegetable 191
  ravioli with spinach and three cheeses 198
  salad with tomato and celery 242
peaches
  ice cream, fresh 285
  summer fruits in white chocolate–lime
    sauce 262
peanuts
  dipping sauce 294
  sauce, Pacific Rim chicken with 88
pears
  bruschetta 254
  mixed fruit grill with spiced lemon cream 254
  pizza with pancetta, wilted arugula, and 189
  salad of pork, toasted pecans, and 164
pecans
  butter 204
  salad of pork, pears, and 164
  wood, whole leg of pork over 157
peppers
  black bean salad with corn and 244
  and corn salsa 211
  couscous salad with cucumber, tomatoes,
    and 228
  fusilli salad with mozzarella and 230
  preparing 296
  relish, tea-smoked shrimp with 63
  roasted, fillet of lamb with onions and 173
  -wrapped scallops, brochettes of 58
peppery flank steak 130
pesto
  sun-dried tomato 295
  walnut, mint, and basil 38
pineapple
  African fruit salad 267
  and bananas with butterscotch sauce 261
  relish, beef kabobs with 124
  tropical fruits with toasted coconut 258
pipérade, grilled, halibut with 22

pistachios
nectarines, mascarpone, and 248
-orange biscotti 280
pita toasts, Parmesan 218
pizzas
double tomato 198
with pears, pancetta, and wilted arugula 189
ratatouille 192
plum-raspberry sorbet, crimson 286
polenta wedges 210
pomegranate and star anise flank steak 144
pork. *See also* bacon; ham; pancetta; prosciutto
baby back ribs, hickory-smoked 158
chops, grilled, with fried sage 146
cooking time for 16, 17
dry marinade for 293
loin, hoisin 159
loin, salt-brined 154
loin with Madeira 152
ribs, mustard-glazed 150
roast, orange-and-ginger-glazed 160
salad of pears, toasted pecans, and 164
satay, curried 160
sausages, mustard-glazed, with sauerkraut
relish 165
spareribs, simple 154
spareribs, Vietnamese style 163
tenderloin and country bread skewers 163
tenderloins with guacamole 152
tenderloin with dried-fruit chutney 151
whole leg of, over pecan wood 157
portobello mushrooms on salad greens 190
potatoes
fans, grill-roasted chicken with 78
and lamb skewers 179
salad, creamy red, with celery seeds 234
salad of grilled lamb, garlic mayonnaise, and 175
salad with sun-dried tomato cream 242
skewers, herbed two- 220
with sun-dried tomato pesto 215
pound cake
kabobs with chocolate-coffee sauce 257
with raspberry sauce 250
prosciutto
trout with sage and 51
-wrapped figs stuffed with smoked
mozzarella 157
Provençal chicken on skewers 77
Provençal dressing, lamb and eggplant brochettes
with 174
Provençal mussels with garlic bruschetta 54
pudding, melba summer 271

quail, thyme and mustard 105

radicchio and Belgian endive with shaved
Parmesan 212
raspberries
-blackberry gratin 273
melba summer pudding 271
-plum sorbet, crimson 286
sauce, pound cake with 250
three-berry cobbler 268
ratatouille
from the grill 184
pizza 192
ravioli with spinach and three cheeses 198
red ginger slaw 230
rhubarb-strawberry sherbet 289

ribs
hickory-smoked 158
mustard-glazed 150
short, all-American beef 133
short, Korean 142
spare-, simple 154
spare-, Vietnamese style 163
rice tabbouleh, brown 238
romesco sauce 62, 197
rotisserie Cuban chicken with orange, mint, and
garlic 80
rotisserie grills 9
rotisserie rib eye with crispy crust 144
rum
foil-wrapped oranges in 252
-raisin bananas with ice cream 257

safety 11, 16
saffron lamb kabobs 169
saganaki 222
sage, fried, grilled pork chops with 146
salads
bean, mixed, with balsamic dressing 224
beet, with orange-tarragon vinaigrette 234
berry and banana 267
black bean, with peppers and corn 244
bread, Italian, with tomatoes and basil 227
brown rice tabbouleh 238
butter lettuce and tarragon 241
cabbage, with cumin seeds 228
Caesar 236
chickpea, with olives and herbs 238
couscous, with cucumber, peppers, and
tomatoes 228
cucumber, orange-and-miso-glazed sea bass
with 44
cucumber, with dill 244
eggplant 202
fruit, African 267
fusilli, with sweet peppers and mozzarella 230
green, mixed 233
of grilled lamb, potatoes, and garlic
mayonnaise 175
pasta, with tomato and celery 242
of pork, pears, and toasted pecans 164
portobello mushrooms on greens 190
potato, creamy red, with celery seeds 234
potato, with sun-dried tomato cream 242
slaw, red ginger 230
steak, Far Eastern 122
tuna, Mediterranean 36
watercress and orange 227
salmon
and asparagus, lemon-dill 43
fennel-marinated 40
with mustard glaze and Asian vinaigrette 48
and scallop skewers, bacon-wrapped 52
skewers 44
with sour orange and red onion mojo 35
salsas
corn and pepper 211
orange 48
tomatillo 27
tomato 215
verde 135
sandwiches. *See also* burgers
eggplant and fontina 196
lamb, with feta and cucumber salad 180
steak, with chive butter 129
satay, curried pork 160

sauces
basic barbecue 294
butterscotch 261
chocolate-coffee 257
Midwestern barbecue 294
Niçoise 72
peanut dipping 294
red and white barbecue 293
romesco 62, 197
spiced lemon cream 254
spicy mop 293
sun-dried tomato pesto 295
tapenade 215
tarragon mustard 206
walnut, mint, and basil pesto 38
white chocolate–lime 262
sausages
mustard-glazed, with sauerkraut relish 165
turkey, with chutney mustard 110
scallops
brochettes of roasted pepper–wrapped 58
cooking time for 17
and salmon skewers, bacon-wrapped 52
sea bass, orange-and-miso-glazed, with
cucumber salad 44
sesame flank steak 139
shellfish. *See also individual varieties*
grill, mixed, with lemon-lime butter 56
with romesco sauce 62
sherbet, strawberry-rhubarb 289
shrimp
with charmoula 55
cooking time for 16, 17
with garlicky tomato glaze 59
and mushroom skewers 66
peeling and deveining 298
tea-smoked, with sweet-and-hot pepper
relish 63
Thai, on lemongrass skewers 60
skewers. *See also* brochettes; kabobs
bacon-wrapped scallop and salmon 52
country bread and pork tenderloin 163
herbed two-potato 220
lamb and potato 179
lemongrass, Thai shrimp on 60
Provençal chicken on 77
salmon 44
shrimp and mushroom 66
vegetable, with romesco sauce 197
s'more bars 279
snapper with cilantro butter 24
sorbet
crimson plum-raspberry 286
mango 289
Southwestern barbecued chicken 70
soy-ginger marinade 292
spinach, ravioli with three cheeses and 198
squab, herbed butterflied 101
squash. *See also* zucchini
acorn, stuffed 186
mixed vegetable pasta 191
summer, and mushrooms, stuffed 192–193
star anise and pomegranate flank steak 144
strawberries
berry and banana salad 267
mixed berry tart 258
-rhubarb sherbet 289
three-berry cobbler 268
succotash, summer 241
summer fruits in white chocolate–lime sauce 262

summer succotash 241
swordfish
   drizzled with balsamic-butter sauce 28
   with lemon, garlic, and olive oil 40–41
   with lime and cilantro sauce 37
   Middle Eastern, with lemon and thyme 35
   with tomatillo salsa 27

tabbouleh, brown rice 238
tacos, spicy Cuban tuna 47
tandoori chicken 82
tangerines, grilled, chicken paillards with green
   onion oil and 97
tapenade 215
tarragon mustard sauce 206
tart, mixed berry 258
tea-smoked shrimp with sweet-and-hot pepper
   relish 63
teriyaki chicken 85
Thai shrimp on lemongrass skewers 60
tikka, lamb 176
tofu, crisp, with oyster sauce 186
tomatillo salsa, swordfish with 27
tomatoes
   brown rice tabbouleh 238
   couscous salad with cucumber, peppers,
      and 228
   glaze, garlicky, shrimp with 59
   and green onions 207
   grilled, hamburgers with 118
   Italian bread salad with basil and 227
   pasta salad with celery and 242

peeling and seeding 298
pesto, sun-dried 295
pizza, double 198
Provençal chicken on skewers 77
salsa 215
   stuffed with eggs and anchovies 232
   vegetable skewers with romesco sauce 197
tropical chicken breasts 85
tropical fruits with toasted coconut 258
tropical papaya boats 265
trout with prosciutto and sage 51
truffles, orange ice cream with 282
tuna
   with beet relish 24
   fresh, pasta with 47
   salad, Mediterranean 36
   tacos, spicy Cuban 47
turkey
   breast, stuffed 112
   breast with ancho rub 110
   brined 109
   burgers with apple-mint relish 112
   cooking time for 16, 17
   grill-roasted 102
   kabobs with peanut dipping sauce 106
   sausages with chutney mustard 110
   thighs, hickory-smoked 105

vanilla bean sabayon 250
veal
   chops, Valdostana style 136
   cooking time for 16, 17

loin chops with tarragon, mushrooms, and
   cream 140
vegetables. *See also individual vegetables*
   grill, mixed 195
   pasta, mixed 191
   ratatouille from the grill 184
   ratatouille pizza 192
   roasted autumn 208
   skewers with romesco sauce 197
   with two dipping sauces 215
vermouth, duck with orange and 98

walnuts
   –cappuccino brownies 276
   cookies, oatmeal, date, and 279
   pesto, mint, basil, and 38
watercress and orange salad 227
white chocolate
   –lime sauce 262
   and macadamia nut blondies 276
wine
   barbecue sauce 293
   marinade 292
   –scented leg of lamb 169

yogurt-curry marinade, chicken thighs in 72

zucchini
   ratatouille from the grill 184
   ratatouille pizza 192
   stuffed mushrooms and 192–193
   vegetable skewers with romesco sauce 197

Credits

AUTHORS

Brigit Binns: Pages 35, 44, 47, 48, 60, 72, 72, 80, 80, 90, 97, 109, 121, 135, 144, 144, 146, 154, 157, 157, 163, 163, 176, 189, 200, 202, 212, 222, 230, 250, 252

Lora Brody: Pages 250, 262, 264, 265, 267, 268, 268, 270, 271, 273, 273

John Phillip Carroll: Pages 22, 24, 24, 27, 27, 37, 40, 43, 44, 52, 59, 63, 66, 75, 75, 77, 78, 78, 82, 85, 85, 87, 87, 93, 94, 94, 97, 98, 101, 101, 102, 105, 105, 106, 106, 110, 112, 112, 116, 118, 118, 121, 123, 124, 128, 129, 130, 133, 139, 140, 143, 149, 150, 152, 152, 154, 160, 160, 165, 166, 169, 169, 170, 170, 179, 184, 186, 192, 195, 196, 200, 206, 207, 208, 216, 218, 218, 220, 221, 254, 261

Emalee Chapman: Pages 77, 93, 234

Lorenza De' Medici: Page 230

Joyce Goldstein: Pages 30, 30, 33, 33, 35, 36, 38, 40, 47, 51, 55, 62, 122, 124, 127, 132, 136, 136, 139, 140, 142

Barbara Grunes: Pages 28, 29, 38, 48, 54, 60, 65, 66, 70, 82, 88, 88, 109, 110, 130, 158, 159, 173, 186, 190, 191, 192, 198, 198, 200, 202, 204, 208, 210, 211, 215, 248, 254, 257, 257, 258, 258, 261

Kristine Kidd: Pages 274, 274, 276, 276, 279, 279, 280, 281

Emanuela Stucchi Prinetti: Pages 227, 228, 232, 233, 236, 241, 242, 244, 267

The Scotto Sisters: Page 176

Sarah Tenaglia: Pages 282, 282, 285, 285, 286, 286, 289, 289, 291

Joanne Weir: Pages 56, 58, 65, 151, 164, 173, 174, 175, 179, 180, 180, 197, 217, 224, 227, 228, 237, 238, 238, 241, 244

Diane Rossen Worthington: Pages 215, 234, 242

PHOTOGRAPHERS

Noel Barnhurst: Front cover, pages 20, 34, 42, 45, 46, 49, 50, 61, 68, 73, 81, 91, 100, 108, 114, 134, 145, 147, 156, 162, 177, 182, 188, 201, 203, 205, 213, 223, 246, 253

Joyce Oudkerk Pool: Pages 28, 29, 39, 54, 71, 88, 89, 111, 131, 158, 159, 190, 191, 192, 199, 208, 211, 249, 256, 259

Allan Rosenberg: Pages 23, 24, 25, 26, 27, 30, 31, 32, 33, 36, 37, 38, 40, 41, 53, 55, 57, 58, 59, 62, 63, 64, 67, 74, 75, 76, 77, 79, 83, 84, 85, 86, 87, 92, 93, 94, 95, 96, 99, 101, 103, 104, 105, 106, 107, 110, 112, 113, 117, 118, 119, 120, 122, 123, 124, 125, 126, 128, 129, 130, 132, 133, 136, 137, 138, 139, 140, 141, 142, 143, 148, 150, 151, 152, 153, 155, 160, 161, 164, 165, 167, 168, 169, 170, 171, 172, 174, 175, 178, 179, 180, 181, 185, 187, 193, 194, 196, 197, 206, 207, 209, 210, 214, 216, 217, 218, 219, 220, 221, 225, 226, 227, 228, 229, 231, 232, 233, 234, 235, 236, 237, 238, 239, 240, 241, 242, 243, 244, 245, 251, 255, 260, 263, 264, 265, 266, 267, 268, 269, 270, 271, 272, 273, 274, 275, 276, 277, 278, 279, 280, 281, 282, 283, 284, 285, 286, 287, 288, 289, 290

Additional food photography: Allen V. Lott

Stylists: Sandra Cook, Heidi Gintner, Sandra Griswold, Carol Hacker, Susan Massey

Assistants: Noriko Akiyama, Elizabeth C. Davis, Arjen Kammeraad, Jennifer McConnell, Karen Nicks, Ann Tonai

SPECIAL THANKS

Donita Boles, Wendely Harvey, Ruth Jacobson, Melinda Levine, Kathryn Meehan, Annette Sandoval